In Search of the Immortals

IN SEARCH OF THE IMMORTALS

MUMMIES, DEATH *and the* AFTERLIFE

HOWARD REID

ST. MARTIN'S PRESS ★ NEW YORK

www.stmartins.com

ISBN 0-312-28006-8

First published in Great Britain by Headline Book Publishing

First U.S. Edition: August 2001

10 9 8 7 6 5 4 3 2 1

In memory of Robin Rusher and Peter Silverwood-Cope

Acknowledgements

Many people have made critically important contributions to the chapters of this book, some in person, others through their writings. Victor Mair was my principle guide and mentor to the mummies of the Taklamakan along with his colleagues Wang Binghua and Lü Enguo in the field. Jeannine Davis-Kimball and Charlotte Roberts shared many revealing insights and were brilliant travelling companions. Jeannine's work on the nomads of Central Asia has been of enormous help in getting to understand the Pazyryks. Sergei Rudenko's book (*Frozen Tombs in Siberia*) formed the backbone of Chapter Two, just as P.V. Glob's classic work (*The Bog People*) provided much of the core information for the Bog People. Joann Fletcher, another wonderful travelling companion, guided me with consummate skill through the maze of ancient Egyptian ritual and cosmology. Mike Eddy, Conrado Martin and Raphael Gonzales were brilliant guides to the enigma of the Guanche peoples. Don Brothwell was enormously generous with his time while organizing the re-examination of the Cambridge Guanche mummy.

In South America I am deeply indebted to Sonia Guillen and Adriana Von Hagen for the enormous help and insights they provided me with, and for arranging for *El Ingles loco* to ride to the tomb site at the Lake of the Condors. Sonia's PhD thesis is a mine of information on all the mummies of the world, as well as the Chinchorro· in particular, and Bernardo Arriaza's boundless enthusiasm and superb writings gave me the keys to these the oldest and most complex mummy-makers of them all. My understanding of human sacrifice was forged by Patrick Tierney while my perception of Near Death Experiences was greatly enhanced by discussions with Susan Blackmore and Paul Badham.

Charles Furneaux (Editor of Channel 4's *To the Ends of the Earth*) was responsible for getting me stuck in the middle of the Taklamakan desert, where I conceived the idea for this book, and was kind enough to support my research in South America, the Canaries, Morocco and Egypt. My agent Mark Lucas has been his usual tyrannical but acutely insightful self throughout the whole process of getting this book into print. His penchant for meting out a 'good (mental) whipping' for slack prose certainly got me on my toes at an early stage in the writing process. I am assured that underneath it all he is, in fact, a gentleman at heart. By contrast, my editor Doug Young has always been the soul of charm and tact while making innumerable positive contributions to the text as it emerged. My copy editor Barbara Nash has done a wonderful job cleaning up the manuscript and is always a pleasure to work with.

Much of the time in the field I travelled with my film team, now all old and trusted friends. Ian Charlton, Jerry Pinches, Chris Bairstow and Steve Higgs never flinched when the going got tough and produced superb results. Heartfelt thanks for their rock-like support and ongoing interest in the worlds of the mummy people. Deep thanks are due, too, to Fiona Wilton, Tara Lee and Pippa Dennis for superb assistance at various times both with the book and the films. Last, but foremost, I want to thank my wife Val and my three daughters Amie, Leila and Maya for putting up with me as I wandered deep into Unknown Country, sometimes on the other side of the world, sometimes just a few feet away in my study.

Contents

Introduction

There is something *very* strange about standing next to a fellow human being who has not been alive for thousands of years. This is a *real* human, not a model or statue. It is very much here, yet not here. It both attracts and repels; looks more asleep than dead. We tend to associate death with pain and suffering, forgetting the repose death can bring, and our fascination goes even deeper than that. Is it that by refusing to return to dust and ashes, mummies have somehow succeeded in cheating death?

When visiting the British Museum, children always seem to make for the Egyptian mummies first, then clamour to peer at 'Pete Marsh', the peat bog body from Lindow Marsh in Cheshire. And in the past few years both academic and popular interest in mummies has exploded. Books, articles and, above all, TV programmes have poured on to the page and screen to satisfy popular demand. Yet little has been produced which attempts to go beyond the purely physical remains and question what the mummies meant to the people who made them. Why did so many ancient peoples want to preserve their dead in the first place?

In this book I want to address these fundamental questions and by doing so I hope also to cast light on why we, in turn, are so fascinated by them and what they mean to us. I have approached these questions from several perspectives – from the anthropological and psychological to the purely spiritual. There is a spiritual dimension to understanding other people's lives, deaths and visions of the afterlife which allows me to draw on my own experiences of death – and my quest to come to terms with it. At this level, this book is also an account of my own journey into the Valley of Shadows.

Mummified human remains, ranging from 10,000 years to just a few years old, have been found all around the world. Many of these bodies are chance preservations. The Ice Man found in the Alps in 1991 died there by accident 5,200 years ago. A German soldier shot in a peat bog during the Second World War was found well preserved a few years ago. There are also isolated cases of individuals or small groups of people who have been intentionally preserved – many of the popes, Lenin, Mao Tsedung, Eva Peron, some Japanese noblemen and Zen Buddhist monks, to name but a few. Fascinating though these cases are, they are not the products of cultures who held that post-mortem preservation was important both for the dead themselves and for the surviving members of their societies. This book concentrates on those mummies which give us a glimpse into the worlds they once inhabited; into their lives, deaths and destinations beyond death.

Dictionaries define a mummy as any preserved human or animal body but, for most people, the term implies an element of intent: people preserving their dead because they wanted to. Yet in most of the times and places where mummification cults flourished, climatic conditions caused natural mummification before people began to elaborate on the process. The archaeological record shows a spectrum of events from purely chance preservation right through to the fully-planned and religiously-motivated preservation of people as practised by the ancient Egyptians. Between these extremes, people have adapted and modified the natural process in many different ways, from the simple application of embalming ointment to the removal of all flesh and its replacement with sticks, padding and earth – as the first mummy-makers did 9,000 years ago.

INTRODUCTION

~~~

Why should people want to preserve the bodies of departed relatives, loved ones or even enemies? The reasons vary enormously and are often little known or understood – not surprisingly, because, with the exception of the Egyptians, most mummy-makers were not literate and left no written records. But both the bodies and the circumstances surrounding their deaths provide clues to the beliefs of the people concerned. My aim in this book is to look beyond the masks of the preserved dead for the ways in which mankind has viewed death and the possibilities of an afterlife. In so doing, I hope to broaden our own perspective on mortality.

Concern with death is certainly as old as modern humanity, maybe older. Like speech and intelligence, it defines us as human. Some archaeologists maintain that the neanderthals (*Homo sapiens neanderthalis*) buried their dead, covering them with red ochre and possibly even placing flowers and fragrant herbs in their graves; and certainly the earliest anatomically-modern humans (*Homo sapiens sapiens*) buried their dead.

Both oral traditions and the earliest written records conceive the transition from life to death as some form of journey. Typically, the human soul sets out on a new path towards the sunset, into the darkness or underground, to face a series of trials and eventual deliverance in the land of the dead. This journey finds expression throughout history and across the cultures of the world. Its universality seems to be confirmed by countless recent reports of a phenomenon known as the Near Death Experience (NDE). The development of ever-more effective resuscitation skills has meant that millions of people living in the 'modern' world have returned from the brink of death, and many report visionary journeys that closely resemble those first described by their ancestors millennia ago. There are extraordinary parallels between ancient belief and contemporary experience at the gates of death.

Near Death Experiences share some basic characteristics. The first is that all who experience them maintain that they were real experiences. Unlike dreams, they have no surreal qualities: they *really* happen. Most people find them wonderful, even ecstatic experiences; a few are intensely frightened by them.

Typically, the victim of a traumatic event – heart-attack, car-crash, near-drowning or acute haemorrhage – loses consciousness, then apparently regains it. There then follows a series of events, some or all experienced by the victim. The first of these is that the victim becomes aware of his or her being, but in a displaced position. This is known as the Out of Body Experience (OBE), where the conscious self of the victim looks down at his or her body from above and observes the attendant activities going on all around. These usually comprise attempts to resuscitate the victim.

The scene below then dissolves and the victim enters a long dark tunnel. At the far end there is a bright, glowing light. Free of all pain, the victim becomes a traveller and sets off towards the light at the end of the tunnel. As the light envelops the traveller, he or she discovers a totally new landscape, often described as heavenly. Here, the traveller may meet deceased relatives or loved ones and commune with them. Some meet a benign 'Being of Light'. According to individual faith and cultural background, this Being may be called God, Buddha, Christ or a similar divine title.

Communing with this Being, some travellers then experience a total recall of all the events of their life on earth. After this, those undergoing Near Death Experiences either decide themselves or are advised by the spirit-beings that their time on earth is not yet complete and they should return and re-enter their bodies 'below'. They then return and revive, finding themselves once more in the waking world of the living. We know no more of those who do not return, but most faiths maintain that they journey on.

The elements of the Near Death Experience share many characteristics with the oldest 'religion' known to mankind – shamanism, which has been practised for thousands of years all over the world. Many experts believe that the systems of belief which inspired our ancestors to

4

INTRODUCTION

〰〰

decorate great caves, such as Lascaux and Altamira, as long as 30,000 years ago were in essence shamanic. Even today all native Americans, both in the north and south of the continent, who continue to adhere to traditional beliefs, practise shamanism. It was also practised throughout Northeast Asia as far as Central Asia, in Tibet and throughout Southeast Asia before the rise of world religions such as Buddhism and Islam. China's oldest religious system, Taoism, finds its roots in shamanism. Practised by both men and women, shamans train themselves to go into trances, usually with the help of drumming or chanting, sometimes with the aid of psychoactive drugs. In altered states of consciousness the shaman's soul travels through a tunnel eventually emerging into another world, where the shaman may encounter spirit-beings and receive messages from them. They may be seeking the causes of misfortune or sickness in the waking world or searching for the causes of death. In some societies living shamans go to this other world to find the wandering souls of the newly dead and guide them to their eternal resting places in the afterworld. We will be encountering shamanism many times in this book, but for the present it is only important to note that in ancient times shamanism was extremely widespread and, in essence, posited the existence of other spirit worlds which could be visited beyond the confines of normal, waking life.

Close encounters with death are not restricted to abnormal states of consciousness. When I was eighteen years old I was involved in a car-crash while on holiday in Spain. Peter, the owner of the car, was killed two minutes after I traded seats with him. I was thrown out of the vehicle on to the tarmac at about 110 k.p.h. Even though the events took place in seconds, the experience seemed to go on for much longer. I clearly remember that I had time to work out that the car must be just behind me – rolling – and likely to land on top of me. As I skidded along on my side, my skin grazing the tarmac, I decided I should wait until I had slowed down sufficiently to get upright, then run to escape being crushed. Occasionally, I opened my eyes to see if I had slowed down enough to get up, and finally I managed to do so. By the time I had taken a few paces, I saw the car lying upright in the ditch ahead of me. It had not rolled, but spun right round me.

A couple of hours later, the *guardia civil* confiscated my passport and ordered me to write a statement of what had happened. This was Franco's Spain and niceties were not extended to walking-wounded tourists. In my shocked state, I found the best way to envisage what had happened was to replay the events in my mind as if from above. What I had actually seen was the huge front wheel of the truck loom up in front of me, heard a huge bang, and, next moment, I knew I was on my side skidding down the road. Experiencing all this from above, I could see it rather in the way that police helicopter cameras track joy-riders until they crash. I saw our open-top sports car pulling out to overtake the truck, then the truck starting to turn left in front of us. At impact, the tail-end of our car slewed round to the left, flicking me out on to the road, and spinning on until it came to rest in front of me. The slewing motion had catapulted Peter, who was sitting across the small back seat of the car, out sideways. The back of his head hit the kerb as he landed.

The experience taught me a great deal about the traumatic side of death. It also contained two elements which seem to me to reveal some aspects of coming very close to death. First, at the moment when I was closest to death, unsure whether I would live or die, time seemed to elongate considerably. Second, in trying to make sense of the events I found the easiest way to piece it together was to detach myself from the action and, as it were, look down on it from above. This, of course, is exactly what happens to people who experience Out of Body Experiences. I should stress, however, that this did not happen to me — I did not go out of body *during* the crash, but afterwards I did find it the easiest way to make sense of the event.

I learnt then that in close encounters the experience of life and death can become entwined. I did not learn until much later in life that this process of entanglement can become much, much more severe. In March 1993, my best friend Robin Rusher died very suddenly of a heart-attack. He was forty years old and had two small daughters. I had introduced him to his wife, my wife's best friend, and we lived in and out of each other's pockets. Our two families were together almost every day, we took holidays together and there was little we did not share with each other. His death devastated everyone close to him. Desperately trying to work out what had happened to him, I found myself trying to make sense of the trauma we were all going through. Gradually I came to realize that, almost unwittingly, I had set out on an inner journey – a quest to face death and discover what might lie beyond it. I soon found that I was far from the first person to make this journey.

The oldest written story in the world is the Babylonian epic of Gilgamesh, inscribed on clay tablets in Mesopotamia around 5,000 years ago and doubtless recited round camp-fires for many centuries before then. It tells of the adventures of the legendary king Gilgamesh and his best friend and soul-brother Enkidu. After Enkidu's tragic death, Gilgamesh determines to travel to the afterworld to discover what has happened to his friend. The fourth segment, entitled 'The Search for Everlasting Life', begins:

> Bitterly Gilgamesh wept for his friend Enkidu: he wandered over the wilderness as a hunter, he roamed over the plains; in his bitterness he cried, 'how can I rest, how can I be at peace? Despair is in my heart. What my brother is now, that shall I be when I am

dead. Because I am afraid of death I will go as best I can to find Utnapishtim whom they call the faraway, for he has entered the assembly of the gods.' So Gilgamesh travelled over the wilderness, he wandered over the grasslands, a long journey, in search of Utnapishtim, whom the gods took after the deluge: and they set him to live in the land of Dilmum, in the garden of the sun: and to him alone they gave everlasting life.

When I first read these words, it was as if a voice was calling out directly to me from 5,000 years ago. Gilgamesh's feelings and reactions to the loss of his best friend were exactly the same as my own. His account of his journey in the afterworld both fascinated me and forewarned me of the complexities to come.

The Gilgamesh epic gives a very thorough account of the Sumerians' vision of the afterlife, but the act of preserving the dead was not part of their cosmology or ritual practices. As I mentioned earlier, none of the world's great mummifying cultures except the Egyptian has left behind a written record of why they routinely preserved their dead. All I had to go on, in my search for the paths that they may have intended to tread beyond life, were cryptic clues in the form of the bodies themselves, their attire and tomb accoutrements, and some accounts by ancient travellers and chroniclers. Patterns, however, did emerge from these clues.

I first saw the Bog People in 1986. Eleven years later I met the mummies of the Taklamakan desert in Central Asia. It was on this trip, bouncing around endlessly in a bus through the desert, that I realized it would be interesting to write a book about the mummy-making peoples of the world. At that time, I saw few connections between the various cultures, but as I looked deeper I found more and more links between them. Some of these connections are to do with history and ethnicity;

INTRODUCTION

others with the shared nature of human experience – similar responses to the same problems in unconnected times and cultures.

Standing next to the near-perfectly-preserved bodies of the ancient Europeans of western China I felt empathy, not fear or revulsion. They were dead, but they were also here and now – utterly real. They seemed almost to beckon, to invite me to return with them to their world. So I set out on the path already trodden by Gilgamesh, Orpheus, St Paul, Dante, Hieronymus Bosch, Blake and countless other wandering souls.

Part One
The Old World

Chapter 1

Central Asia
the riddle
in the sands

In March 1989 archaeologist He Dexiu was surveying a remote corner of the Taklamakan desert (the so-called 'desert of no return') in China's westernmost province, Xinjiang. The heat thumped down on him as he crossed a dry stream bed and climbed a small rise not far from the village of Zagunluq. All around him the coarse grey-brown sand stretched away to the horizon, melding there with the dusty air. Scanning the surface with his binoculars, He Dexiu detected a small ruffle about 200 metres away. It looked like a crumpled piece of sacking. Scrutinizing the area more carefully, he could just pick out slight depressions in the sand a metre or so across — tell-tale signs for an archaeologist that the sands had been disturbed by digging.

As he drew closer to the 'sack', he realized that what he had seen was an orange fabric. Beside it he could make out a cascade of fair wavy hair. As he closed in on it, he found himself peering at a mummified woman. Her face was plastered with sand and mud and her eyes were empty sockets. She had no arms below the elbow and her legs were missing, but her clothes were finely woven and in amazingly good condition. Her lovely hair looked freshly combed.

Finding intact mummies on the surface is extremely rare anywhere in the world and, in the past, some discoveries have been wrongly identified

— assumed to be recent exhumations and hastily reburied. But He Dexiu could tell right away that the woman lying before him had died a long, long time ago — about 3,500 years ago in fact. Her clothes and hair were all the clues that he needed. In the preceding ten years Chinese archaeologists had found similar mummies all round the edges of the Taklamakan.

Searching the area carefully, He Dexiu was soon convinced that he was in an ancient cemetery and decided to come back later with colleagues to carry out a proper dig. They began by gently cleaning and freeing the woman's body from the sand. Inspection of her pelvis made it probable that she was less than twenty-five years old — the ends of her pubic bone displayed the characteristic ridge-and-furrow pattern of a young woman.

After she was removed, He Dexiu suspected that she was, in fact, lying over the site of another grave. The workers continued to dig slowly and carefully, and soon came upon a little bundle of red fabric bound firmly round two tiny feet.

Lying head down in the sand was a baby boy, wrapped in swaddling clothes. Four little milk teeth had recently erupted in his lower jaw, making him eight to fourteen months old. Someone, perhaps his mother, had plaited a red-and-yellow woollen braid to a lock of his sandy-coloured hair, just as children like to do today. A braided woollen strap was passed under his chin and tied at the top and back of his head. These straps are common on mummies in this area and in many other parts of the world. They are there to keep the mouth shut after death. But it had slipped down and rigor mortis had left the baby's mouth wide open, frozen in a silent shriek as agonizing as Edvard Munch's famous painting *The Scream*.

The child was wrapped tightly in a red gauze-like cloth, then in a beautifully worked shawl that had first been dyed red, then had bright yellow circles added — some of the oldest batik work ever discovered. Unwrapping it, He Dexiu found the baby's tiny hands, fists firmly clenched. Scrutinizing the child's face, he thought he could see mucus coming from his nose and even traces of tears on his perfectly preserved eyelashes.

Gently placing the baby boy with the young woman, the workers continued to dig and soon came to a layer of reeds and branches – the cover of the main grave. They were in good order, carefully placed to stop loose sand falling into the tomb. He Dexiu knew that this grave had not been disturbed – grave-robbers never bother to put tomb-covers back properly.

Carefully lifting off the covering, they measured, annotated, labelled and took photographs of each stage of the process. When they reached the row of logs which formed the roof of the tomb they lifted them out cautiously, letting as little rubble as possible fall into the grave. The central log was from a really big tree and had a bas-relief carving on it – the outline of a hand or, perhaps, a lick of flames.

Immediately below this symbol was the head of a woman, aged about forty. As the dust settled after the last roof-logs were removed, He Dexiu found himself staring down at an almost perfectly preserved woman who looked as if she had died just a few days before. She lay on her back, her face staring up at the magic symbol on the log. Her right hand was raised above her chest, the fingers arranged in a curling, spiral-like formation. Her legs were bent beneath her, so that her feet almost touched her thighs. A stick had been placed vertically under each of her legs, holding her knees upright. Some time during the 3,000 years she had lain there, her head had become separated from her body. He Dexiu gently replaced it in position. Her clothes were finely woven in brown, purple, beige and red wool. She wore felt socks and deer-skin boots, the fine soft fur outermost. She lay on a beige mat which displayed a dazzling array of differing weaving skills. Elaborate scroll-patterned tattoos adorned her fingers, wrists and the backs of her hands. She was wearing eye-shadow, possibly even face-powder. Her long and beautiful greying fair hair lay in braids around her head, with strands of red sheep's wool plaited into them. Her long fingernails were in perfect condition, indicating she was not someone who had laboured long and hard with her hands. The tattoos and her fingernails suggested she was a shamaness, someone very important, a dignitary.

An idea began to form in He Dexiu's mind. The young woman he had discovered on the surface had no legs or forearms, and looked as if her eyes had been gouged out. The baby appeared to have been buried alive, its clenched fists, tears and the terrible screaming mouth attesting to an agonizing death. Yet the woman in the main grave epitomized the serenity of death – grace, beauty and elegance radiating from her. Could it have been that when this great priestess had died, her kin had decided to sacrifice the baby and the younger woman (perhaps a slave or war captive) to her memory, to give her company and assistance in the afterlife? If so, it would explain why the younger woman had been abandoned on the surface and the baby thrust head-first into the grave shaft. But, as He Dexiu knew so little about the ways of life and death of these people, such ideas would have to remain speculative.

He climbed down into the grave, carefully lifting the woman up to the light, to inspect her more closely. Explaining how he had felt when embracing this perfect woman from before the dawn of history, he said: 'That moment as I held her in my arms and looked at her lovely face, I knew she was the most beautiful woman I had ever seen. I knew then that if she were alive today, or if I had been alive 3,000 years ago, I would most certainly have asked her ... I would most certainly have made her my wife.'

The beautiful lady now rests in He Dexiu's museum in the town of Korla on the northern edge of the Taklamakan desert.

Zagunluq cemetery yielded up a further seventeen bodies, most in the same incredibly fine state of preservation. Three of these mummies – a mature man (the 'sun man'), a woman and another infant – were shipped to the provincial capital, Urumchi, and displayed there in the archaeology museum.

THE RIDDLE IN THE SANDS

A short while later an American scholar, Professor Victor Mair, saw them and was the first foreigner to realize their significance. Professor Mair specializes in ancient Chinese history and was intimately familiar with the earliest written accounts of the peoples who inhabited the lands to the west of China in ancient times. The accounts were not flattering – they wrote of barbarians who looked like monkeys – but they were quite detailed. These wild people had large noses, blue or green eyes, long faces and red or blond hair. The men had beards and some were said to be hairy all over. These descriptions were clearly aimed to distinguish the 'pure' Chinese from the 'impure' barbarians, but the details they provide are all characteristics of Western Europeans.

When Victor Mair first saw the mummies he was as amazed as He Dexiu: 'I just couldn't believe my eyes. I mean, they looked as if they had died just a few days ago. I was really fascinated, riveted. I knew right from the start that I just had to tell the rest of the world about these amazing finds.' He knew he was looking at the embodiment of the barbarians in the early Chinese accounts of the wastelands of Central Asia. But at that time few had heard of the mummies and no one knew exactly who they were, where they had come from or what eventually happened to them. The enormity of the puzzle attracted Victor intensely and, over the next decade, it drew in a host of Chinese and international scholars all bent on solving the riddle in the sands.

Spectacular though He Dexiu's finds were, he was not the first researcher to discover mummies in the sands of the Taklamakan. At the beginning of the twentieth century, European adventurers and explorers had scoured this section of the great Silk Road seeking the treasures of the great Buddhist cities and temples which had flourished there two millennia before. Thousands of paintings, sculptures and manuscripts were shipped back to Europe on horses, mules and camels for examination and 'safe keeping'. The saw-marks and blank spaces on the walls of the temples are still clearly visible today.

Foremost among these adventurers was Sir Aurel Stein, a Hungarian-born British archaeologist and explorer, who made many trips to the region. On one trip he excavated a grave and was startled to find two very European-looking bodies in it. The woman, it has been noted, looked like an Irish peasant, the man like a Bavarian burgher. He took them to be travellers who had somehow wandered into the desert and perished there. After taking a couple of photos, he reburied them.

In the first half of the twentieth century, China was in turmoil and the westernmost part of the country was effectively abandoned by central government. It became the fiefdom of a succession of warlords until Mao Tsedung's Communist party took power in 1949. Stung by China's humiliation, first by the colonial powers then by Japan, Mao was determined to prove to the world that China was the cradle of ancient civilization. He ordered a major programme of archaeological research, stressing the need to show that landmark inventions, such as the wheel and metallurgy, had originated in China and then spread to the rest of the world. Although this major programme took place all over China, emphasis was inevitably placed on the western part of the country as it was from there that inventions must either have been imported or exported to and from Europe.

The big questions for Mao's archaeologists, therefore, was how and when did people from the Chinese homeland begin to make contact with the peoples to the west, in Central Asia and ultimately Europe? When and how did trade relations begin to link the hearts and minds of the ancient peoples? It was thought then that contacts between east and west did not occur until the Silk Road was established around 100 BC because of the formidable barrier inhibiting these links – the Taklamakan desert.

The Taklamakan is one of the most inhospitable places on earth and

THE RIDDLE IN THE SANDS

〜〜

the furthest point from any seashore on the entire Eurasian landmass. A place of immense extremes – temperatures can reach 72C in summer and plummet to -34C in the winter – Aurel Stein describes the ink freezing in his pen as he struggled to write his notes there one winter evening.

Looking at the region on a map, it seems that the desert sands reach the edge of the Tien Shan mountains ('Celestial Mountains') to the north and the Tibetan plateau to the south, but the landscape is more complex than that. Snow falls on the mountains to the north and south, and in the spring it melts and runs down the slopes to the edge of the desert. There, most of the water disappears underground. A few miles into the desert the water resurfaces, generating a string of oases – narrow strips of green in the pinks, greys and browns of the sands. In some places, the water continues to flow into the desert, but eventually all the water sources peter out without any real outflow. Evaporation levels are among the highest anywhere in the world. This means that all the minerals and salts washed into the desert in the mountain rainfall are not carried away downriver but remain in the sands. In earlier aeons, the desert was a shallow sea which eventually dried out, leaving huge deposits of salt in many parts. So the desert sands, always dry and alternately ferociously hot or bitterly cold, are also very salty – perfect conditions for the preservation of soft human tissues.

The oases which fringe the desert are relatively evenly dispersed, forming a chain of water-points all round its north and south sides. There are some gaps – occasionally we drove for 50 or 60 miles between oases – but there are few places where two or three days' hard walking does not take an explorer from one water source to the next.

So the possibility for human colonization of this region, albeit hazardous, has existed for millennia, as long as people stuck to the chain of oases on the desert fringe.

We know that people did work their way along the oasis chains from about 10,000 years ago but, apart from some stone implements, the first colonists left little behind them to provide clues about who they were or where they had originated.

In 1978, archaeologist Wang Binghua decided to excavate a cemetery just outside one of the small oasis villages on the northern fringes of the Taklamakan. Chinese administrators called it *Wupu* ('number five village') and the site had probably been occupied by people for at least 4,000 years. Wang's finds there revolutionized scientific thinking about the original populations of the region. The local people call it *Qizilchoqa*, 'Red Hillock', after a distinctive geological formation next to the village.

Wupu is about an hour's drive from Hami, a large market and industrial town, but the rhythm of life in the village feels far from modern. The dirt streets and alleyways throng with people, donkey carts, sheep, goats and the inevitable sea of bicycles. Everyone moves at a leisurely pace, the air filled with human voices calling greetings, exchanging gossip, chiding children and shooing animals. The mud-brick houses are arranged with courtyards to the front, large airy rooms to the sides and rear, and they have high ceilings supported by whole tree trunks. Nowadays there is some electricity but most houses have their own wells providing cool, clear but often salty-flavoured water. The women wear bright-coloured clothes and the men embroidered hats. Small naked boys glisten as they swim and play in the irrigation ditches which thread their way through the village. The villagers are Uyghurs, an ethnic minority group who speak a form of Turkish. Their looks are a blend of east and west – some have long faces and noses with hazel or even blue eyes, others have the high cheekbones, rounded faces, narrow eyes and sleek black hair typical of Mongoloids. Most are a mixture of both.

The Uyghurs are known to have inhabited this region since at least 700 AD, so when Wang Binghua began to dig in the cemetery outside the village he was expecting to find a similar, ethnically mixed population. Walking up the slight incline to the cemetery, he could see at once that it was a large one. There were clear depressions in the sand every few metres and, standing on them, he could feel that the sand was softer, less compressed than on the ridges between the graves. His initial survey plotted the sites of more than 300 graves. Scattered around the surface were fragments of cloth and rope, a few wooden bowls and spoons, even a chunk of a wooden cart-wheel. Clearly, some of the graves had been looted but most looked undisturbed.

Opening a grave in *Wupu* is not difficult. I watched this in 1996. Using local labourers, the archaeologists first dig down for about half a metre in the loose sand, exposing the 'roof' of the tomb. A layer of rushes and brushwood provides a sand-tight seal over a set of large timbers, carefully cut to length. The cut-marks of the bronze axes used to trim the logs 3,000 years ago are perfectly clear, as if they had been hewn just a few days ago. After brushing the timbers clean and measuring, photographing and sketching each one, the archaeologists gently lift them clear of the grave. As shafts of light enter the chamber, dust obscures the base of the tomb about 1.8 metres below the surface. You can see that the tomb has been lined with mud bricks forming a rectangular shaft 1.2 metres long and 0.7 metres wide. If the roof has not done its job and sand has fallen into the tomb, the corpse in most cases will have decayed and there will only be a skeleton surrounded by some grave goods and rotten fabrics. If the roof has remained sound then, as the dust settles, you first see a pair of knees, legs bent under the body touching the thighs, then perhaps an arm and a hand, and finally a face and torso. In *Wupu* some of the bodies lay on their sides, others were on their backs staring upwards.

After just a few days of the first dig at *Wupu*, one thing was clear to Wang: the vast majority of the people preserved in the desert sands were not of Mongoloid or Chinese descent, they were Caucasoids and looked like Europeans. Most had long faces and noses, and their hair colours ranged from blond to reddish and many shades of brown. Their clothes, too, bore little resemblance to the Chinese dress-style of 3,000 years ago.

Over the last twenty years, Wang and his colleagues have excavated about 200 graves in *Wupu*. These have yielded around thirty mummies, which means that about one grave in six contained a preserved body. One particular grave was removed in its entirety and reassembled in the provincial archaeological museum in nearby Hami city. This provided the chance to look closely at both its occupant and the objects placed with her when she died.

According to Charlotte Roberts, the biological anthropologist travelling with us, the mummy was of a girl about eighteen years old. Her face had high cheekbones and a small nose, but her hair was fair and she had an over-bite (her upper front teeth overlapped her lower teeth, not meeting edge to edge). The over-bite, characteristic of European populations, is uncommon among Mongoloid peoples. As Charlotte inspected the girl's hands, I was reminded of my old friend Peter Silverwood-Cope who told me: 'Always look at the hands and fingers. They tell you so much about what people do, how they express themselves, how they feel.' The girl's hands were very small and thin and she had extremely long fingernails. This showed that she was not in the habit of doing hard manual work, such as food preparation, collecting firewood or farm work. This implied that she had either held a social status which exempted her from manual labour or for another reason had been unable to work for some time before her death. The experts agreed that her body looked very emaciated, but were not sure if this was the result of post-mortem desiccation or a long period of illness before she died. Our Chinese hosts would not allow us to examine the body physically or to remove any of her clothing, so the cause of her death remained unresolved.

THE RIDDLE IN THE SANDS

〜〜
〜〜

Her clothes were made of finely woven cloth but looked faded and grubby and we could see some darns and patches on them so, unlike the woman He Dexiu had found dressed in her best attire, she had gone to her grave in ordinary workaday clothes. Overall, the impression I had was of a young woman whose life had slowly faded away, possibly from some wasting disease. Perhaps her family had expected her death and laid her to rest with little pomp and ceremony.

But she had not been neglected in death. Just by her right hand there was a wooden water bucket with a perfectly preserved piece of unleavened bread balanced on its top. At her side lay a leather halter or bridle for a donkey and a lot of leather strapping, presumably a donkey harness. There was even a little whip made from a wooden switch with a leather thong attached to it. Beside it lay a small textile bag. We could not see what was inside it, but guessed it contained her personal effects, possibly even some make-up as we had seen black sticks of 3,000-year-old eye-shadow recovered from other tombs. So she had food, water, personal effects and the means to make a journey – a journey into the world beyond death.

Hundreds of other items have been recovered from the *Wupu* cemetery: ceramic pots of many shapes and sizes, wooden bowls and basins – with and without feet – some of them apparently made almost in miniature; wooden spoons, a cart-wheel and spindle whorls for spinning wool. There was even a pair of tiny wooden dolls, dressed in miniature clothes. There were felt blankets and a huge array of clothing, from finely cobbled leather boots with tongues, leather straps and copper studs to heavy woollen coats and fine shirts, kaftans, dresses and trousers. Polished stones had been pierced to make necklaces, and copper and bronze worked for earrings and bracelets. There was also a beautifully carved bone comb with superb scrolling patterns incised on it. The design reminded me of the crests of waves in an angry sea or the swirling edges of fast-moving clouds. We would come across this motif many times as our research continued. Metalwork ranged from large bronze cooking cauldrons through to needles and knives. The curator of the Hami museum, Jacob Satuola, was especially fond of a beautiful little tool-kit all laid out on a braided woollen belt. It consisted of a whetstone in its leather pouch, two bronze blades, a metal punch and the knife handle, each set in its own little leather pouch. Perhaps they had once been the property of a leather worker.

Among the more exotic objects were polished bronze mirrors, some in leather cases and cowrie seashells. The latter immediately caught my attention as the nearest seashore is at least 2,000 miles from the Taklamakan. Here was tangible evidence that these people must have been at the heart of long-distance trade networks.

Wupu's grave goods were so plentiful and diverse, it seemed almost as if all of life was here in this 3,000-year-old cemetery. It certainly was not a problem for the excavators to build up a detailed picture of how life must have been in the little oasis all those years ago. The picture that emerged was of a sophisticated and diversified society.

The people who lived here were village farmers. They grew crops and raised animals – sheep, goats, donkeys and horses. At least some of them were also skilled artisans. There were leather workers producing finely tooled boots and shoes, some from sheepskin, others from deer hide, as well as harnesses, saddles and heavy sheepskin jackets for the bitter winters. Carpenters made everything from household utensils, such as spoons and bowls, through to cart frames and solid wooden wheels and, of course, the 'roofs' of the tombs. The wood looked as though it was worked mainly with axes and adzes, not saws or lathes, though some of the work was finely done.

It is not yet clear whether metal ores were mined, smelted and alloyed in the Taklamakan or whether the people traded in raw ingots from elsewhere, then cast and worked copper, bronze and later iron themselves. They certainly knew how to work metals with great skill. There were also people skilled in working stones, both finely for jewellery and more crudely to produce whetstones. Potters produced a huge array of different vessels, from large cooking pots and jugs to very fine tiny cups and pots, some probably only used on ritual occasions. In one area, the potters had developed specially reinforced bases to their pots so they could be placed directly on a fire without cracking. You can still see charring on the pot bases today. The same people also decorated their pots with elegant designs in white and red.

Throughout the region, people had learnt to compress sheep's wool to make felt for use as blankets and padding for saddles, but above all these people were superb weavers. Besides mats and little baskets, made from reeds and willow, they produced some of the finest woollen textiles ever discovered from that era. They used the natural colours of their sheep, from white through many shades of brown to black, and dyed the wool in a huge range of colours – yellow, red, purple, turquoise, blue, magenta and many more. They wove tartan-like patterns, checks and pin-stripes as well as plain cloth, natural and dyed. The range of different weaving techniques employed on just one baby's shawl was described by textiles expert Dr Elizabeth Barber as a 'tour de force'. These people clearly revelled in their skills with the loom.

Looking closely at these superb cloths with expert help, I began to see that there is something very deep, very magical about weaving – something supernatural which, at this stage in my research, I didn't fully understand. The spindle whorls perhaps provided the first clues. Some of these were decorated with the same whirling cloud or wave-like patterns that we had seen on the comb. Spinning the whorl round and round creates a thread, a fine strong line from a mass of loose fluffiness. Crossing these fine strong lines together creates a pattern, a web. It is almost as if the texture of life itself is forming in front of your eyes, with its warp and weft. We will return to these ideas in Chapter Seven when we look at the incredible textiles produced by the mummy peoples of the coastal deserts of Peru around 2,000 years ago.

More certainly associated with the supernatural were the polished bronze mirrors found in a few of the graves at *Wupu*. One of them, clearly a cherished possession, was kept in a beautiful little leather case. In one way, these mirrors probably played the same practical role they do today. We know these people wore make-up, so vanity has been around for a long time. But throughout Central Asia, Siberia and in China itself, mirrors have played a key role in religious activities for thousands of years. In ancient China they were used to expose and scare off demons and evil spirits.

Today the shamans of Siberia still use mirrors in their rituals. It seems that ever since people first discovered their own reflections – probably initially in water – they wondered: is that really me or someone or something else? And is this image of me in another dimension, another world? Are our reflections, like our shadows, somehow evidence of another dimension to our existence?

What can be safely deduced from anthropological records is that shamans have long believed that mirrors, like lakes and pools and caves, are entry points to spirit worlds. Shamans have taught themselves to pass through the looking glass into these other worlds. There they may search for the soul of a sick or dead person and effect a cure, or comfort a bereaved family with news that the soul of the deceased has arrived safely at his or her destination.

During the period 1500 BC to about 800 BC, when the mummy people were buried in cemeteries such as *Wupu*, shamanism was the basis of religious practice throughout Central and Eastern Asia. And, as the Taklamakan lies at the very centre of the 'Old' World (the Eurasian landmass), it is hardly surprising that these first desert oasis people drew their metaphysical insights from shamanism.

Besides human remains, the early people of the Taklamakan left more than enough in their graves to give us a good picture of how they lived and from this evidence we can make some informed guesses as to how they saw life and death.

The first question to tackle is that of job specialization. It is clear from the quality of the goods produced that many of these people were fine craftsmen and women with a very wide range of skills, but were there people who specialized and made a living solely from their crafts? For me the evidence suggests probably not, because food items, farm implements and the like were found in almost all the graves. I never heard of a grave which had been 'kitted out' with only one specialist set of tools and products, which would infer that it was, for example, the grave of a potter or an ironworker. It seems more likely that almost everyone farmed and reared animals to provide the basics for subsistence, and that most people had specialist skills which they would practise during 'down time' from farming and herding. This, in turn, suggests that there would have been a lot of local trading between specialists and that the people had, therefore, developed a sense of relative values for the objects they produced. Trade and exchange was an important feature of the internal dynamics of these societies and provided a framework for the people to enter into trade relations on a much larger scale, as the cowrie seashells mentioned earlier attest. So, even in these early times – a thousand years or more before the rise of the Silk Road – these people were part of a web of trade networks that linked people throughout this region, sharing not just objects but ideas, and perhaps even languages, over thousands of miles.

Within any one group, such as the people of *Wupu*, there is little evidence of social stratification, of the emergence of a noble or royal level of society. There are no great burial chambers filled with fine objects which we would assume to be the tomb of a great chief, nobleman or king. But close scrutiny of some of the best preserved bodies does suggest that not everyone worked with their hands for a living. Graceful hands, with long carefully manicured fingernails, such as those of the beautiful woman He Dexiu unearthed, cannot be sustained if you have to grind corn, weed fields, knead bread and cut and carry firewood every day; the same can be said of the exquisitely preserved sun-man and his wife in the Urumchi museum who have delicate hands, long fingernails, and fine painted designs on their faces. Their clothes, too, are of excellent quality and their graves contained many well-made artifacts. All this suggests that these people were not ordinary workers, but people from an élite group of leaders or perhaps ritual experts. We will return to the role of such people in the next chapter when we look at the 'Ice Princess' of Siberia. For now, it is sufficient to say that there is evidence from neighbouring societies to suggest that such women may have been shamanesses who were treated with great respect by their people. The fact that women seem to be treated as men's equals in death suggests that the same would have held true in life. So, overall, this seems to have been an egalitarian society with some specialization and a lot of exchange.

One 'absence' Victor Mair pointed out to me is the almost total lack of weaponry in the graves. Some wonderful recurved bows and fine sets of arrows have been recovered, but the points on the arrows are clearly for hunting small game, not shooting people. There are almost no swords, axes, spearheads, helmets or armour in the tombs, so, unless these were objects deemed unsuitable for the journey into the afterlife, it seems that these were peaceful people with few enemies. In essence, they were traders not raiders.

Although we may now have a picture of life in the Taklamakan, the finds that the archaeologists have unearthed raise almost as many questions as they answer. The mummies of the Taklamakan date from 1800 BC to about 300 BC, but how did they get there? Where did they come from and how might they be related to the people who were then spreading into Western Europe? One piece of evidence is especially puzzling: both the tartan-like patterns, and the actual loom type and weaving techniques employed are closely related to the techniques and patterns of textiles produced by the Celts and other North-western Europeans at this time. There is little doubt once you have seen one or two mummies that these people also looked very similar to the Celtic and Germanic peoples of Europe. Although there is furious debate about the point of origin of the Indo-European peoples, the consensus is that they originated somewhere to the east of Europe and migrated westwards into Europe and south into India and Southwest Asia. But the evidence from the Taklamakan now suggests that there may have been a more generalized diaspora of these first Indo-European peoples.

A more specific mystery concerns the production of very fine textiles in this area. It is generally agreed that the climate of the oasis villages is not conducive to the production of sheep with fine wool, yet the textiles found there are of superb quality. So if the wool was not being produced locally, where was it coming from? Similarly, the massive cart-wheels and a few very large wooden bowls had been made with timbers which seemed too large to have grown in the oases.

The answers to some of these questions may lie with one unique grave in the *Wupu* cemetery. Although this did not contain a mummy, it held an array of implements and clothes which were quite different from those used and worn by the local people. There were items of saddlery, woollen clothes and unspun fine wool. Most telling was a felt hat which had a tall curved top in the shape of a cock's comb, and ear-flaps and draw-strings to secure it firmly in winter. Jeannine Davis-Kimball, an expert on the archaeology of Siberia and the steppes, immediately recognized the hat as belonging to a Saka nomad, the people who roamed the plains in those days.

It was around this time that a really major revolution swept through Central Asia: the advent of horse-riding. The horse had been domesticated around 4000 BC and used as a draught animal and source of meat and milk, but in this part of Asia it was not until around 800 BC that people first learnt to ride horses. The immediate effect was to greatly increase any traveller's range. On foot, a lightly-laden fit man, walking hard and long, can cover maybe twenty-five miles a day, but he cannot keep that up day in day out for weeks. On horseback, a rider can cover thirty miles or more without stressing the horse; and with a change of mounts to hand can cover enormous distances in short times. Once a nomadic horse culture had developed (as it did on the plains of North America nearly 2,000 years later) not just individuals but entire human groups could move around incredibly quickly. This allowed people such as the Saka of the steppes to expand their range enormously. It also gave them the speed to exploit pastures which were only useable at certain times of the year.

In the Taklamakan region, the archaeological record shows the sudden arrival of nomadic peoples in the high grasslands to the north of the desert just a few years after the advent of horse-riding, and there are still nomads there today.

We had already been impressed by the echoes of the past that we found in the oasis villages where people still farm, make food and tools in ways very similar to ancient times, so we decided it was time to try learning about the past from the present in the high pastures. Victor's friend Lü Enguo offered to guide us – a great bonus as he is one of China's leading experts on the ancient nomads of the region. Until very recently, the area he decided to take us to had been totally closed to foreigners, but the Chinese authorities reluctantly agreed to let us be some of the first outsiders ever to visit the region.

THE RIDDLE IN THE SANDS

The climb up the mountain pass was spectacular, though the road was in appalling shape. About halfway up, our bus was suddenly embroiled in a huge herd of horses, cows and yaks being driven up to the high pastures by Kazakh herders, just as their forebears had done for almost three millennia. The air rang with snorts, bellows and whinnies as the animals shied from the vehicles and the shouting herders drove them on uphill. Blasts on the horn were not enough to shift some of the animals, so I took to slapping the passenger-door with my hand. The rapid bangs terrified the yaks, and moved all but the most obstinate cattle.

After a full day's drive struggling up the mountains, the vehicles suddenly came out of a high valley into an enormous open plain. A very long way off snow-capped mountains fringed the high pastures, but the foreground was a vast green emptiness. There were a few nomads camped at the top of the valley, but we could see that the grass at this entry-point to the pastures had already been grazed low by earlier arrivals in the spring. Climbing down from the bus after an hour of bumping over a road made more of potholes than asphalt, we were suddenly totally enveloped in silence. Nothing except the faintest murmuring of a small brook stirred up there. There was no birdsong, no insects, no breeze – nothing. I had only ever heard a silence like this when I was with the Tuareg in the Sahara. It is at once deeply calming and slightly alarming to ears which are accustomed to filtering out at least ten decibels of constant background noise. It was cold, too, even in mid-June. From about October until May the passes are blocked by snow and temperatures can drop to -50C. Bumping on, we eventually reached a crumbling government out-post where we were to stay the night: filthy rooms, dodgy food, suspect laundry and antique rusted plumbing – par for the course in rural Xinjiang.

Early next morning we set out off-road over the plains to visit the nomad camps. This part of the high pastures is occupied by Mongols who probably overran it during the time of Genghis Khan and opted to stay there. Though ethnically distinct from the ancient nomads, we could soon see that their adaptation to the environment is almost identical to the earlier people. They live in round felt tents known as *yurts*. The felt is hung on a wooden lattice-work with a conical roof and the tent has flaps which can be raised or lowered to regulate the temperature inside, like wigwams. These ingenious structures provide spacious weatherproof houses, yet they can be dismantled and moved in minutes on the back of a camel, horse or in a cart. The entire structure is held together with incredibly strong spun or braided woollen ropes, identical to the ones we had seen in the 3,000-year-old-graves at *Wupu*. A local woman showed us how to make them. Taking a handful of raw wool, she twirled it along her thigh a couple of times, doubled it and twirled it again. Almost instantly she had a piece of cord that was strong enough to tether a horse or fix a set of tent-poles on to the back of a horse or camel.

Lü Enguo had already shown us some amazingly well preserved saddles, bridles and saddle ropes and, although the construction of the saddle was different (the Mongols use a wooden saddle frame whereas the ancient saddle was just stuffed leather padding), there were numerous similarities between ancient and modern. My eye was caught by the near-identical bone toggles at the back of the saddles used to attach blankets or other travelling gear. Once again, we were impressed by the extraordinary continuity between the ancient and modern up there in the high pastures.

But what impressed us most was the sheer size of the grasslands. They stretched for hundreds of kilometres within the mountains. Because of the severity of the winters and the extremely rapid changes in the seasons, this vast area could not have been inhabited until people had learnt to ride horses. Chatting with the nomads, we soon learnt that they had special pastures for each of the four seasons and that they had to move within each season, too. The distances involved could not have been managed on foot. Even when mounted, the nomads had to winter their animals on the edge of the desert, as they still do today.

There can be no doubt that the advent of horse-riding gave people access to vast swathes of land that they had never been able to use before. Furthermore, I had learnt while filming in the US Rocky Mountains that high pasture is much more nutritious than lowland grass. Presumably the greater strength of the sun in the rarefied air increases photosynthesis which, in turn, gives the grass greater nutritional value. The nomads' animals, especially their hardy little horses, were in superb condition, sleek and fat from the mountain grasses. One afternoon we stumbled across a group of herders shearing their sheep and could see that their animals had fine thick coats.

Living from the products of herding alone presents difficulties, however. An unbalanced diet, consisting solely of meat and dairy products, can lead to nutritional problems. The nomads we met all ate a lot of bread with their cheese and meat. They bought flour when they sold their animals and wool, a pattern which the archaeological record shows to have existed since nomads first penetrated these lush high pastures.

So who were the early people who mounted their horses and drove their animals to the high pastures? Were they outsiders who came in from the Steppes, or did some of the villagers from the desert oases change their lifestyle and take to tents and the way of the wanderer? This mystery remains unsolved. Searching for clues, Lü Enguo suggested we make two further visits to archaeological sites. The first was to a nomad cemetery called Charwigal that he had excavated some years ago. It lay at the foot of the mountains, at the point where two major trails led from the desert directly up to the high pastures. Immediately to the south was a small oasis with a plentiful and permanent water supply, the site of the nomads' winter quarters.

IN SEARCH OF THE IMMORTALS

A bone-jarring ten-hour bus ride down the mountains brought us to the site around 8 p.m. Back in the desert, the landscape was suddenly all browns and greys again. A heavy dust permeated the late evening light, making it soft and ghostly. The land was strewn with large stones worn smooth in the course of their watery passage from the mountains to the desert floor. The nomads had used these to line their circular burial pits and capped the tombs with larger flat slabs. The pits were much larger than the ones we had seen at *Wupu* and Lü explained that many had been multi-occupied. He had found up to fifteen skeletons in the largest tombs, which he took to be family vaults. There were hundreds of tombs arranged in rows and many of them had an interesting feature: beside the main tomb there was a much smaller chamber, maybe half a metre across and a metre deep. In most of these he found one or more horses' skulls. It seems the nomads sacrificed the animal when its owner died, perhaps to provide transport for their journey into the afterworld.

The second site Lü took us to was very different. At the head of a lush green valley in a lower part of the 'Celestial Mountains' there is a spectacular cliff face fifty or more metres high. Erosion has etched exotic patterns into its surface, giving it the look of an elaborate temple. At its base there is an overhang creating a large rock shelter and on this smooth rock face is an array of bas-relief carved figures of women, men, children and animals. The figures were highly stylized and there were traces of red and white paint on some of them, suggesting that they were probably decorated when they were first made, around 1000 BC. The female figures were all given tiny wasp-like waists and most seem to be wearing hats with twin feathers pointing upwards. Their arms are held out horizontally in line with their shoulders, one forearm and hand pointing upwards, the other down – almost certainly a dancing posture. Victor was amazed to see these figures. He had recently come across near-identical images on pottery excavated in Bulgaria and the Ukraine, thousands of kilometres to the west of the 'Celestial Mountains', dating from about 2000 BC.

There are fewer images of men, but almost all of these display enormous erect penises, more like a stallion's than a man's. One such member points directly at a long row of children, making the association of the site with fertility rituals virtually certain. We were looking at some of the earliest and most explicit erotic art I had ever seen.

Most of the figures are about a metre and a half tall, near life-size, and a few of the women are depicted horizontally, as if lying down or having fallen to the ground. This suggested to Jeannine that the women would dance themselves into a frenzy then fall to the ground entranced, as still happens today in many of the seances of shamanic and ecstatic religions.

The faces of the figures, stylized though they are, have distinct characteristics. They are oval-shaped with long straight noses, almond-shaped eyes and quite heavy eyebrow ridges. We all felt that they were drawn from Caucasian sources, not Mongoloid stock. So these early nomads were probably European-type people too, like their neighbours in the oases below.

Besides the people there is a wonderful depiction of two stallions rearing up face to face, their forelegs locked in battle, doubtless competing for mating rights. This is a well-known ancient Indo-European motif. Another horse-shaped animal, which Lü Enguo took to be a tiger, has been marked with stripes all over its body. An even more enigmatic figure seems to have a female human body with a head like a monkey, with large ears and nostrils.

Lü Enguo had excavated the base of the site, but it had yielded almost nothing. So it was probably not a habitation site but a special holy place to be visited perhaps in midsummer, to dance, to make love and ensure the vitality and recreation of people and animals.

Looking out over the lush green hills, the breeze carrying the tinkle of cowbells and the jangle of harnesses from the Kazakh herders camped below us, it was easy to slip backwards in time. 'It's easy to feel the spirit, the potency of this place,' Lü Enguo murmured. 'You can see why they would have wanted to come up here – it all feels so alive.'

It was true – especially for us after weeks of tracing the shadows of life through the dusty barren wastes of desert cemeteries and dark museums. Standing there, witnessing these loin-stirring scenes of life, conception and creation, was deeply invigorating.

The road back to Urumchi passed through stunningly beautiful country, the scattering of hills in all shades of pink, yellow, orange and green. I remember a shimmering lake with water of light grey-green. But most of all I recall the dust and the potholes. There were more holes than surface on that road and it took nearly five hours to complete the 120 or so kilometres back.

As we bumped and lurched, I tried to map out exactly where we had got to in our explorations. We knew that the first mummies were of people who lived as farmers in the oases of the Taklamakan; that even from the earliest days these people seem to have had some contact with outsiders; we knew that a thousand years or so after their first appearance in the archaeological record, a new *modus vivendi* appeared and mounted nomads herded their animals in the high pastures immediately to the north of the desert in the Tien Shan mountains. We did not know if these people were oasis farmers who opted to change their lifestyle to become nomads after the advent of horse-riding, or if they were outsiders who moved into the area from the Steppes.

Either way, both groups, it seems, were in contact from the earliest times; they traded with each other, maybe intermarried. There's no evidence of conflict between the two groups and both were probably ethnically Caucasian, though a note of caution should be added here. Classifying people ethnically from skeletons alone is neither easy nor certain. A leading geneticist has recently pointed out that there is often more genetic difference between two very different members of the same ethnic group than there is between similar members of two apparently distinct groups: two very different Caucasians may have less in common genetically than a Caucasian and a Mongolian. This whole question of racial or ethnic origins and identity remains a hotbed of scientific dispute.

Chinese archaeologists have put a lot of work into trying to determine the ethnicity of the peoples of those times and they consider most inhabitants to be Caucasian or mixed Caucasian-Mongolian. What seems most likely is that, while the core of the desert farmer/nomad herder population was Caucasian, intermarriage both to the west and the east laid the foundations for the ethnically-mixed populations who still inhabit the area today.

The beginnings of this ethnic admixture roughly coincide with the dawn of written history. Around 500 BC, peoples of the east and west started to write. Herodotus, the Greek historian renowned as 'father of history, father of lies', turned his attention to Central Asia and at the same time the first reports of the 'barbarians of the west' began to appear in Chinese annals. This is Victor's specialist area and he read me a description of the people of the region, referring to about the third century BC: 'They lived in tents. They followed the grasses and the waters. They had considerable knowledge of agriculture. They owned cattle, horses, camels, sheep and goats. They were proficient with bows and arrows.'

So it seems from this source that the ways of life of the two peoples were beginning to blend together, perhaps with even more interaction and intermarriage between the two groups. 'Do you want to see what these guys were really like?' Victor asked me in a whisper. 'Well, maybe you can – Lü has got about five of them locked up in his store-room at the Institute. The only outsider he's let see them is me and they're amazing.

IN SEARCH OF THE IMMORTALS

I'll see what I can do.' Moving to the back of the bus, he lowered himself into the seat next to Lü's and began a whispered conspiratorial conversation. This wasn't really necessary as they were the only two people on the bus who could speak Mandarin.

A couple of days later we were at the Institute and Lü decided to show us the mummies. They were indeed amazing. Although not quite as well preserved as the people from Zagunluq, they were still very impressive. One of them, a woman, wore an enormous conical hat, maybe seventy centimetres long. She was dressed in furs and wool, and wore a sort of hair-net. Some of the men seemed to have buckskin-type clothes. Perhaps most extraordinary of all, one man had two large cuts on his chest which had been sewn up with horse-hair sutures. All around the bodies were funerary goods and offerings. As at *Wupu*, there were little wooden bowls filled with a variety of grains, seeds and nuts. There was also jewellery and other personal items, a magnificent recurved bow, a set of hunting arrows and a superb suede bow-case cum quiver to house them.

Once again, there is evidence from the goods found in the graves that these people were also long-distance traders, though they probably did not know that at the far ends of their trade links things were changing very fast. By 300 BC, at the western end of the Eurasian landmass, classical civilization was emerging all round the shores of the Mediterranean, growing, pushing ever outwards. To the east, China was reaching the end of the 'Warring States' period, where rival kingdoms ceased fighting and a single unified empire was born. They, too, were bent on exploration and expansion. At around the same time the Lord Gautama Buddha was preaching in India, his messages beginning to slip out of the sub-continent along the tracks and trails leading to Central Asia. And, standing at the crossroads of these great interflows, at the heart of Asia, was the Taklamakan desert and the people whose mummified bodies we were now looking at.

THE RIDDLE IN THE SANDS

Just eighty kilometres from the place where Lü found these bodies, a great city was being born. At that time there was probably only a large village at Jiaohe, a spectacular site overlooking a deep and fertile river valley right by the modern city of Turfan. By 100 BC there were 600 houses there, by 200 AD there were 1,500 houses. The Chinese arrived around 350 AD and the city prospered as the camel caravans plied the great Silk Road, bearing silk from China to Europe, and returning with silver from Rome. Jiaohe was not just a trade post, it was a great centre for scholarship and learning where people from all over the Old World met and shared ideas, knowledge and technology. It flourished for more than 1,000 years, until it was put to the torch by the mighty Genghis Khan, and trade and travel between east and west became principally maritime.

But who built and populated these great cities and temple complexes which sprung up along the Silk Road? Victor is convinced that the descendants of the mummy people were the creators of these extraordinary structures. That they had suddenly been caught up in the vortex of new ideas and technologies flooding through the area is certain, and the most recent Sino-Japanese excavations in the Taklamakan are revealing Caucasian-type mummies dressed in Chinese silk clothes, accompanied by lacquer-ware and Chinese coins – all clear evidence of Chinese influence.

The Chinese, however, were not the only people to make their way there. To get a first-hand look at the people who lived in this area at the time of the Silk Road, we decided to visit a famous temple complex called 'The Cave of the Thousand Buddhas' at Kizil – a slight misnomer as there are, in fact, hundreds of distinct caves, all decorated inside with images of the many incarnations of the Buddha. The scenes depicted on the walls are not only drawn from Buddhist texts. The artists also found inspiration in the great diversity of peoples who passed through the temple complex. The caves date from about 200–700 AD, providing a spectacular visual record of the peoples of those times. Here there are hunting scenes using identical recurved bows to the one that Lü Enguo found in a mummy grave; pictures of mounted warriors carrying long swords and bow cases, like the one we examined in Lü's office; and some tall conical hats like the one Lü's mummified lady wore in her tomb. So it is clear that warrior nomads, such as the Saka and Scythians, visited this region. There were also thousands of faces which scholars of classical Indian and oriental art would be familiar with – the artistic style typical of the early Buddhist tradition. To my eye, some of these figures were clearly Mongoloid, while others seem to represent a mixture of Oriental and Indian features. Perhaps more surprising there are also distinctly European faces which seem to be drawn in the style of classical Greece or Rome. Their presence seemed more plausible when our Chinese hosts explained that a delegation from the Roman Empire had passed through here on their way to try to reach the Chinese capital. The last group we saw were essentially Persians. Their clothes – kaftans, baggy britches and boots or sandals – are very distinctive, and many of them had red beards and brown or fair hair. This startled me at first because, thinking of contemporary Iranians, my mind's eye sees black hair and bushy black beards. But the word Iran derives from Aryan (meaning 'noble') and it is known that in those times Iranians had much more European-like appearances than they do today.

However, the people we were seeking were not the exotic strangers who had passed through the temple, but the local people who had built and maintained it. When a monk wanted to have a cave made and decorated, it seems he would seek the sponsorship of local dignitaries. As a mark of respect, he would also in some cases instruct the artist to paint likenesses of the sponsors at worship in a specified position in the cave, usually on the sides of a narrow passage at the back. At least one of these sets of pictures has survived to the present, but the cave which houses it is about 6 metres above the ground, accessible only by scrambling up the cliff face then up an ancient rickety ladder. Thereafter, a very narrow ledge traverses the cliff face which can only be crossed by hugging the cliff.

In this remote and unrestored cave there are images of the four sponsors – local people. Their clothing was distinctly Iranian in style, with patterns on their kaftans which Victor identified as 'Pearl Roundel'. Their hairstyle was very specific, centre-parted with little coifs over each side of the forehead, suggesting it might have been curly. All four had neatly-kept beards. Three had red hair, the fourth was fair. They all had tika marks – attesting to their devoutness – in the centre of their foreheads, and their faces, although damaged by non-Buddhist zealots, had that serene quality so often found in sacred Buddhist art. Despite this oriental gloss, it was obvious to us that these people were ethnically Caucasoid.

It was the beauty of the artwork in places like the 'Cave of the Thousand Buddhas' which first attracted explorers such as Aurel Stein and Sven Hedin to the Taklamakan at the turn of this century and the huge empty spaces on the walls of many caves were mute testament to their work. Excavating at various sites along the Silk Road, Stein also unearthed huge collections of scripts, some written on thin wooden boards. Although most were in known languages, one of them was very peculiar. The writing was a form of Kharoshti, one of the known Indian scripts, but the letters did not add up to words in any of the Indian languages. However, because the script was known it didn't take scholars long to decipher the new language. They called it Tocharian and it is now thought to be the language of the 'sponsors' we were looking at on the cave walls. It came as little surprise that it is an Indo-European language, though it does have some strange characteristics. It seems that, overall, it is more closely related to the languages of Western Europe than it is to neighbouring Indo-European languages such as Sanskrit and Iranian.

So, if these descendants of the mummy people spoke a variant of Indo-European that was closely linked to Western Europe, does this mean that the mummy people originated in Europe and migrated thousands of miles to the Taklamakan? Not only their language, but their physical appearance, weaving techniques and designs, and many other aspects of their material culture – even the strange dancing women on the rock face – do seem to tie them in closely to Europe, but that doesn't necessarily mean that they came from there.

Another explanation for these curious links lies in the history of Indo-European language and its speakers. There is a furious debate in archaeology and linguistics as to the origin point of this phenomenally successful language family. According to one school, the first Indo-Europeans originated around eastern Anatolia, in what is now Turkey and Georgia. Others trace the homeland to the northeast of that point, in the Caucasus or on the Pontic Steppes between the Black Sea and the Caspian. Either way, no one is proposing that the Indo-European homeland was as far east as the Taklamakan. So a plausible explanation for the Tocharian language enigma is that when the Indo-European diaspora began and the people spread out from their point of origin, most went west, towards and into Europe. But others, the ancestors of the Tocharians, went east, making their way eventually into the oases of the Taklamakan. There they survived in relative isolation until the upheavals of first horse-riding then the Silk Road transformed their lives, though not their language, for ever.

As the archaeological record stands at the moment it seems that, in most areas of the Taklamakan, no mummified bodies have been found after about 200 BC, though in 1996 archaeologists working in the south and east of the desert found mummies with Caucasoid physical characteristics who were dressed in Chinese embroidered silk clothing. These seem to date to 100–200 AD, so we do not really know yet when the mummy record ceases. One possibility is that with the rise of the Silk Road and the wholesale adoption of Buddhism in the region, funerary practices may have changed, with cremation replacing burial of the dead. There is also evidence to support the view that from the last centuries BC there was a steady encroachment of ethnically Mongoloid peoples pushing into this area from the east. They may have displaced the original Caucasoid peoples or absorbed them through inter-marriage or both. A cemetery near Turfan, dating from the sixth to ninth centuries AD, has yielded hundreds of naturally mummified corpses. They are all Mongoloid.

The key question that remains is, did the Caucasoid funerary tradition of preserving their dead come to an end or was there no tradition in the first place? Was the mummification accidental rather than intentional? For example, the Alpine Ice Man's bodily preservation (see Appendix) was entirely due to the right natural conditions. The same could have been the case in the Taklamakan where none of the bodies had been eviscerated, nor had incisions been made to pad parts of the body to retain the appearance of 'living'. Some Chinese archaeologists do claim to have found signs of a fatty substance, containing animal proteins, spread on the skin of some of the Taklamakan mummies, but its purpose is not certain. So, technically, these are 'natural' mummies. In my view, however, that does not necessarily mean that the people were unaware that the bodies of their deceased relatives would survive. The graves in this area are shallow and easy to open, and in neighbouring nomad cemeteries some vaults were multi-occupied. The fact that many of the bodies were laid to rest with straps round their heads to prevent the mouth opening and the tongue protruding post-mortem, shows that these people were aware of what happens to a body after death. Similarly, the placing of wool plugs in the nostrils would probably have been to prevent cranial fluids flowing over the face and disfiguring it. The evidence from the Taklamakan then suggests that it would be over-simplistic to try to label the mummification processes as either 'natural' or 'artificial'. Rather, the picture building up in my mind is of a variety of subtly different approaches to the preservation of the dead.

I believe that the people of this region were well aware that their ancestors' bodies would survive underground and that they took steps to see that they were laid to rest with their future comfort assured. They didn't develop more elaborate mummification techniques because they didn't need to. These are certainly the best preserved mummies discovered anywhere in the world – and Victor is not exaggerating when he says they look as if they have been buried for only a week or less.

What the people actually felt about their preserved ancestors and how the existence of the mummies affected their afterlife beliefs we will probably never know because there are no written records. The huge array of grave goods recovered from their tombs, however, does give some clues as to how they felt about the afterlife. First, at least up until the arrival of Buddhism in the region, they seem to have adhered to the shamanic belief system so widespread throughout this part of Asia. In essence, this posits the existence of other worlds, or at least other dimensions to the world of the senses. The spirit or soul may travel to these worlds in life and will certainly travel there in death. So there is a continuity and linkage between the worlds of the living and the worlds of the dead. Second, the huge quantity and variety of ordinary goods found with the mummies suggests that these people saw afterlife in the next world as largely an extension of life as it was lived in the desert oases. They equipped the dead with the essentials for a life extended beyond death, rather than preparing them, say, to meet some supreme being or to enter heaven or hell.

THE RIDDLE IN THE SANDS

As yet no settlement sites of these ancient villagers have been found or excavated, but I strongly suspect that they lived in houses made with mud bricks, just as they lined their tombs with bricks. Similarly, they would have supported the roofs of their houses with wooden beams, just as the tombs are roofed. So the tomb is a miniature house, a tiny world for the dead to rest in. Although we do not yet have proof of these points, the fact that today's villagers build their houses with mud bricks and roof them with hefty beams lends support to these ideas.

The fact that many of the tombs are oriented east – west suggests that, like many other ancient cultures, the peoples of the Taklamakan felt deeply about the sun. The sun symbols on the temples of the Urumchi 'sun-man' bear further witness to this notion. However at the very ancient graveyard in Loulan, the tombs are different. There, great concentric circles of logs have been set into the sand, with the graves at their centre. Could these, too, be sun symbols? With such scant written testimony we can only speculate, but it does seem likely that these people equated the daily rhythms of the rising and setting of the sun with the human cycles of birth, life, death and, perhaps, rebirth. This notion, as we will see throughout this book, is extremely ancient and widespread.

The journey to the Taklamakan and the Tien Shan was hard and wearisome, but it was also deeply revealing. We had travelled back in time to the very points where archaeology and history first meet and embrace, to times where you have to use your own intuitions to seek grains of truth in a patchy and sometimes inconsistent factual record. And even when documents do exist, they are often written from afar and based on hearsay. They may also carry political slants which suit the interests of the parties they are written for, regardless of the observed truth. Piecing together this sort of jigsaw puzzle is fascinating and I found myself increasingly drawn to this era, where the dawn of history lies half-lost in the mists of time.

IN SEARCH OF THE IMMORTALS

〰

The first and most important lesson I had learned on this trip was that the people of these ancient times were much more connected to one another than I had ever imagined. We tend to equate remoteness with isolation, especially in the times before ancient civilizations forged major means of communication such as the Silk Road. Yet here, 2,000 miles away from the sea, the people had cowrie shells 1,000 years before the Silk Road came to be.

Admittedly cowries, with their vulva-like open jaws, have inspired special fascination in many cultures all over the world — and may have been the first form of money — but the shells we saw must have passed along chains of human hands for thousands of miles. Where objects travel, so do ideas; where languages meet, there is overlap and communication is possible. So, even thousands of years ago, the human world was tightly woven with webs of trade and exchange of objects, ideas and knowledge.

Another deceptively simple point became clear to me on the trip to the Taklamakan: the chances of any human soft tissue surviving intact for thousands of years are very slim, even in near-ideal conditions. Only one body in six survived in *Wupu* cemetery and so far the Chinese have only found about 100 mummies from the hundreds of thousands of people who must have died in that desert over the millennia.

Looking at a map of the old world and mentally picturing the points where mummies have survived, I saw just a few pinpricks spread out over the vast empty space — Northwest Europe, the Canary Islands, Egypt, the Taklamakan, Siberia. But did that mean that these were the only peoples who practised mummification? Or does it mean that these are the only places where mummies have actually survived down to the present? In South America I actually witnessed the destruction of mummies which had survived for 10,000 years before freak flooding swept them away in 1998. History records the near-total destruction of the mummies of the ancient Canary Islands and of the Inca Empire at the hands of the Spanish. So both natural conditions and human intervention can destroy in moments bodies that have been perfectly preserved for thousands of years.

Recalling the huge threads of human communication which wove their way across the face of the ancient world, I began to wonder if the few scattered dots of known mummy-makers are, in fact, just the tips of many icebergs. Could the knowledge and practice of mummification have been even more widespread than we are at present aware? With this thought in mind, I determined to start tracing links, looking for connections, filling in the gaps.

The most obvious next port of call was a few hundred miles to the northeast of the Taklamakan border, across the Altai Mountains in what is now southwest Siberia. Around 500 BC a people lived there who loved to ride, hunt, tend their herds and to immortalize their ancestors. But, unlike the mummy people of the Taklamakan, these people were not cut off or isolated. They were part of a confederation of people which stretched right into the heart of Europe. And they all made mummies.

Chapter 2

Siberia
ice mummies
of the nomads

Getting from Europe to Xinjiang province in western China is one of those nightmare journeys you wish you never had to make. You fly from one side of the world to the other, then half way back again – sixteen hours or so to Beijing, then six hours back to Urumchi. I first made the trip in February 1988. I was heading for the Altai Mountains on the Russian border to see what life was like for the Kazakh nomads in the dead of winter.

A local flight took us to Altai city, a small town still closed to foreigners. Because our visit was under the auspices of the UN World Food Programme, a major reception had been arranged for us by the town council. They were nearly all Han Chinese from eastern and central China, as were our minders throughout the visit. The high point of our reception was to be a formal dance in the town hall. I am no great shakes at ballroom dancing at the best of times, let alone on the wrong end of two days of air travel, but our minders stressed that this event was being held in our honour and it would be bad form not to show up.

Copious supplies of warm beer flowed round our table as the band struck up the first fox-trot. Four young women strode over to our table, smiled, bowed, then politely but firmly hauled us on to the dancefloor. The Kazakh girl who picked me wore high shiny leather boots, a thick woollen jersey and a scarf over her hair. Her face was oval-shaped, her eyes hazel-coloured and her nose was long and narrow. Only her straight shiny hair looked Chinese. Her hands felt strong but they were not calloused by long hours of manual work. She guided me, stumbling, round the dance floor with precision and authority, just as men are meant to in ballroom dancing. I had read somewhere that Herodotus got his notion of the 'Amazons' from the women of Central Asia and I was beginning to see why.

Next morning, we loaded up a convoy of jeeps and set off for a remote Kazakh winter camp where the Green Gobi Desert butts up to the foothills of the Altai Mountains. With a snow-plough in front for the last thirty miles, we made it to the village just before dark. It was bitterly cold, around -15C. As we got out of the jeeps, several men on horseback rode over shouting greetings and waving their arms. They looked very fat but in fact they were wearing thick felt leggings, heavy padded coats and beautiful fox-fur hats tied securely under their chins. The horses were small and shaggy, but they looked tough and moved well.

Ushered inside our most senior host Ablaikhan's mud-plastered house with a flat roof, we hastily stripped off several layers of excess clothing. The room had two low platforms on either side covered in embroidered carpets, cushions and bed-rolls, and elaborate hangings adorned the wall space. One small window let in a little light, and in the centre of the room a metal stove provided ample heat. For an hour after we arrived, a steady stream of people passed through to greet us and chat. The men were big and powerful, even after their felts were off. They spoke loudly and directly, willing us to understand their Turkic dialect. The women, too, were forthright, staring us directly in the eyes and wringing our hands firmly. They seemed pleased and amused by these strange winter visitors.

It was impossible not to be struck by the contrast between our Kazakh hosts and the Han Chinese officials who accompanied and interpreted for us. The Han were always quiet and obsequious, and you could never tell what they were thinking or plotting. The Kazakhs seemed to wear their feelings on their faces and expressed them through their bodies with total openness. I could easily see that the Han thought this crude house and these vulgar people barely tolerable. The Kazakhs, for their part, seemed to treat the Han with a sort of jovial contempt.

As the night set in, about a dozen men gathered in the room and conversation got under way. The Chinese produced some *maotai* – rice spirit – which was greeted with whistles of delight by our hosts. The conversation swung almost at once to the Kazakhs' favourite topic – horses. All evening we talked horses. What made a good one, what colours were best, the difference between race-horses and work-horses, and so on. At one point I asked how they broke their horses, and received only quizzical looks in reply. So I rephrased the question: 'How do you get a horse used to the saddle?' Their reply revealed that they considered the idea of breaking a horse totally unnecessary. 'Just keep the young horse near to you for a few weeks,' they said; 'feed it, talk to it. After a while, put a blanket on its back, then a bit later a saddle. They'll soon let you climb up on them after that.' This was obviously true. I spent the next few days with their horses and, compared to animals 'broken' in the Western style, I found them wonderfully calm and easy to handle.

At around midnight, the women brought in a huge cauldron of boiled mutton. A sheep had been slaughtered in our honour. We ate the unsalted meat with hard dough bread which had been made months before and stored throughout the winter in underground pits. A few bits of wild onion and garlic flavoured the broth. Salty tea helped to wash down the greasy meat and the dry bread. It all sat rather uneasily on the copious doses of *maotai*.

The next day, Ablaikhan introduced us to his pride and joy – a magnificent eagle perched on his arm. It was hooded and periodically let out piercing shrieks. Its colouring was almost identical to the golden eagles seen in Scotland, but I believe it was a Steppe eagle. Ablaikhan put the bird on a perch and took off its green velvet hood. Its eyes were fiercer than any I had ever seen before – or since. Pitiless, merciless, defiant eyes. Ablaikhan, a man of maybe sixty with dark but gentle eyes and a small goatee beard beneath his fox-fur hat, explained that the bird was only a year old and he was training it to hunt foxes. He planned to go out the next day and invited us to join him.

Early next morning, another hunter appeared on his horse. He held a short stick in his right hand, the end propped into a notch on his saddle. Sitting on his right arm was another magnificent eagle. Ablaikhan joined him and, with his hooded bird resting on his padded arm, we set off. An hour or so from the village, we met up with two men who had an extremely angry desert fox on a chain. This was to be a training exercise for Ablaikhan's eagle, so, when the order was given, the men released the fox which scampered away through the snow. Lifting the hood from his eagle, Ablaikhan urged his horse forward and launched the bird into the sky. It circled a couple of times, saw the fox and came at it in a low swoop. As it was about to strike, the fox turned on it, trying to bite the bird and box it away with its front paws. The young eagle landed, looked momentarily perplexed, then with a few high hops above the fox landed on top of it, pinning the creature to the snow. Victorious, the eagle spread its wings, held the fox firmly down and screamed in defiance. By then we had dismounted. I looked at the eagle's eyes and saw again that steel-cold merciless glare – the perfect look of the hunter, the bringer of death to the prey, the transformer of life into sustenance. Ablaikhan placed his foot on the fox, hooded the eagle, coaxed it up on to his arm and passed it to the other hunter. Then he picked up the fox by its back legs. To my surprise it was still alive, snapping and snarling. Swinging it in a full circle, Ablaikhan crashed its skull down on to the frozen ground, killing it instantly. He then tied it behind his saddle, remounted and took his eagle back from his friend. The two of them rode slowly back to the village, bearing a fresh pelt for a fine new hat and meat for their birds' dinner.

I came back to visit Ablaikhan and his family the following June. By then they had migrated high into the Altai Mountains with their herds, to wonderfully lush mountain pastures. They were living in a fine yurt. The air was wonderfully fresh and clean, all the animals looked fat and the people happy and well. We had come to attend a wedding ceremony with more than 600 guests, all of them mounted. There were long-distance horse races, bouts of wrestling and a game which is the ancestor of polo. In this, two mounted teams do battle, a sort of mounted wrestling, to gain possession of a headless sheep. After two days of partying, the guests returned to their camps scattered throughout the mountains.

Though harsh in the winter, the way of life of these mounted nomads seemed wonderful to me. What I did not know then was that this very same lifestyle had persisted almost unchanged for nearly 3,000 years. All the things I was seeing and doing could just as easily have taken place around 400 BC, with one important exception. While today's Kazakhs follow Islamic tradition and bury their dead in cemeteries, two and a half millennia ago the people of the Altai Mountains mummified their dead leaders and placed the bodies in the centre of huge ceremonial mounds. Permafrost enveloped them and they became ice mummies.

The Russian Czar Peter the Great had a passion for the artwork buried in these ancient tombs and ordered many funeral mounds, *kurgans*, to be opened and the contents sent to him in St Petersburg. Today the Hermitage there, retains his collection, although it is not on display.

Looting of the huge tombs continued over the centuries, but it was not until the 1920s that a trained professional began to investigate them. Sergei Rudenko started out as an ethnologist and spent many months living with and studying the Kazakhs before he became drawn to the great funerary mounds scattered throughout their territory. He always maintained that his intimacy with contemporary Kazakh lifestyle was of immeasurable help when it came to interpreting the contents of the ancient *kurgans* he excavated.

As the only means of travel in Siberia at the turn of the century was by horse, Rudenko spent much of his life mounted, a great advantage when it came to excavating the graves of the nomads, as they sent their dead nobles into the afterlife with plenty of steeds to carry them there, and Rudenko was able to distinguish their age, sex, usage, and so on. The valley where Rudenko did most of his excavations was called Pazyryk, and that is the name he gave to the ancient peoples who lived and died there around 400 BC. His finds were absolutely astounding. Even though all the tombs he opened had been robbed, he uncovered a culture whose artistic achievements rival any of the great ancient civilizations which were beginning to flourish at that time. Perhaps because they never became literate and their heyday slipped past before they were described by the earliest chroniclers, the richness of Pazyryk culture was almost totally ignored by both experts and the broader public until a few years ago.

In 1990 a Russian archaeologist, Natalya Polosmak, began new excavations in the Pazyryk region – this time in a valley called 'The Pastures of Heaven'. Her first three seasons yielded little to compare with Rudenko's finds, but in July 1993 she found an undisturbed tomb. At its heart lay the totally frozen body of a young woman. Now famous, this woman is known as the 'Ice Princess'. Two years later, the team found the frozen body of a young man, apparently killed in battle by a huge blow to the stomach. He is known as the 'Ice Warrior' or the 'Horseman'.

The graves, mummies and the funerary customs of the Pazyryk are now well documented. One fact stands out starkly about these remote Siberians: they and their people were *not* isolated. They saw themselves as part of an extensive network of like-minded peoples, mounted nomad-herders and warriors whose domains stretched from the Black Sea in what is now Romania, as far as the frontiers of the Chinese empire to the east, and quite probably as far as the Bering Sea, the very ends of Asia, in the northeast.

Pazyryk art also shows very direct connections with worlds which lie way beyond the bounds of their mounted nomad neighbours. So it is important to understand the networks of communication which linked the peoples of the Old World around 400 BC.

In Chapter One we saw how these nomads seem to have moved into grazing lands in the mountains to the north of the Taklamakan shortly after horse-riding spread to this region, around 800 BC. They were in contact with the farmers of the desert oases in Central Asia and very probably traded their meat, dairy products and wool for agricultural products. They were also entering into the phase characterized as 'trade or raid' with the Chinese. Some of the nomad tribes were highly organized militarily and well capable of mauling settled Chinese communities if provoked. China itself, was divided into three rival kingdoms, but there were already many urban centres and the people could write and make records of their neighbours to the west and north. In this area the nomads are referred to by Western scholars as Saka or Sarmatians. Contact with China, though volatile, centred around trade though there were also exchanges of women as brides and for the paying of tribute. Exchanges went both ways; that is, the Chinese sometimes gave brides to the nomads and vice versa. They also made lavish presents to the nomads, who particularly loved silk. The Chinese, in turn, greatly coveted the fine horses reared by some of the nomad tribes.

To the south and southwest, the nomads came directly into contact with the peoples of what are now Iran and Iraq. The Persians and Babylonians, themselves highly organized urban societies, were in direct contact with ancient Egypt and with the peoples of India, and Persian influence seems to have been especially strong on the nomads' art traditions. To the west, the nomads were known collectively as the Scythians. By the fifth century BC their westernmost outposts were directly in contact with the Greeks, who had pushed up the Black Sea from the Aegean and made colonies there.

Herodotus, the Greeks' most famous chronicler, was born around 490 BC and provides us with some of the first written accounts of the Scythians, whom he claims to have visited around 460 BC. There are always doubts about the credibility of Herodotus's observations because he clearly enjoys reporting gossip and hearsay, exaggeration and innuendo as bald fact. But in his writings on the Scythians he does on the whole seem to be reliable. Archaeological finds have borne out many of his descriptions and some passages correlate quite closely with Chinese records from the same period.

When describing things like one-eyed peoples or group-sex sessions, Herodotus often covered himself by making remarks, such as 'I do not believe this tale; but all the same they tell it, and even swear to the truth of it'. But he was utterly forthright when describing Scythian mortuary practices:

> When a king dies they dig a great square pit, and, when it is ready they take up the corpse, which has previously been prepared in the following way: the belly is slit open, cleaned out, and filled with various aromatic substances, crushed galingale, parsley-seed and anise; it is then sewn up again and the whole body coated over in wax.

The body, according to Herodotus, was then carried in a wagon from tribe to tribe of the Scythians. As it passed, people wept, cut pieces from their own ears, shaved their heads, gashed themselves in the arms and face or drove arrow heads through their left hands. Eventually the corpse arrived at the Gerrhi, the most northerly and remote of the Scythians.

> Here the corpse is laid in the tomb on a mattress, with spears fixed in the ground on either side to support a roof of withies laid on wooden poles, while in other parts of the great square pit various members of the king's household are buried beside him: one of his concubines, his butler, his cook, his groom, his steward and his chamberlain, all of them strangled. Horses are buried too, and gold cups, and a selection of his other treasures. This ceremony over, everybody with great enthusiasm sets about raising a mound of earth, each competing with his neighbour to make it as big as possible.

A year later, according to Herodotus, another ceremony took place where fifty of the dead king's finest horses were killed and set upright on top of halved cart-wheels which had been set in the ground. Next, fifty of the king's most loyal subjects were strangled, gutted, stuffed with chaff then sewn up again. Finally, the bodies were impaled on poles and set on the backs of the sacrificed horses placed all round the outside of the tomb. Once these rituals had been attended to, the final act of mourning was a purification rite:

> They wash their heads with soap and their bodies in a vapour-bath ... On a framework of three sticks, meeting at the top, they stretch pieces of woollen cloth, taking care to get the joints as perfect as they can, and inside this tent they put a dish with red-hot stones in it ... They take some hemp seed, creep into the tent and throw the seed on the hot stones. At once it begins to smoke, giving off a vapour unsurpassed by any vapour-bath one could find in Greece. The Scythians enjoy it so much that they howl with pleasure.

IN SEARCH OF THE IMMORTALS

The places where these rituals were performed were clearly sacred for the Scythians. Having given his description of their funeral rites, Herodotus returned to his historical narrative, the account of the Persian king Darius's attempt to conquer the Scythians. Darius pursued the Scythian king Idanthrus all round Scythia, but Idanthrus refused to engage in pitched battle. Hugely frustrated, Darius eventually dispatched a rider to the Scythians asking them why they kept running away. Idanthrus's reply is revealing:

> Persian, I have never run from any man in fear; and I am not doing so now from you. There is, for me, nothing unusual in what I have been doing, it is precisely the sort of life I always lead, even in times of peace. If you want to know why I will not fight I will tell you: in our country there are no towns and no cultivated lands; fear of losing which, or seeing it ravaged, might indeed provoke us to hasty battle. If, however, you are determined upon bloodshed with the least possible delay, one thing there is for which we will fight – the tombs of our forefathers. Find those tombs, and try to wreck them, and you will soon know whether or not we are willing to stand up to you.

Here, then, is the credo of the mounted nomad, summarized so perfectly by Herodotus that he could almost have heard the Scythian king saying it. Free of the encumbrances of material life, unfettered by ties to land or buildings, the nomad is free to roam as he will. The only things he holds sacred and inviolable, which he will defend and preserve at all costs, are the tombs of his ancestors.

Herodotus claimed that his knowledge of the Scythians was first-hand, from visiting them near the Black Sea. He may have learnt about their funerary practices there, although he also implies that the royal tombs were far away to the north or east – at least in a land where the trees needed in the construction of the coffin, tomb walls and roof were plentiful. Generally, when Herodotus describes peoples, such as the Indians or the tribes of North Africa, the further his reports were from his sources the more fantastical they became. But, as already mentioned, this does not seem to be the case with his descriptions of the Scythians. Although he stated vaguely that the royal tombs were in the 'most northerly and remote of Scythian tribes', he was absolutely confident – and, as it turned out, extraordinarily accurate – in reporting the details of Scythian royal burial.

When Sergei Rudenko opened the first of the Pazyryk tombs, he knew immediately that he was looking at what Herodotus had recorded. Even though all the graves had been looted, there was no doubt that the layout and contents were almost exactly as the Greek historian had described: the tombs even contained the triangular sticks, felt covers and little bowls containing pebbles and burnt hemp seeds used in the purification rituals. The bodies of the entombed nobles had been eviscerated, embalmed and 'stuffed' in the way that he had said. Meals were set out for the deceased and many horses had been sacrificed both in the royal tombs and in adjacent chambers, in the 'afterlife stables'. Being an expert himself, Rudenko was able to identify both elderly work-horses and superb young thoroughbreds among the sacrificed animals. The tombs had, indeed, been covered over with many layers of poles, then capped with great mounds of earth and rocks in an attempt to keep looters out.

Because the bodies were left on the surface, there is no surviving evidence of the ritual killing of horses and human 'riders' a year after the king's death. However, as Herodotus was so accurate on other counts, I am inclined to take his word for this. Some of the tombs Rudenko opened also contained more than one human remain, which may infer the ritual killing and interment of a living spouse, servants and so on with the dead king.

The archaeological confirmation of Herodotus's accounts is an enormous help. It is also extremely important for understanding how widespread mummification practices were in the ancient world. That Herodotus, standing on the Black Sea just a few hundred miles north of classical Greece, could describe mummy burials which we have now found more than 2,000 miles to the east, gives the lie to the idea that there were only isolated pockets of mummy-makers scattered around the ancient world. Besides acknowledging the veracity of Herodotus's descriptions, Rudenko also claims that around 450 BC not only the Egyptians but also the Assyrians, Medes and Persians were preserving their dead, too. The very word 'mummy' comes from the ancient Persian word for pitch, an original ingredient in the embalming process. So, at that time, it seems we can say with confidence that people were mummifying their dead in Eastern Europe and North Africa, throughout Asia Minor, right across the Central Asian steppes, all around the Taklamakan desert and probably as far as the Gansu corridor (the gateway to China), and at least as far northeast as Siberia. This represents perhaps half of the entire landmass of Eurasia (see map on page 171).

The Scythians, like the Tocharians of the Taklamakan and, by 500 BC, almost all the peoples of Europe, spoke Indo-European languages. Herodotus mentioned that most Scythians lived in white felt tents (like today's *yurts*) and all were excellent horsemen and archers. He noted that one of the Scythian tribes, 'The Budini, a numerous and powerful nation, all have markedly blue-grey eyes and red hair'. He went on to describe the infamous Amazons, a distinct tribe of women-warriors who, after being defeated by the Greeks, became sexually entangled with the Scythians. After a major migration eastward, the Amazon women are said to have settled down with their Scythian husbands and became known as the Sauromatae. These people, he tells us, retained the ways of the Amazons:

> The women of the Sauromatae . . . ride to the hunt on horseback, sometimes with, sometimes without, their men, taking part in war and wearing the same sort of clothes as men . . . They have a marriage law which forbids a girl from marrying until she has killed an enemy in battle. Some of their women, unable to fulfil this condition, grow old and die unmarried.

Although this may be a bit of Herodotus hype, it is certainly endorsed by the pride, independence and superb equestrian skills of today's nomad women, as well as the tombs of several high-ranking nomadic women who were buried alone 2,500 years ago. In some Sarmatian women's tombs there were iron swords and daggers, bronze arrow heads and even whetstones to sharpen their weapons. These, surely, were the graves of women-warriors.

So Herodotus, 'father of history, father of lies', seems to have been telling a good deal of truth about the peoples of the Steppes and beyond. But this century's Russian archaeological finds paint a picture far more complex than he would have us believe. For besides the basics of the tombs, bodies and grave goods and chattels, these ancient chambers yielded up an extraordinarily complex vision of otherworlds and after-worlds presented in breathtakingly beautiful artistic forms.

The tombs themselves were made with logs, very probably in imitation of the log houses the people lived in during the winter. In the tomb 'house', the walls were adorned with felt hangings, colourfully illustrated with animals, people and exotic mystical beings – most of them combined forms of animals. The floors were covered with superbly

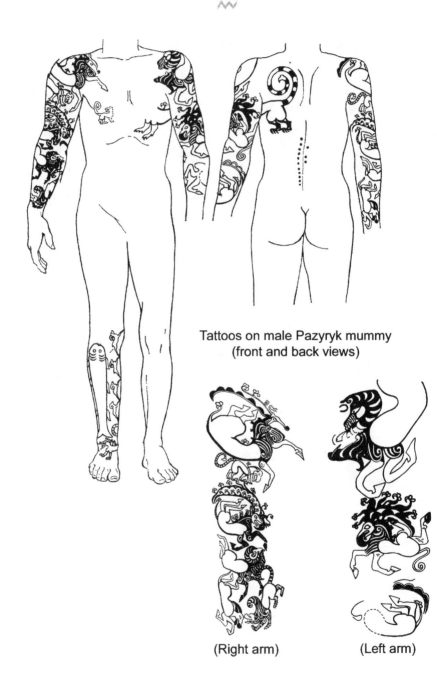

Tattoos on male Pazyryk mummy
(front and back views)

(Right arm)   (Left arm)

decorated woollen carpets. One particularly beautiful example has a deep red background with beige figures on it. Besides complex geometric patterns, a set of thirty mounted warriors ride round the four outside edges of the carpet. Each rider and horse is depicted in great detail: the rider in multi-coloured clothes, the horse's saddle-cloths and harnesses in fancy coloured trappings. They encircle twenty-four superb deer, probably elk, whose markings are highlighted with yellow and white, their horns a glowing golden hue.

Little tables with detachable legs were set on the carpet. The legs, carved as springing lions, fitted into sockets on the base of the table so that they could be dismantled easily and carried away on a horse or in a cart. On the tables were oil-lamps and wooden bowls containing meat. By the platform – in the 'bed' where the coffin lay – there were leather or fur pouches and flasks, some of them decorated with leather cut-out images of cockerels or mythical beasts locked in combat.

The bodies in the coffins also lay in their clothes – these, too, often decorated. One man's kaftan has a wonderfully elaborate set of deer's antlers sewn up each side of the back section; a woman's pink leather boots are adorned with glass beads and crystals of iron pyrites which looks like gold. Many elaborate head-dresses have also been recovered, from both male and female graves. Some are decorated with cockerels, others with abstract patterns. The Ice Princess was found with an enormous headpiece still in place. Built around a wooden frame, this was a metre tall. In other tombs Rudenko found women's pigtails, a wooden head-dress with a pigtail attached and even a false beard with strings to tie it to the face. There were also silver and bronze mirrors, the former certainly made in China, gold earrings and elaborately worked buckles, clasps and brooches.

The Ice Princess wore a beige silk shift, with maroon piping, next to her skin. The silk apparently came not from China but from India. She had thigh-length riding boots and a dress made from sheep and camels' wool in three colours. Around her neck, she wore a necklace of carved camels and her head-dress bore little carvings of an ibex and a griffin.

The decoration did not end with jewellery; many Pazyryk bodies, including the Ice Princess and the 'Warrior', have extremely elaborate tattoos on their bodies. These were made by pricking the skin with sharp needles and either rubbing soot into the holes or dipping the needles into the dye before pricking. Rudenko found the most elaborately tattooed body in 1948. Although it was not well preserved, enough of the designs had survived to provide a good impression of just how elaborate it must originally have been (see illustration on page 62).

Rudenko believes the body was that of a chief. His lower right leg, both of his arms and some of his chest and back bore tattooed images. Originally his lower left leg also bore tattoos, but this was so badly damaged by tomb-robbers that they are not now discernible. Along his spine, in the middle of his back, there are a series of dots which reminded me of the Ice Man's tattoos (see appendix). Patterns of black dots or bars like these are not uncommon on mummies from cultures which practise tattooing, and are generally interpreted as being there for medical reasons.

The tattoos on the Pazyryk chief's back suggests that they may have been applied to relieve back-ache. But the other patterns are of a very different order. On his right shin, a fish rises from his ankle to his knee. It is a river fish, probably a catfish or sturgeon as it has a little moustache of barbels around its mouth. Below it, running all round his ankle, is a dragon-like being, a fanged and winged monster which has three birds' heads arranged like a mane on its neck and a long feline tail like a tiger's. In front of the monster's face there are several more dots like the ones on his back, which may have been placed there to relieve ankle pain. Running up the inside of his calf is a beautiful set of four mountain rams or goats in full flight. Their hooves touch each other, making the four into a single composition.

Wrapped around the left side of his chest is a magnificent beast which starts just to the left of his backbone, over his shoulder blade. Here, there is a great spiral of tiger's tail the tip of which is a bird's head. Powerful haunches with fierce claws support the rear end of the back. The beast's body curls under his armpit then out across his left pectorals with another bird's head emerging from the beast's back. Sadly, the head of this great carnivore has been lost but, opposite it, on the right pectoral, there is a smaller figure with a spiral tail, powerful carnivore body and wolf-like head.

The most elaborate and best preserved motifs are on the chief's arms. His right arm is covered with tattoos from wrist to shoulder. Just above his wrist there is a donkey, or maybe an onager (wild ass), galloping but with its back legs twisted right round as if it is taking a high-speed fall. It faces down the arm, towards his hand, which accentuates the impression of a fall. Beside the onager, also facing downwards, is a winged monster with the same tiger's tail and long sharp claws as the monster on his chest and back. It faces the onager and could be attacking it. Above these two is a superb ram with great spiralled horns and heavily fleeced neck and chest. Its back legs are also twisted round so that they are pointing upwards. Above the ram is a deer with very long and elaborate antlers. The tines on the antlers are all birds' heads. It has a row of four birds' heads along its back and one at the end of its tail. Like the ram below, its chest and forelegs have been darkened and decorated with stripes, swirls and spirals. The deer's face has been transformed by substituting a fearsome eagle's beak for the muzzle. As with the onager and ram, the front legs appear to be in full flight but the rear legs have been inverted upwards into a great twisted leap. Above the deer, almost perching on the bird-head tines of his antlers, is a feline monster very like the one on the chief's chest, with the tiger's tail ending in a bird's head. Interestingly, like the carnivore monster on his wrist, this beast is upright in a walking or maybe a crouched position, as if it is stalking a prey. At the top of his arm, spread out over his shoulder, is another magnificent deer, again with its head and chest darkened, its rear legs inverted and bird heads as antler tines. Again, its long tail ends in a bird's head.

His left arm, as mentioned, is not as well preserved, but it contains three figures. On his forearm he has a deer, again with its rear legs in the air. In the centre, another deer, well preserved and magnificently portrayed, rear legs inverted and head blackened, the antler tines once again transformed into birds' heads and the muzzle reshaped as a huge eagle's beak. Above the deer is another ram or mountain goat, not so well preserved but clearly styled in the same way as all the other animals.

These tattoos are probably the most elaborate works of body-art to have survived from ancient times anywhere in the world. They are particularly impressive because they literally encase the naked body of a man who knew that he would be carrying them with him into eternity. The chief's body, like all the Pazyryk bodies, had been deliberately and carefully mummified; and the tattoos carry powerful messages about who this particular man was.

But tattoos, intimate though they are, are far from the only artwork left behind by the Pazyryk. Much of their finest and most complex art is associated with their horses. They covered saddles, bridles and harnesses with the most wonderful decorations, some gold-plated. One particularly striking and gorgeous technique was the fastening of an entire set of gilded antlers to an elaborate bridle-cum-headpiece which their horses wore, turning them into deer-horses. This wealth of artwork provides good clues to the meanings of the tattoo systems on the human bodies.

When I first saw this treasure trove I was amazed and perplexed. I had absolutely no idea that an obscure nomad tribe, tucked away in the

ICE MUMMIES OF THE NOMADS

Siberian wasteland, could produce works of such stunning quality. The complexity of the imagery meant that it was going to be hard to interpret, to 'read', yet it is all highly codified, almost standardized, so there had to be messages embedded in it. As always, the safest first step is to go back to simple observations about the lifestyle and the quality of human experience among these people so many centuries ago.

First, the Pazyryk were master horsemen and horsewomen. They were extremely skilled herders and warriors who were particularly renowned as archers. They were also evidently skilled hunters, probably mostly hunting from horseback. The mountains, grasslands and forests of Siberia supported a considerable range of wildlife. Among the wild herbivores were elk, deer, reindeer, roebuck, hares, onagers, mountain goats and sheep, wild boar, squirrels and saiga antelope. A myriad of birds hung in the air – cranes, swans, grouse, ptarmigan, geese and all the little song-birds. And, of course, there were birds of prey: eagles, owls and hawks. Carnivores included snow leopards, tigers, wolves, wildcats, lynxes, foxes, ermine and pine martens. It seems the Pazyryk hunted almost all these animals and not just for their meat. For example, in the mummification process, after they had removed the brain they filled the cranial cavity with the fine soft fur of the pine marten.

To be a good hunter, you have to study and understand the prey's behaviour. I spent two years with the hunting people of Amazonia and I learnt something new almost every day about the animals of the rainforest and how to catch them. My hunter friends, the Maku, took great delight in their skills and spent much of their leisure time talking about animals and hunts, present and past. This extraordinarily rich knowledge and experience moulded their world view, and their visions of the worlds of the spirits and of the afterlife. These visions are not static abstracts, they are highly dynamic supernatural systems which live alongside the world of waking normality. I think similar things must have been going on in the heads of the Pazyryk.

Returning to the tattoos, it is very clear that these are not simple representations. *All* of the animals have been transformed in some way or other. They are all 'spirit animals' if you like. Furthermore, they are transformed in consistent ways. Deer have bird-head antler tines and eagle heads. Almost all the carnivorous beasts have striped tails with a bird's head on the end and so on. Fantastical though they are, the images are none the less based on real animals and depict two categories – predators and prey. The depictions are mostly of wild animals, but there are also quite a few of domestic animals, including their beloved horses. The prey are the animals with their rear legs twisted upwards. The reason for this is immediately clear from a beautifully coloured felt appliqué saddle-cover found in one of the tombs. This depicts a flying eagle-griffin forcing a terrified wild ram to the ground. The ram's rear legs are twisted upwards as the weight of the flying monster knocks it down. Its head turns back in a terrified stare as it realizes it is doomed. I had witnessed such a moment when the eagle took the fox in the wintry snows. It is the moment just before death for the hunted, the moment of triumph for the hunter.

If you shoot a running animal from the side with an arrow or a heavy-calibre bullet just behind the foreleg, the animal will take the same posture depicted on the tattoo as it turns to look at the entry wound and simultaneously goes down. This, of course, is exactly what the tattooed chief would have seen as he hunted on horseback.

I bet he was right-handed: right-handed people hold the bow with the left hand and draw the string and arrow with the right hand. The right arm aims the arrow at the prey. The chief's right arm has friezes of carnivores pouncing on their prey tattooed on it, while his left arm just has prey animals on it. So, to me, his tattoos call upon the spirit hunter-animals to guide his aim. Sympathy here seems to lie with the predators: victory is certainly theirs, even against the literal 'flight' of the deer, as symbolized by the birds' heads on their antlers, backs and tails.

The great carnivore beast wrapped round his back and chest has been placed there, in my view, to protect his heart. The fish is placed at the bottom of his legs just above his ankles, almost the lowest part on his body, representing the depths where fishes reside in the real world. Running up his leg are mountain goats which may well represent stamina and agility – qualities he would want from his own legs. Again, at the lowest part of his body around his ankle, yet another feline monster seems to stand guard, perhaps protecting him from the dangers which lay on or under the ground.

Besides the carnivores, the deer is a highly important symbol. When Natalya Polosmak thawed out the Ice Princess in 1994 she found two fine tattoos of deer on her, both executed in near identical style to the tattoos on Rudenko's chief. The deer tattooed on the Ice Princess also has birds' heads on its antler tines, and its back and rear legs are twisted into the 'point of death' posture. Yet, unlike some other women's tombs in this region, the Ice Princess had no weapons in her grave nor any other signs of warrior status. So her tattoos are probably not intended to be hunting charms. As this highly stylized motif appears throughout Pazyryk art, including two superb carved wooden statues found by Rudenko, it seems likely that the deer symbol holds meaning of a more generalized form than mere game animals.

Looking closely at them, the most striking feature is that the size of the antlers is always exaggerated so that they sweep majestically back above the animals' backs in a curve which is nearly symmetrical with the fleeing animal's belly. The remains of both red deer and reindeer have been found in Pazyryk graves – to my eye, the spirit deer look more like reindeer, but it was not species identification which mattered to these artists. Their concern was to capture certain qualities of the animal. Deer are, of course, extremely swift-footed and the impression that the artwork gives is always of speed. The birds' heads seem to confirm this idea of 'flight'. But the antlers are probably more important. Every year after the rutting season, deer shed their antlers and regrow them every spring. In many cultures this ability to lose a part of the body and regrow it is seen as a magical process, a type of rebirth. My Maku friends in Amazonia consider snakes to be immortal because they can slough off their skins and emerge new and fresh. Interestingly, the words for skin sloughing also mean menstruation, where a woman renews herself and her fecundity every month by losing a part of herself. There are echoes of these concepts in the use of deer as symbols, animals who hold the secrets of 'death' and 'rebirth' and of fertility. Finally, antlers are also basically weapons which deer use in sexual combat and in self-defence. So perhaps these renewable defensive charms provide an element of protection for the human bearer. Overall, though, it seems to me that deer were special, sacred animals for the Pazyryk and that by depicting them so frequently on their bodies and tombs, the deer spirits became their companions in the afterlife. That they should choose to adorn their horses, their most cherished animals, with antlers to transform them into deer-horses seems to confirm this view.

Other prey animals were also important to them, especially wild goats or sheep whose spiralling horns perhaps also symbolized protective power. Cocks are often used decoratively, once again with the emphasis placed on their combs, which sweep backwards from their heads in wave-like ripples. There is a wonderful head-dress which has many leather cut-out cocks strutting around on the crown of the head, and a fine earthenware bottle decorated with cut-out leather cockerels all round its centre. All of these animals have natural 'head-dresses' of their own — the quality, perhaps, which led the Pazyryk to give them special status. We know the Pazyryk adored hats and headpieces and that the Ice Princess was wearing an enormous headpiece, over a metre tall, when she was found. If you live in Siberia or anywhere in the Steppes you most definitely need headgear. When I was out on the eagle hunt with the Kazakhs a wind suddenly got up. I had the ear-flaps of my fur hat turned up and the wind shot into my ears like a frozen dagger. Adorning the head has also been a sign of sacredness since the dawn of time. In our own society hat styles are used to denote rank, status, occupation and holiness, and often incorporate exotic animal furs, bird feathers, jewels, badges and the like to define the 'message' the hat bears more precisely. The Pazyryk, it seems, were drawn to animals which carried similar messages on their heads. Spirit animals should evidently wear hats.

Besides the herbivore prey species, there are also many depictions of carnivores – predators like ourselves. Prominent among the realistic carnivores are lions. This is both strange and revealing because lions do not exist anywhere near the Altai Mountains in Siberia. Far to the south, in India and parts of the Near East, there were lions and they were, of course, potent symbols in ancient Egypt, Babylonia and Persia. So their prominent depiction in Pazyryk art demonstrates that the people had powerful links with, at the very least, the peoples of Persia. The fame of the 'King of the Beasts' had unquestionably reached Siberia by 500 BC.

Along with lions, there are tigers, leopard-like animals and wolves, but by far the most recurrent carnivores are not representations of any one species. Rather, most are composite, heraldic spirit animals. Some are familiar – griffins with the bodies and claws of lions, and the wings and heads of eagles; or minotaur-like animals with lion bodies and bull heads. Others are less so – winged monsters with feline bodies and snarling wolves' heads.

There are not many human representations. The figures which do appear on carpets, wall hangings and horse bridles show people who look European rather than Asiatic. Clothing, hairstyles and the artistic style of presentation all have a marked Persian feel. This is a little surprising as archaeologists' examinations suggest that the Pazyryks were, in fact, of mixed Caucasoid and Mongolian stock. This, in turn, suggests that artistic influences probably derived from the Persian/Iranian peoples living far to the southwest.

One particular figure, of applied felt on a felt wall hanging, seems to say it all for me (see photograph between pages 86 and 87). It is of a sphinx-like figure, half man half lion. His face is extraordinarily Persian, with a large nose, bright oval eyes, dark bushy eye brows and a fine upturned handlebar moustache. He sports a brown, curved pigtail at the back of his head and has an embroidered coiled turban covering his head. His ears, in bright pink, are unquestionably deer's. A magnificent pair of multi-pronged antlers sprout from the top of his head, balanced but not symmetrical, in pink and grey. He has two short arms which end in three-fingered hands. His light blue body is so lithe it might almost be the body of a leopard or racing dog. In the small of his back are planted fine wings – pink, grey and light blue feathers, some with straight black tips. They are echoes of a fine pair of swans on a different felt wall hanging, whose wings also have black tips. His tail, also in pink and grey, flares out like a great fan at the end. His feline feet end in three sharp light-blue claws.

This part-human spirit-being is graced with the vision, intelligence and manual dexterity of a human; the sharp hearing, martial protection and fertility of the deer; the powerful flight of swans and the feral power of the leopard in body and hind quarters. The tail, a pure fantasy, passes through his rear legs and fans out under his belly, both balancing the picture aesthetically and hinting strongly at sexual potency. There is much in this picture: an incredibly strong visual statement which cries out down the centuries and across the barriers of muteness enveloping this lost wordless civilization. To me, it seems to be a statement of an ideal. It says

ICE MUMMIES OF THE NOMADS

〰〰

'Look at me. I am all you could ever hope to be. I am man and nature, beauty and power, a superbeing built from all that is finest in the world around me.' In short, I suspect that this superbeing is the symbol of the goal of the Pazyryk afterlife journey, the way we should all end up if we are lucky after death.

This reverence for nature does, of course, have extremely ancient roots. It can be traced back as far as the magnificent cave art of 30,000 years ago, but it is rarely expressed in the way of the Pazyryk where the aspects of many beings are compressed into one creature. Yet this type of symbolism was very prevalent in the world's ancient civilizations. Think of sphinxes, minotaurs, griffins and phoenixes. These mythic spirit-beings abound in the minds of ancient Egyptians, Greeks, Babylonians and Persians.

There are two other symbols which the Pazyryk seem to have revered. Their art is often adorned with images of the lotus, the holy flower of ancient India and Egypt. In ancient Egypt it stood for regeneration and rebirth, for Buddhists it represented purity. Yet this tropical water-flower did not exist in the wild mountains of Siberia. The other symbols found in Pazyryk tombs, as in the Taklamakan, are cowrie shells. These, of course, come from the sea, thousands of miles from Siberia. The cowrie shell, with its vulva-like appearance, is often associated with fertility. The presence of the cowrie and the lotus is, for me, absolute proof that ancient chains of thought linked the peoples of the Old World over vastly wider areas than is normally assumed. The Pazyryk expressed these chains of thought symbolically. They also performed symbolic acts with the bodies of their dead, by preserving them. They were doing this at almost exactly the time when Herodotus lived and wrote. He himself claimed to have visited both the Scythians around the Black Sea and ancient Egypt. He knew of both people's mummification practices. Though he was among the first to set his observations down on paper, he can hardly have been the first curious traveller to have moved between Egypt and Central Asia. To my mind, then, it seems probable that at the very least the Egyptians knew of Scythian mummification practices and vice versa.

This is not to say that one culture got their mummification practices from the other. If that did happen, then it would seem likely that the ideas travelled from Egypt northwards and to the east, as Egyptian mummification practices are a good deal more ancient than anything yet discovered in Central Asia. But it seems safe to assume that these two great mummy-making cultures were aware of each other and shared an ideology which embraced the preservation of the dead.

There are a good deal of differences between the ways the Egyptians and the Pazyryk set about preparing their dead for the afterlife and many of these are related to the very different environments the two peoples inhabited. When the Pazyryk buried their dead, they built their tombs along an east – west axis and arranged the bodies accordingly, the head at the east end and the face looking west towards the setting sun. They probably believed that the afterworld lay in that direction, an idea they shared with the ancient Egyptians. It is interesting, though, that the Pazyryk seemed to care a good deal less about the sun than the Egyptians and the peoples of the Taklamakan. Sun-worship, so bound up with the annual cycle and the fertility of plant life, often plays a central role in agricultural societies. The Egyptians and the people of the Taklamakan were both farmers and sun-worshippers. The Pazyryk, however, were herders and hunters, depending for their livelihoods on wild meat and the produce of their herds. I am sure this is why they filled their supernatural worlds and the world of the dead with animal imagery.

The Pazyryk mummification process shares quite a few features with its Egyptian counterpart. Both peoples extracted the brain, the Egyptians by removing it through the nose, the Pazyryks by trepanning a hole in the skull. Both peoples also removed all of the internal organs by cutting open the bodies and refilling the cavities with various materials for preservation and to retain the shape of the body. In Egypt, from the twenty-first dynasty onwards (around 1000 BC) the embalmers removed, treated then replaced the internal organs in 'packages' inside the bodies. The Pazyryk do not appear to have done this. But the biggest difference between the two traditions is that the Pazyryks made major incisions in the bodies and sometimes removed as much of the musculature as they could. For example, all the surviving bodies have been opened right across the back from shoulder to shoulder, then right down the back from the neck to the buttocks. In many bodies, the neck, face and buttocks have also been extensively cut open, either for the removal of flesh or for insertion of preservative materials, possibly salt. Both arms and legs have been slit open from top to bottom for the same reason. All these incisions were then sewn up with great care.

The ancient Egyptians also made slits in their bodies to insert either 'packing' or preservatives or both, but on nothing like the scale practised by the Pazyryks. If anything, then, the Pazyryks used more complex techniques of mummification than the Egyptians. The reason for this may be related to both ritual practices and practical necessities. Whereas the natural conditions for preservation are extremely good in Egypt – hot dry climate, salty desert sands – they are not as good in the Black Sea area where the Scythians lived. Though cold in the winter, the Steppes of Central Asia do not undergo the extremes of temperature characteristic of the Taklamakan. Nor is the ground salty as in Egypt and the Taklamakan. These special conditions greatly enhance the likelihood of the survival of preserved bodies. The fact that no mummies have survived in the Black Sea region of Scythian territory is almost certainly a result of unfavourable climatic conditions. We know they mummified their dead, but the bodies have not survived. In the Altai Mountains, where the

Pazyryk lived, sub-surface permafrost played the same role as sand and salt elsewhere, making the preservation of human and animal remains possible.

The Scythian case, however, was complicated by cultural factors. Whereas the Egyptians set about the mummification process shortly after death, Herodotus tells us that Scythian royalty had to be taken from place to place for mourning rituals for a very long time before the bodies were interred. He also states that the burial rituals took place either in the spring or the autumn, again implying that corpses may have had to remain above ground for weeks or even months. There is corroborative information for these reports from the archaeological record. It is only possible to excavate holes deep into the ground in Siberia at the end of the summer when the soil is in its most thawed state. Even then, you encounter permafrost a few metres down. This, of course, was the secret the Pazyryks had discovered – that if you could preserve the dead for the months that they were above ground – not a problem if a dignitary died in winter but much more difficult if they died in spring or summer – then you could get them into the ground where they would rapidly become deep frozen for eternity.

Once the body arrived in its tomb, relatives may have tended it for some time before it was closed up – certainly long enough for the requisite grave goods to be installed with it, and perhaps a ritual meal shared between the living and the dead. The presence of the little wigwams, where hemp seeds were burnt in the tombs, also suggests that the rites of post-mortem purification were performed there. These rites provide important clues to the Pazyryk attitudes towards death. That they should perform acts of purification means that they recognized death as a dangerous polluting event. That they should choose to purify themselves by taking mind-altering drugs is also revealing. Like most of the nomads of Central and West Asia, Pazyryk men and women smoked hemp (cannabis) in their everyday lives. They also used a narcotic called ephedra. Although these drugs are not hallucinogens, they do markedly alter consciousness. Using them in a ritual context means that the states induced are characterized by the people as sacred. Although nowadays we tend to associate drug use with social deviancy this was not the case in the ancient world. Herodotus remarked that the Scythians' 'steam baths' made the people ecstatically happy. He may have been right. People such as the Pazyryk induced ecstatic feelings to expunge the grief which death generated. In many other cultures around the world mind-altering substances are used to heighten sensitivity to supernatural powers, and death is precisely that. So it seems that the Scythians and Pazyryk used their stimulants to cross the barriers between life and death, and to communicate with the spirit beings which inhabit the otherworlds beyond the frontiers of the living.

In Chapter One the archaeological evidence suggested that the people of the Taklamakan – farming neighbours and traders with nomads, such as the Pazyryk – essentially saw the afterlife as an extension of this life. The Pazyryk funerary customs and art suggest that they followed a different path: their journey to the afterlife was on horseback, but their companions on the journey, or perhaps the beings of the otherworld where the journey took place, were a pantheon of mystical creatures. The stories they tell are of predator and prey, of the sheer exultation of the hunt, of the ways in which death transforms the living but nourishes them, too. And in the deer, the lotus and the cowrie, life rejuvenates and fertility brings life anew.

As we shall see throughout this book, reverence for ancestors was the most important single incentive for preserving the dead: in essence, looking after the dead ensured that the living would thrive. There is no doubt that this was a fundamental belief for the nomads of Central Asia. Indeed, caring for the dead was so important that, according to

IN SEARCH OF THE IMMORTALS

∿∿

Herodotus, some tribes sacrificed the living to ensure their well-being. As the Pazyryk tombs show, horses routinely accompanied the dead on their afterlife journeys. Herodotus, as already mentioned, claims that wives, concubines and servants were strangled and placed in the tombs of the dead, and also provides a graphic description of a far more gruesome form of human sacrifice by the Scythians:

> One man is chosen out of every hundred [prisoners of war]: wine is poured on his head, and his throat is cut over a bowl; the bowl is then carried to the platform on top of the [sacred] woodpile and the blood poured out over the sacred scimitar.

There is, as yet, no archaeological evidence to confirm the existence of such practices. But there is evidence, in the form of preserved human beings, of similar practices taking place during those times thousands of miles to the west, in the marshes and peat bogs of Northwest Europe.

Chapter 3

Northwest Europe
bodies
in the bogs

Late in the afternoon of 8 May 1950, archaeologist P.V. Glob was giving a class at Aarhus University, Denmark, when he was called to the telephone. It was the local police in a small village in central Jutland. Could he come at once to the scene of a probable murder? He gathered up his bag and set out at once. Later he recalled the events of the following hours, as if they were a turning point in his own life.

He had been summoned to Tollund Fen, a peat bog in the vale of Bjaeldskov. The afternoon was overcast with grey thunder-clouds scudding in from the west. As he arrived at the edge of the valley the sun burst through the cloud cover for a few moments, bathing the valley in warm light, bringing everything to life. A sunken cart-track wound its way through ancient woodland – firs, willow, wild cherry, blackthorn, crab apple and aspen – a landscape little changed for thousands of years. The track led down to Tollund Fen, where people had cut peat to use as fuel for as long as anyone could remember. Two local farmers had gone to the Fen the day before to cut their winter peat supply, which would need the summer months to dry out once it had been sliced from the bog. Wielding long spade-like turf-cutters they first sliced straight down into the peat then cut out horizontal blocks and tossed them to the surface. Removing a block nearly three metres below the surface, they suddenly found themselves staring at a face so perfectly preserved that they assumed he was a recent murder victim. They called the police.

This was not the first time the police had been called to Tollund Fen. Twelve years earlier another body had been found just 82 metres from the new discovery which had proved to be 2,000 years old. That is why the police called the archaeologist before they set out for the scene of the 'crime'.

Despite the eerily perfect state of preservation, Glob knew at once that the body was ancient. He lay on his side on his damp bed, his eyes closed and lips slightly pursed, 'as if', Glob noted, 'in silent prayer'. He had no beard, but his chin and upper lip were covered by stubble, perhaps two days of growth since his final shave. His expression was utterly serene, bringing to Glob's mind a quote from Gilgamesh, the legendary king and hero of the ancient Babylonian epic: 'The dead and the sleeping, how they resemble each other.' A pointed leather cap, finely stitched, covered his short hair. It was held in place by a leather drawstring tied firmly under his chin. He wore a leather belt round his waist, but was otherwise naked.

The removal of a lump of peat over the man's throat changed the image irrevocably. It revealed a raw-hide noose drawn around the man's neck so tight it must have strangled him. This was indeed a murder, but it had taken place 2,000 years ago. In the fading light, Glob realized that he was looking at a major archaeological discovery: possibly the best preserved Iron Age European ever found.

A team from a nearby museum arrived at first light next day and set about building wooden 'walls' round the body, then slipping boards underneath it. Finally, they packed peat all around and over the exposed parts of the man, and nailed a lid on the case. The complete peat-filled box weighed nearly a ton. No crane could be got anywhere near the site, so the team had to man-handle it on to the back of a horse and cart. The tremendous struggle proved too much for one member of the team who collapsed with a heart-attack and died on the spot. It seemed to Glob that the spirit of the bog was claiming its due: an ancient body taken, a new life forfeited in return.

The area where they found Tollund Man is rich in archaeological sites. Among the earliest settlers in the region were the 'Battle-axe People' who invaded Northwest Europe around 4,000 years ago. Speakers of an Indo-European language, they hailed from the Steppes of Central Asia and may originally have been related to the peoples of the Taklamakan, perhaps even to the ancestors of the Pazyryk. The 'Battle-axe People' pressed deep into Northwest Europe and are commonly held to be the ancestral peoples of Scandinavia – tall, fair and light-skinned like their descendants today.

Tollund Man had met his fate in the peat bogs of Jutland around 100 BC. Throughout this period, from the late Stone Age, through the Bronze Age and down to Tollund Man's era, the Iron Age, the people built funerary mounds and tumuli to honour their dead. The earliest historical records note that the peoples of this region set the bodies of their leaders on funeral pyres then interred their bones. Around the time of Christ this practice changed and the people began to bury their dead in graves with grave goods. Burying the dead in peat bogs was certainly not the norm, yet, during the last two centuries, over 100 human bodies have been recovered from peat bogs throughout the wetlands of Northwest Europe – and most of them seemed to have suffered death by unnatural causes.

As I began to find out more about the Bog People, I realized I was entering a world which was peopled by Celts, my own ancestors, a world whose physical properties I knew intimately. Yet it was also a world far more exotic in many ways than anything I had encountered in Amazonia, Africa or China.

Today, few of us would think of marshes and peat bogs as shrines or holy sites, but they are mysterious, treacherous places where black waters ooze noxious gases, threatening to suck us under if we put a foot wrong. Indeed, there is evidence that some people did precisely this, slipping into bogs never to be seen again. Bodies have been recovered with their arms stretched forward, hands grasping at heather or sticks as if trying to haul themselves out. In Russia in 1850, a woman who committed suicide was cast into a peat bog, and there are several cases of felons being thrown into bogs after execution. A medieval soldier was found in a German bog. He had been hanged with two dogs strung up by their hind legs beside him. The man's thighs and stomach had been badly bitten as the dogs tried to break free. Near Berlin, a wooden barrel was found in a bog. Its inside was studded with nails which had pierced the man who lay within. Perhaps most gruesome of all, a man was found near Brandenburg who had been scalped and had the skin stripped from his back. In his hands, he clutched his own lips and ears. In 1955, the body of a German soldier killed in the Second World War was recovered from a peat bog. His clothes had almost totally disintegrated, but his body was well preserved.

Peat bogs have been the recipients of human bodies throughout history, but there is a concentration between approximately 700 BC and 200 AD, and these have come to be known as the 'Bog People'. They have been found in western Ireland, northwest England, Holland, Germany and especially Denmark. They share one stark common characteristic: they all seem to have been deliberately put to death.

The rope around Tollund Man's neck was so tight it left a deep furrow in the skin of his throat and the sides of his neck but not at the back. From this, the pathologists examining him concluded that he had been hanged before being cast into the bog. His stomach was well preserved and contained the remains of a meal eaten twelve to twenty-four hours before he died. It consisted of gruel made from barley, linseed, gold-of-pleasure and willow-herb seeds, along with smaller amounts of at least thirty varieties of wild seeds, including violet, hemp-nettle, fat hen, black bindweed and mustard. Most of these seeds would have grown among the cultivated cereals and may have been harvested at the same time as the main crops.

Two years after his discovery, another body was found in a bog near the village of Grauballe in Jutland. Grauballe Man's throat was slit from ear to ear, he had been struck a fierce blow on his right temple and his left shin had been broken. He was naked and, like Tollund Man, had also eaten a gruel of cereals and wild herb seeds just before he died. His gruel contained an even wider range of seeds, about fifty different varieties, some of them not grown locally. There were also traces of meat and animal hair in his stomach.

Between 1946 and 1948, three bodies were found in a bog called Borre Mose in Jutland – a man and two women. The man was naked, the back of his skull crushed and his right thigh broken. He had died from hanging or strangulation, the hemp rope still held in a slip-knot around his neck. The two women were covered by capes or skirts. One woman's right leg was broken, and both women seem to have been attacked around the head before they were put in the bog. Two other women, found elsewhere, show no physical signs of violence, but both were pinned firmly to the bottom of the bog with stone weights and heavy logs. It is assumed they died by drowning. Another young girl was found naked, with half her hair shaved off and a blindfold bound tightly over her eyes. She, too, had been weighted down in the bog to drown.

The most recent bog body to emerge came to light in Lindow Moss, near Manchester, England, in 1984. He was a young man of about twenty-five. He wore nothing except a fox-fur band on one arm. He, too, had eaten a porridge of seeds, including spelt, emmer and barley, with traces of mistletoe pollen. He had been struck twice on the crown of his head, the blows smashing his skull. A blow to his back had broken one of his ribs, while a thin cord twisted round his throat had throttled him. Finally, his executioners had cut his throat, severing his jugular vein, possibly as an act of blood-letting.

Faced with these and many more gory accounts of violent death in the bogs, the most simple, pressing question is *why?* These ritual killings were obviously widespread, taking place over nearly a thousand years, but peat bogs were not the normal way to dispose of the dead in those times. Does the discovery of more than 100 bodies in the last 200 years mean that we have now discovered most of the Bog People, or are there yet more bodies? More important, do all bodies cast into peat bogs become mummified, or do only some survive?

The answer to the latter question is now well established. To survive in peat bogs, human (or animal) soft tissue requires very special conditions:

1. The bodies must be placed in deep, relatively still water – deep enough to prevent attack from insects and scavengers, still enough to be oxygen deficient and stop decay by bacteria. Many bog bodies were found in old pits or trenches caused by earlier digging of peat for fuel.

2. The water must contain sufficient tannic acid to preserve the outer layers of the body by tanning. If the water is non-acidic, the bones will survive but the soft tissue will rot.

3. Water temperature in the bog pool must be below 4C, at least for several months after the body is deposited and the 'tanning' process gets under way. Any warmer and the body will decompose.

So, the ideal conditions for mummification are a deep, still pool of black water in the dead of winter. Depositing a body at other times of year, or in different water conditions, may lead to partial preservation, and there are several cases where a complete human skin has been found as an empty shell, all traces of bone, sinew, flesh and organs gone forever. It is more likely, however, that in water that is warm, shallow or low in tannin, the body would have decomposed altogether.

Given that ideal conditions do not pertain all year round, it seems likely that many more people met their fates in the peat bogs than we know of today. Their bodies simply did not survive to 'tell the tale'. In a sense, this complicates the issue. If more people were killed in the bogs than have survived, then the question of 'why?' is even more puzzling.

The bodies themselves tell us a good deal about who the Bog People were, how they dressed, what they ate and how they died. But to discover *why* they died, we need to turn to the world of the living, to the societies which bred, nurtured then killed these individuals.

Northern Europe in the Iron Age was a cold wet world with very short winter days and summer nights where the sun seemed to skim across the horizon, never really setting. Scandinavia, northern Germany and northern Holland were settled by people speaking Germanic languages. They farmed cereal crops, reared animals, hunted and fished. The Romans considered them barbarians, arranged into tribes such as the Cimbri, Angles and Jutes. All members of the 'tribe' owed allegiance to a paramount leader, titular head and warlord. They were fierce fighters, wielding axes, spears and swords – mostly on foot. They did have horses, which they rode and used to pull carts and chariots, but were not renowned as cavalrymen. Their political world revolved around constantly shifting sets of alliances between chiefs and warlords. They fought among themselves and with the Celts, their neighbours to the south. Later they fought, sometimes with stunning success, against the might of Rome. The Romans never succeeded in conquering them, but they did not try very hard. They felt that these cold, mineral-deficient northern lands had little to offer their empire.

IN SEARCH OF THE IMMORTALS

The ancient Germans loved to fight and loved to celebrate. Festivals were held after victories and conquests, and they honoured many gods. The celebration of the rites of war was an integral part of their religious system though for many of them the most important deity was Nerthus, the Earth Mother goddess of fertility.

To the south and west, in what is now southern Germany, the Low Countries, most of France, Britain, Ireland and much of Spain and Portugal, the Celts held sway. Their languages form a major branch of the Indo-European family. Their Germanic neighbours' tongues form another major branch. Although the languages are not mutually intelligible, there is evidence that the Celts and Germans interacted. Trade routes linked many parts of Europe and goods moved quite freely between peoples. Even warfare generated forms of communication between them. If a Celtic army was overrun by Germanic warriors, the Celtic women and children would be absorbed by the Germans, or vice versa. Alliances between the two groups also occurred, cemented by the giving of hostages and the intermarrying of the sons and daughters of the war-lords. Overall, the Celts and Germans knew plenty about each other and led broadly similar lives. All the evidence suggests that they shared common religious beliefs and ritual practices, including occasional ritual killings and the depositing of the victims' bodies in peat bogs.

The Celts had a much rougher time than the Germans at the hands of the Romans. Pushing out from their Italian homelands, the Roman legions systematically overran much of 'Gaul' and subjected the natives to their rule. After a shaky start in Britain in 55 BC (Caesar evidently did not 'come, see and conquer', as he claimed), the Romans had overrun most of England by about 50 AD, forcing the Britons either to yield, take refuge in Cornwall, Wales and Scotland, or emigrate to Brittany or Ireland. It may well have been Roman influence, followed

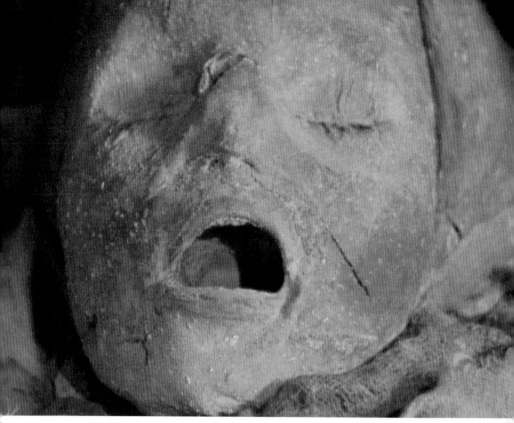

This 8-14 month old baby boy was found buried head down in the sand in the Zagunluq cemetery in the Taklamakan desert. His discoverer, He Dexiu, believes the child may have been buried alive *(Ian Charlton)*

The almost perfectly preserved body of a mature woman, dating from about 1500 BC, was found in her tomb below the body of the baby boy in the Zagunluq cemetery. Coloured wool has been inserted into her nostrils to absorb any fluids which might otherwise have damaged her face *(Ian Charlton)*

One of the best preserved mummies found anywhere in the world, the 'Sun Man' was also discovered in the Zagunluq cemetery. Tall with fair hair and Caucasoid features, his fine quality clothes and carefully maintained fingernails suggest he was a man of high social status *(Jeffery Newbury / Discover)*

The Kazakhs of Central Asia have been hunting foxes with eagles for centuries. Though linguistically distinct from their ancient forebears, their lifestyle as nomadic herders essentially continues traditions which have thrived in this region for 3000 years *(David Beatty / Robert Harding)*

A mounted warrior carries a bow in its case suspended on his saddle. Applied felt decoration on a wall-hanging from a Pazyryk tomb *(Novosti / London)*

This applied felt wall-hanging found in a Pazyryk tomb in southwest Siberia which dates to around 450 BC, depicts a fabulous spirit-being, a winged and antlered half-lion, half-human figure. The human face is clearly not Asiatic, the large nose and 'handlebar' moustache being more reminiscent of Persian art *(Novosti / London)*

The Pazyryk loved to decorate their horses and harnesses with superbly-crafted icons and imagery. This antlered horse's headpiece would originally have been covered in gold leaf *(Novosti / London)*

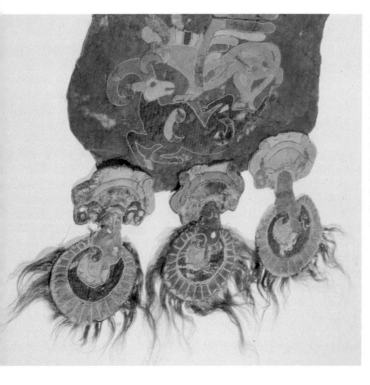

A fabulous griffon figure, with the body of a lion and head and wings of an eagle, over-powers a ram in flight, causing its rear legs to turn upwards as it is struck (detail from a Pazyryk saddle cover, c.450 BC, Siberia) *(Novosti / London)*

Grabaulle Man was found not far from Tollund man in 1952. His throat had been cut, his right temple had received a fierce blow and his left shin bone was broken. He may therefore have been a victim of 'triple killing' *(Jan Friis & Torben Peterson / Bonniers / Inst. of Anthropology & Archaeology, Moesgaard, Denmark)*

Tollund Man, perhaps the most famous of all the bog bodies, was found in 1950 in a peat bog in Jutland, Denmark. Though he looks serene in death, he had been hanged before being cast into the bog *(Jan Friis & Torben Peterson / Bonniers / Silkeborg Museum)*

Windeby Girl was found in a peat bog in northern Germany in 1952. She shows no signs of injury or having died before she was placed in the bog, but probably drowned, her naked body pinned to the bottom of the bog with heavy branches. Her hairband had been bound tightly round her head as a blindfold *(Jan Friis & Torben Peterson / Bonniers / Archäologisches Landesmuseum, Schleswig)*

This scene from the famous Gundestrup cauldron shows a god standing at the head of the tree of life, holding a large cauldron. Beside him is a dog, symbol of death. The lower row of warriors approach the god and are either sacrificed or baptised in the cauldron, then reborn as mounted warriors who ride away along the upper row *(Werrer Forman Archive / National Museum, Copenhagen)*

This painting on papyrus depicts the 'Opening of the Mouth' ceremony, the final act before the entombment of the mummified body in ancient Egypt. The body, standing upright, is touched on the mouth with ritual implements to restore the ability of its *ka*, o spirit, to speak. An attending priest wears the mask of Anubis, the jackal-god *(British Museum)*

The other aspect of the human spirit, the *ba*, was depicted as a human head with bird body in ancient Egypt. The *ba* was free to leave the mummified body and had to make the dangerous journey through the underworld to the Hall of Judgement, where Osiris would decide its eternal fate *(British Museum)*

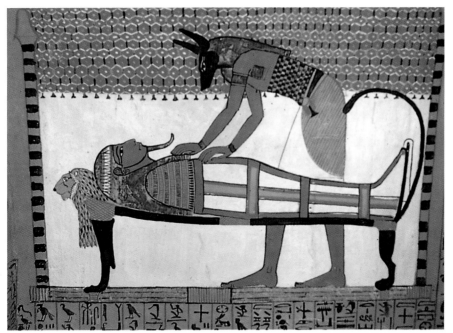

Anubis, the ancient Egyptian jackal-god, 'invented' mummification when he helped to reassemble the scattered remains of Osiris, god of the underworld, so he could be brought back to life to inseminate his wife, Isis *(Jenny Pate / Hutchison)*

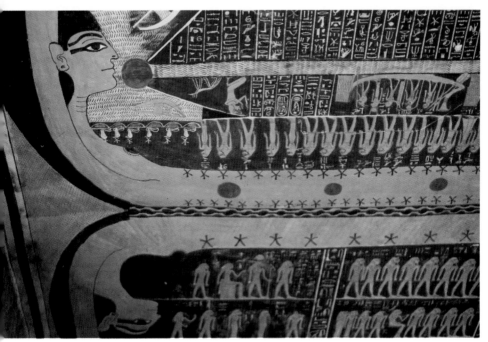

he sky goddess, Nut, spans the entire ceiling of the burial chamber of the great rock-cut mb of Ramesses VI. She is represented in dual form as the skies of day and night. very night the sun-god Re must travel through her body, metaphor of the underworld, d be reborn from her vulva each morning *(R.Ashworth / Robert Harding)*

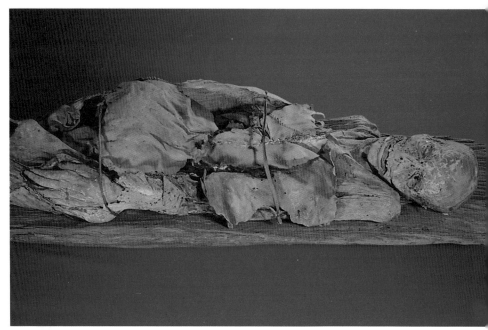

This Guanche mummy, still wrapped in its goatskin shroud, came from a cave in San Andrés, near Santa Cruz de Tenerife *(Archaeological Museum, Tenerife)*

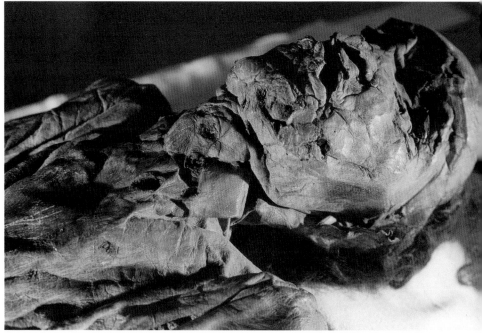

The face of the Cambridge Guanche has clearly been injured, but before he was examined with a CT scanner in 1998 it was not known if the facial injuries had been the cause of death. The scanner revealed massive damage which would have killed him instantly. Carbon 14 dating revealed that he had lived in the Canary Islands about 650 years ago *(Paul Stokes / Channel4)*

shortly by Christianity, which brought the custom of bog killings to an end, at least in England.

History begins in northern Europe with the arrival of the Romans because the Celts and Germans were not literate before then. Their first records, combined with archaeological evidence, allow us a glimpse through the veil of pre-history in search of clues to the enigma of the Bog People. The search becomes easier as we move forward to the time when, under Roman influence, the Celts learned to read and write. Their legacy is an extraordinarily rich array of myths, legends and religious beliefs, along with some stunning works of art.

Written sources provide vital clues about the Bog People. The Roman historian Tacitus, writing in 98 AD, gave the first detailed account of the peoples of northern Europe in *Germania*. Tacitus was, of course, looking at these people from the Roman perspective and his writing should, therefore, be viewed rather in the way that we view the 'truth' of, say, Victorian explorers travelling in Africa. It suited the Romans to see the peoples of northern Europe as barbarians with savage habits because this provided a pretext for their subjugation and civilization. Nonetheless, many of Tacitus's observations have been confirmed by subsequent archaeological investigation, and his book contains many fascinating hints which might relate to the Bog People.

In the early chapters he describes the country as 'covered either by bristling forests or by foul swamps', and the people as going about naked or clad only in short capes fastened with a brooch or thorn. Only the most wealthy wore tight-fitting undergarments. He notes that the people had silver cauldrons which had probably been presented to their chiefs when travelling abroad. Their main weapon was a short spear and a protective coloured shield. He continues: 'To throw away one's shield is the supreme disgrace, and the man who has thus dishonoured himself is debarred from attendance at sacrifice or Assembly.' Many such survivors from the battlefield have ended their shame 'by hanging themselves'. The Assembly also judged criminal charges and ordered capital punishment: 'The mode of execution varies according to the offence. Traitors and deserters are hanged on trees; cowards, shirkers and sodomites are pressed down under a wicker hurdle into the slimy mud of a bog. This distinction is based on the idea that offenders against the state should be made a public example of, whereas deeds of shame should be buried out of men's sight.' Unfaithful women received treatment which has echoes among the bog bodies – their husbands cut off their hair, stripped them naked and turned them out of the house, flogging them all through the village. Tacitus noted that all important men were burned on funeral pyres when they died, their remains buried in mounds of turf. Thus far, Tacitus's evidence suggests strongly that the people cast into bogs were, in essence, condemned criminals and perhaps unfaithful wives.

Having given his general description, Tacitus then made sketches of the more important Germanic tribes. Among them, he mentioned the Suebi, renowned for their elaborate hairstyles. He tells us that only free men are allowed to comb their hair sideways across their heads then gather it into an elaborate knot above the ear. It is known as the 'Sueban knot'. Several of the bog bodies had their hair tied in the Sueban knot, indicating that they were free men, not slaves.

The most senior clan of the Suebi were the Sennones and their seniority was confirmed in a sacred and highly revealing rite:

At a set time, deputations from all the tribes of the same stock gather in a holy grove hallowed by the auguries of their ancestors and by immemorial awe. The sacrifice of a human victim in the name of all marks the grisly opening of their savage ritual . . . No one may enter the grove unless he is bound by a cord, by which he acknowledges his own inferiority and the power of the deity. Should he chance to fall he may not raise himself or get up again, but must roll out over the ground. The grove is the centre of their whole religion.

More intriguing even than the implication that human sacrifice took place in these sacred groves, is the fact that all participants were bound by cords and if they fell they had to stay down on the ground. In case after case of the bog bodies, the victim had his or her legs broken shortly before death. This would, of course, have brought the victim to the ground in the way that the rite prescribes. It is also worth recalling the sacrificial acts which took place far to the east, among the Scythians of the steppes and their cousins the Pazyryk. There, sacrificial animals also had their front legs bound. The sacrificer then pulled the front legs forward, forcing the animal to the ground. As it fell, he slipped a noose round its neck. Passing a stick through it, he twisted the rope, throttling the animal. At least one of the bog bodies was strangled in exactly this manner.

Tacitus goes on to describe a group of Germanic tribes, including the Anglii or Engels, who would migrate a few hundred years later to an island they would rename as Engellond, or England. They and their neighbours all worshipped the fertility goddess Nerthus, Mother Earth:

They believed that she takes part in human affairs, riding in a chariot among her people. When the goddess sets out in her chariot drawn by cows there is rejoicing and merry-making in every place she visits. No one goes to war and all iron objects are locked away. Peace prevails until the goddess, tiring of human company, retires to her sacred grove once again. After that, the chariot, the vestments and (believe it if you will) the goddess herself are cleansed in a lake. This service is performed by slaves who are immediately afterwards drowned in the lake.

IN SEARCH OF THE IMMORTALS

Most experts who have tried to trace the reasons for the deaths of the Bog People have concluded that either they were judicially executed or were ritually sacrificed. The evidence from Tacitus seems to confirm both these views. He reports that people were killed in the bogs as punishment and that ritual sacrifices also took place in holy groves, which may easily have been wooded areas surrounding lakes, marshes or bogs. He also talks of the drowning of slaves at the end of annual fertility ceremonies. In broad terms, these descriptions are accurately reflected in the physical details which the bog bodies provide. But the match is not perfect. There are no reports of several bodies deposited in one place, as one would expect if the entire slave entourage of the fertility goddess Nerthus had been drowned after cleansing her and her cart. Likewise, many of the bog bodies have finely preserved hands and well manicured finger-nails. Their finger-prints are clear and there are no signs of the calluses, cuts and abrasions normally associated with manual work. In short, these were probably the bodies of nobles or warriors not labourers, slaves or common criminals. So perhaps some of the victims of the bogs were noble prisoners of war.

In Chapter Two I mentioned Herodotus's description of the Scythian practice of sacrificing captives. Another Greek author, Strabo, gives a detailed description of the ritual killing of prisoners by the Germanic Cimbri. His *Geography* dates from the time of Christ:

Among the women who accompanied their war-like expeditions were priestesses who possessed the gift of prophecy... Sword in hand they walked through the camp towards the prisoners, decorated them with garlands then led them to a huge bronze cauldron. Mounting a step they bent over the cauldron and cut each prisoner's throat as he was lifted up to them. Others cut open the victims' bellies and read the omens from their entrails, proclaiming victory in the battle to come.

BODIES IN THE BOGS

Other sources report that the priestesses interpreted the pattern of blood on the cauldron to predict victory or defeat. So there is little doubt that these ancient Germans performed human sacrifices, and ritual blood-letting may well have sealed the fate of Grauballe Man in Denmark and Lindow Man in northwest England. But no reference is made to casting the bodies of the victims into peat bogs. Why should they have done this, and were they aware that the bodies might remain intact in their watery graves?

There are many references to the Germanic tribes revering groves and special stands of trees. They shared these beliefs with their Celtic neighbours. Both groups believed that trees, with their ability to 'die' in winter and be 'reborn' in spring, harboured mystical powers. Living for hundreds of years, trees also span the three fundamental layers of the cosmos, with their roots set firmly in the underworld, their trunks in the world of mortals and their top canopies caressing the heavenly world of the skies.

Written sources tell us little about the Germans' interest in peat bogs, but there is much archaeological evidence attesting to the importance of bogs, marshes and lakes throughout Northern Europe in that era. By the time of the Bog People, water and watery places seem to have been recognized for their purifying and healing powers. Springs, wells and especially thermal water sources were places of pilgrimage and making offerings to the water spirits was a well established practice. In France, two main sites have been discovered where several hundred wooden figurines were immersed in spring-fed ponds. Many of these figurines were not whole human representations, just body parts – legs, arms and heads. Some were naked, others clothed. The implication here is that people suffering afflictions in specific parts of their bodies were offering representations of the affected area in the hope that the water powers would cure them. At Lake Neuchatel in Switzerland, the local people built special wooden platforms from the lake shore to facilitate the hurling of offerings into the lake. The lake has subsequently yielded up hundreds of brooches, weapons, shields, chariots and animal remains. Lake sites in Scotland, Wales, Ireland and on the Druidic holy island of Anglesey were all used in the same way.

But by far the largest caches of votive offerings to watery powers have been found in northern Germany and Denmark. The offerings are very varied, from pottery vessels containing food to jewellery and weaponry, sometimes in prodigious quantities. The skeletons of ten dogs turned up in a Danish bog, cow horns in another, and yet another contained a complete beehive made from the trunk of a beech tree, with its lid and two twig ring-frames for the honeycombs. The Germanic peoples especially favoured the depositing of war booty in their bogs. One Danish bog contained the battle spoils from an engagement estimated to have involved about 200 men on the losing side. The bog yielded up 9 saddles and bridles, 60 swords, 62 daggers, 123 shields, 191 spears, and 203 javelins. Six similar finds in Denmark contained between 15,000 and 20,000 metal objects. In most cases, the offerings were deliberately damaged – swords bent double, points broken and so on, as if breaking and 'killing' these objects was the best way to present them to the gods. In almost perfect confirmation of Tacitus's description of the Nerthus fertility rites, two complete four-wheeled carts were also retrieved from Danish peat bogs.

Wells and deep springs were also sacred sites. The Celts believed that water sources, piercing deep underground, acted as a link between the earth and the underworld. Many of these were associated with healing cults. 'Wishing wells', still common throughout Europe, are almost certainly the remaining vestiges of the early Europeans' veneration for watery places. They still attract us into casting coins into them in return for granting a favour or righting some wrong.

A deeper association with watery places has its roots in ancient shamanic rites which are still practised today. On going into a trance, many shamans seek access to the spirit world by envisioning wells, waterfalls or deep pools. The shaman's soul plunges further and further into the watery abyss until suddenly it 'breaks through' and emerges in the spirit world, bathed in the rich glowing light of this other land. If you are seeking favours or greater knowledge, or wisdom or foresight from the powers of the underworld, it would seem that a direct means of access is straight down into the depths of wells, springs, lakes or maybe even peat bogs.

Making gifts to the watery powers was clearly best effected by placing the offerings directly at the doors of the underworld. Most offerings, specially prepared for the supernatural powers, were rendered useless in the ordinary world by being broken or bent. This deliberate destruction seems to add up to a statement to the gods: 'Here, I give up to you my finest, the things I covet most. No one shall use or see them again but you.' Such offerings included the greatest sacrifice of all, human life, where once again the offerings were ritually mutilated before being consigned to their watery graves.

The finest inanimate offering yet discovered in a peat bog was prepared in just this way. It was very carefully broken into pieces, forming six small piles, and had been placed in deep water around 100 BC. Pieced back together, they formed a magnificent Celtic silver cauldron, found in a peat bog called Gundestrup in Denmark. The superb decoration on the cauldron is both elaborate and controversial. Some experts consider it the key to understanding the mystery of the Bog People.

One of the friezes inside the bowl has been interpreted as depicting human sacrifice. Here, a procession of warriors on foot passes along the tree of life until they encounter a dog, symbol of death. There, a huge god holds the sacrificial victims upside down over a cauldron which collects their blood. The tree of life itself grows from the sacrificial cauldron and, above it, a procession of mounted warriors rides away from the cauldron, as if the sacrificed mortals had been reborn in greater glory.

P.V. Glob had his own theory as to the origins and final destiny of the Gundestrup cauldron. Made originally by the eastern Celts, perhaps somewhere around the Black Sea, he believes it was a battle trophy of the Cimbri tribe who took it back to their Danish homeland after successful fighting in Germany. There, they retained it at their most sacred shrine in Himmerland, a shining testimony to the victories of their warriors. Their fortunes reached a peak in the first century AD when they defeated the Romans in Germany. But after that their luck turned and whole divisions of their army were cut down. In Glob's view it would have been then that the Cimbri decided to 'sacrifice' the great cauldron by breaking it up and placing it in the bog, entreating the watery powers to give them a great victory in exchange for the gift.

In a way, it is not surprising that the Celts and Germans should have held cauldrons in such sacred esteem. Ever since their invention in the Bronze Age, metal cauldrons were highly prized functional objects – holders of liquid and cooking vessels which were much more durable than their ceramic equivalents. In particular, the nomads of the steppes, who moved all their possessions around in wagons or on horseback, found metal cauldrons of great value. As we have seen in the first two chapters, many of the steppe nomads were Indo-Europeans and shared common ancestors with the Celts and Germans. Reverence for cauldrons, chalices and grails might well have been an inherited cultural tradition reflecting the functional importance of such vessels. But for any object to be revered to this extent, it must also be of symbolic value. Cauldrons and chalices are holders of liquids in a confined space, miniature ponds or wells in their own right. They are also the means for transforming food – the essential life-support. They render the raw cooked and the inedible edible. By 'giving' food and drink to the cauldron you make a miniature offering to the watery powers. By 'taking' cooked food or drink from the cauldron, you receive both vital nourishment and the purification and blessings of the watery powers. Make the cauldron from a precious metal, such as silver, decorate it with scenes of the most vital ritual practices, then give it an offering of human blood. This seems to be the heady brew which the prophetesses of the ancient Germans and Celts were using to divine the future.

Two final elements need to be cast into this metaphysical melting pot before we can assess its relevance to the bodies in the bogs. First, the Celts and Germans, like almost every other culture on the face of the earth in those days, held the sun to be the holiest, most powerful deity. In Chapter One, we met the 'Sun Man' of the Taklamakan desert; in Chapter Four, we will see how pivotal the sun was in ancient Egyptian cosmology and ritual. For now, we should note that the sun is universally recognized as the ultimate source of all nourishment, of life itself. But it is not a constant. Every evening it disappears, temporarily 'dies'; every morning it is reborn. In northern latitudes, such as Scandinavia and northern Britain, the duration of its presence varies greatly through the year. In midsummer it is almost omnipresent; in midwinter it seems that it might vanish for ever. Rituals aiming to ensure that the sun 'turned', making the days grow longer rather than shorter, were a central part of the Germano-Celtic annual ritual cycle. As the earthly representation of the sun was fire, autumn and winter rituals centred around fire.

Remnants of these rituals are still with us. Although today we burn a Catholic subversive on 5 November (an exceedingly un-PC thing to do when you think about it) we are also kindling the bonfires marking the end of the Celtic year (1 November). In Scotland today, as soon as the New Year has been seen in, the Scots still go 'first footing', traditionally taking a piece of coal and so passing a new fire from house to house, kindling back to life the new year and the new-born sun.

Along with fire, the sun was also associated with the wheel, and many people were buried with small solar wheels or discs, presumably to provide them with light during their sojourn in the underworld. The association of the sun and wheels, in those times, was extremely widespread, occurring right across Central Asia and parts of North Africa. Even the Gundestrup cauldron bears a prominent image of a goddess surrounded by fabulous animals – elephants, griffins and tigers – and on each side of her are two beautifully worked six-spoked wheels.

Finally, the Celts believed that three was a magic number. Many events in their myths occur three times, and important powers manifest themselves in triple form. The greatest of the goddesses, the divine Earth Mother, is often represented in triple form, bearing symbols of fertility such as babies, fruit and bread. Magical birds also appear in groups of three in both the Irish and Welsh Celtic traditions. They are associated with healing and rebirth in the otherworld. Bulls, admired for their strength and virility, are sometimes depicted with three horns. There is even a figurine depicting a three-horned bull mounted by three women.

There was also a dark side to this triple symbolism. Irish myths tell of King Conaire who encountered sinister harbingers of death in the form of three red-clothed riders on red horses. In an eerie scene reminiscent of *Macbeth*, he then comes across Badbh, goddess of destruction, who appears in the guise of three hideous black hags, naked and bleeding, with ropes around their necks. Most sinister and relevant of all this imagery, the Celts also practised the art of 'triple killing'. One report describes the sacrificial triple killing of an Irish king by burning,

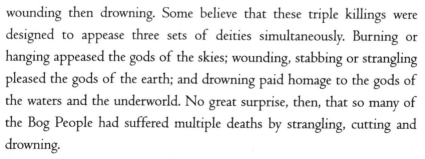

wounding then drowning. Some believe that these triple killings were designed to appease three sets of deities simultaneously. Burning or hanging appeased the gods of the skies; wounding, stabbing or strangling pleased the gods of the earth; and drowning paid homage to the gods of the waters and the underworld. No great surprise, then, that so many of the Bog People had suffered multiple deaths by strangling, cutting and drowning.

A more precise picture is beginning to emerge. At least some of the bog bodies were sacrificial victims, offerings to the Germano-Celtic deities. The ritual meals that Tollund and Grauballe Man had eaten before their death indicate that they died in winter. The gruel they ate was apparently specially prepared, not just a typical porridge. It contained so many wild herbs and grasses that some experts have suggested that these men were being prepared for death to ensure the fertility of the next agricultural season. That their bodies survived at all is further evidence that they died in winter, when the temperature of the tannic waters in the bogs was low enough to prevent their decay. An alternative explanation for the deaths of Grauballe and Lindow Man is that they were sacrificed to the gods of war, the blood from their slit throats used for divining the outcome of battle. Most of them seem to have been subject to some form of triple killing and many have had limbs broken which would have caused them to fall to the ground in the manner prescribed for those about to meet deities. Another angle to this type of interpretation is to see the bog bodies as deliberately 'broken', like so many of the inanimate offerings made to the watery powers in those times. Placing – perhaps sometimes even fixing – the bodies in the deepest parts of the peat bogs, seems a very deliberate act to me. Doing so ensured that the victim was as close to the divine receivers of the offering as possible, as close to the gateway to the underworld as ordinary mortals could reach. It also ensured that the bodies were held in water which could preserve them.

IN SEARCH OF THE IMMORTALS

The question of whether the ancient Celts and Germans knew that the bodies they placed in the bogs would be preserved is rarely addressed, yet for our purposes it is very important. Throughout this book, we come across peoples who believe that the preservation of the bodies of the dead confers special status on them, a kind of immortality. It also often indicates that the individual selected for preservation held high status amongst the living.

There is no written testimony that the Celts or Germans knew that the bodies cast into the bogs would endure. But we do know that these people had lived among the peat bogs for thousands of years and that these places had acquired sacred status as centres of mystical power. The bogs themselves have thrown up the remains of animals and even people who had accidentally fallen into them and expired there. We also know that the Bog People cut peat turf from the bogs for fuel. These people were farmers and stock-rearers, so they are certain to have attempted to rescue animals trapped in the bogs on many occasions and sometimes must have failed. From time to time they must have lost a sheep or calf in midwinter, then found it in almost perfect condition months or years later. People take note of strange events like that and puzzle about how they come about, so there are pragmatic grounds for assuming that the early Celts and Germans were aware of the preservative powers of the bogs.

If this is right, then we can safely assume that the people who placed the bodies in the bogs wished to confer special status on them . We have established that some of the Bog People were people of elevated status when alive, and that it is possible they were captive nobles sacrificed as prisoners of war. Alternatively, they may have been noble criminals, executed for crimes such as cowardice or sodomy, as Tacitus mentioned. But it is also possible that the victims were members of the same tribe as the sacrificers, perhaps even volunteers. This may sound far-fetched, but, over the centuries, cultures in many parts of the world embraced human sacrifice as a necessary, even honourable, part of their religious systems.

Having grown up in the Judaeo-Christian tradition, most of us find the idea of human sacrifice – the giving of life to the supernatural – baffling and abhorrent. Yet human sacrifices occur several times in the Old Testament and Jesus claimed to be a sacrificial victim himself – giving his own life for the good of humanity. The Greeks and Romans, ancient Persians and Indians all performed human sacrifices, as did many of the ancient peoples of South America. One of the commonest forms of human sacrifice was the killing or interment of wives, concubines, servants and slaves at the death of an important leader. This ancient practice still has its echoes in India today with the practice of *Suttee*, where a wife dies on the funeral pyre alongside her husband. Although outlawed decades ago, rumours persist that such deaths still take place. At least one expert on the subject, Patrick Tierney, maintains that in times of natural calamity – tidal waves, earthquakes and the like – children have been offered to the gods in South America as recently as the 1980s.

At the heart of human sacrifice there is a notion of balance, or at least the desire to achieve it. In places where the forces of nature may suddenly become overwhelming, people often strive to find a way to placate the 'anger' of powers which control nature. This idea, central to understanding the role of mummies in South America, will be explored in more depth in Part Two of this book. In northern Europe, 2,000 years ago, people depended upon farming and stock-rearing in ecological conditions which, at best, are characterized as marginal. Successful cropping in these areas was dependent upon a series of factors beyond the control of any one individual. Scandinavia, Scotland and Ireland had cool, wet climates with extremely long winters – climates where the spring had to be good and the summer relatively warm and dry to ensure a good harvest and livestock sufficiently fattened up to endure the winter. A cold spring, rainy summer or sudden cloudbursts at harvest time could spell disaster. When crop failure occurred, the only option was to raid others, to try to secure winter supplies through warfare. So, local conflict between people was another factor shaping the metaphysical thinking of the early Europeans. Both the physical and the social worlds that these people inhabited were precarious.

In essence, these people were farmers who recognized the cycles of generation and growth of plant life, and its ability to lie dormant in seed form throughout the winter only to be reborn each spring. They understood perfectly that these processes were dependent upon the light and heat of the sun and the nurturing powers of water. They knew that if any of these natural forces went awry there would be crop failure which would lead to many deaths, directly by starvation or indirectly through warfare. It could even lead to the total disintegration of a society. But if one person paid the ultimate price – the price of life itself – then this might guarantee the well-being of the rest. This is the logic which underpins human sacrifice: the loss of one for the welfare of all. The Spanish conquistadors encountered this logic in action, high in the Andes, in the sixteenth century AD as we shall see in Chapter Eight. There seems to me to be persuasive evidence that very similar thinking may lie at the heart of the fates of at least some of the sacrifices in the bogs of northern Europe 2,000 years ago. After all, it is one thing to put to death a few captives or slaves, quite another to offer up one of your own loved ones to persuade the gods of your sincerity.

If this were the case, then it also makes a great deal of sense to place the bodies of those who have surrendered their lives in an environment where they will be preserved, where they will continue to exist beyond death. As messengers to the gods, there would be every reason to give them the best chance of rebirth.

BODIES IN THE BOGS

At the moment, it is impossible to determine whether the bodies in the bogs were members of the local community or prisoners of war from other groups, but with the recent extraordinary advances in population genetics this riddle may one day be solved. As it stands, the few garments, hairstyles and the like found with the bodies only indicate that the Bog People were from similar cultures to their executioners. But the clues which the bodies provide do cast light on how the Celts and Germans, our ancient ancestors, perceived the cycles of life, death, rebirth and the afterlife. The picture is further enhanced by the patchy but generally accurate details provided by classical writers.

The Celts and Germans had a clear conscious vision of the otherworld, the land where deities, the souls of the dead and some ogres and supernatural monsters resided. Although this otherworld was distinct from the land of the living, it was also overlapping in time and space. For example, in November, at the turn of the Celtic year, it was held that the spirits of the otherworld could roam the earth and that mortals might stray, or be lured into the otherworld – a timeless place. According to the myths, if mortals strayed into it they were in great danger. Although they might feel that they had only been there for a few moments, when they returned to the mortal world they aged instantly. In one Irish tale, sailors returning from the 'Happy Other-world of Women' are warned not to touch the shore, but one man flings himself into the sea. As he touches the shore, he turns instantly to dust.

Some animals were thought to be able to go between the worlds of the living and the otherworld. As in so many other cultures round the world, birds were identified with the spirits of the dead rising from the mortal body to the heavens above. Snakes, with both deadly venom and the ability to slough off their skins, were potent images of rebirth, death and fertility. Stags were also seen as symbols of regeneration because of their ability to regrow their antlers. Dogs, with their hunting skills, were associated with death.

The Irish believed that the otherworld lay far across the sea to the west, and that it could be reached by a lengthy sea journey. Others thought it was underground, accessed through lakes, wells, bogs or caves. In most circumstances, the otherworld was a miraculous place where feasting was continuous and there was no pain, ageing, disease or decay. Music and beauty filled the air, a world full of magic, the place of immortality. A huge cauldron maintained a constant supply of meat and drink. In these respects, the afterlife world is characterized as an idealized extension of everyday life without the hassle. Lots of partying, no hangovers.

But a new element also enters the equation here. While the Pazyryk hinted through their artwork at an awareness of the possibility of rebirth, the Germans and Celts were much more explicit. In the afterworld there was the 'Cauldron of Rebirth', a great diamond-studded cauldron boiled by the breath of seven virgins. In Irish legend, this cauldron could restore warriors to life if they were cooked in it overnight. Red wine was seen as another source of restoration and rebirth. With its blood-like appearance, wine linked death with rebirth.

A further new element is also apparent from the Celtic materials. While, from what we can gather, the general view of the afterlife was positive for the Scythians and the peoples of the Taklamakan, an element of doubt is clear in Celtic thoughts and writings. The dark side of death is becoming apparent. The otherworld was not always a jolly, festive place; it was also sometimes portrayed as dark, sombre and frightening, especially if mortals should stumble across it. I have already mentioned the blood-red riders and the three naked black hags who tormented a mortal visitor. For me, these aspects of the otherworld all seem to point towards an underworld, which reminds us of the cold darkness of death.

BODIES IN THE BOGS

It was for the journey through this gloomy world that some Celts provided the deceased with solar discs or sun-wheels to light their way. Perhaps it was to this dark gloomy underworld, the world beneath the black waters of the peat bogs, that the sacrificial victim was consigned, to find his or her way directly to the deities, to plead the cause of the living above. If successful, then perhaps the spirit of the victim would be warmed in the Cauldron of Rebirth and be given the chance to inhabit a new body, and live again.

Caesar wrote of the Celts that their priests, the Druids, 'attach particular importance to the belief that the soul does not perish but passes after death from one body to another'. He felt that this led to their disdain of death and their fearlessness in battle. The Roman poet Lucan said that the Celts saw death as merely an interruption in a much longer survival, a stage between one life and the next. This regenerative view of life stretching beyond death provides precisely the ideology which would support voluntary human sacrifice. Very similar metaphysics provided the rationale for human sacrifice in the Andes and comforted the chosen victims there.

There is only a little evidence to show that the Scythian nomads of the Steppes and their Pazyryk cousins had evolved concepts of regeneration or rebirth in their afterlife beliefs. That they believed in the immortality of the human soul and its continued existence after death is beyond doubt. But they seemed to focus their preparations for eternity on the journey to the next world, helping the dead on their way with great elemental forces, such as the sun and moon, as well as simpler material goods, animals and spirit- beings. They may well, too, have feared the darker side of the afterlife journey, but left nothing behind to show us this. Their focus is on an epic journey, as we would expect in a nomadic culture.

IN SEARCH OF THE IMMORTALS

Among the Celts and Germans who were in essence farmers, the seasonal rhythms, the plant cycles of life, death and regeneration, began to influence their visions of human life, death and the afterlife. As with their predecessors, the bedrock of their beliefs was the immortal soul, but they conceived new ways in which it could persist beyond death. The idea that death was a suspension of life, a seed-like state which could be re-activated with the appropriate ritual behaviour, was a core concept. They did not go as far as enunciating a full-blown doctrine of reincarnation, but they certainly felt that life could be restarted, just as the dormancy of winter gives way to the greening and blooming of spring. At the same time, an element of peril and uncertainty entered the equation. Death's darker side is acknowledged and, in extreme cases, was placated with the supreme offering: human life. At a different level, all these ritual observances were essentially aimed to ensure a safe place for humans, alive or dead, within the rhythms of day and night, sun and rain, winter and summer, as they progressed smoothly from year to year.

Far away to the southwest, several thousand years before the times of the Bog People, another apparently isolated culture had been elaborating its visions of precisely these same processes. The conclusions they reached, the visions they formulated and the rituals they evolved, seem at first glance to be totally distinct from the world views of our ancient European ancestors. Yet, as we shall see in the next chapter, there are strange echoes, harmonic chimes, to be found between the peoples of Bronze- and Iron-Age Europe and the spectacular achievements of the peoples of ancient Egypt.

Chapter 4

Egypt
land of immortality

The first things to really catch my attention in Egypt were the birds, thousands of them, in every shape, colour and form, scattered all over the west bank of the Nile opposite Luxor. We had taken a little ferry boat from our hotel on the east bank and crossed the 'strong brown god' of the river early on our first morning in Egypt. That crossing from east to west, made thousands of times millennia ago by the ancient Egyptians, still signals a shift from one world to another. Behind us on the east bank was a bustling town: cars hooting, traffic-lights blinking. Rows of enormous Nile cruise-ships, laden with elderly European tourists, were jostling on their moorings, obscuring a river bank of mostly concrete quays and walkways.

In front of us on the west bank was hardly a building to be seen. The river met the land with a fringe of water plants, little hummocks of grass and a scattering of bushes and palm trees. The land rose lazily from the river, a patchwork of water meadows and irrigation canals with the occasional low mud-brick house on higher ground. A man brought three camels down to the water to drink. A woman first washed some clothes then her baby at the water's edge. Two fishermen in a shallow boat encircled a clump of rushes with a nylon net, then beat the water with their paddles to frighten the perch out of their havens. Every bush on the bank housed kingfishers, mostly a beautiful black-and-white variety. The water's edge teemed with waders of every shape and size. The fields were full of egrets and ibis. Overhead, crows flapped effortlessly from place to place; occasionally a hawk flashed through the blue. In the fields, I could hear the constant babble of sparrows and small songbirds. The pulse of the city, airports, cabs and customs officers dissolved, replaced by the timeless rhythm of life lived in much the same way for 6,000 years.

Accompanying us on this my first visit to Egypt was Dr Joann Fletcher, Egyptologist *extraordinaire*. Under flaming auburn hair, her searing dark brown eyes were highlighted by eyeliner. Her skin is very pale, so sensitive to the sun that she carries a black parasol wherever she goes in Egypt. Her clothes are almost always black and a large silver Egyptian wadjet eye invariably adorns her left lapel.

When she was barely able to read, her parents gave her a book on ancient Egypt, igniting a passion which has never been sated. She first visited the ancient sites when she was fifteen. Now in her early thirties, she has been back whenever she has had the chance. Her knowledge is encyclopaedic. In normal conversation she is relaxed and chatty, her Yorkshire brogue playing on the dour humour of her home county. But the moment the word Egypt enters the conversation, there is an intensity in her face and an authority in her voice. As we drifted along the banks of the river that morning I sensed I was in the hands of a very fine guide, someone who could lead me through the labyrinth of the most sophisticated mummy-making culture the world has ever known.

Egypt is unique in the annals of mummy-makers because, from very early on indeed (at least by – possibly earlier than – 3000 BC), the Egyptians could write and, almost from the outset, recognized the power of the written word. Unlike the accountant-type records of the scribes of

LAND OF IMMORTALITY

Mesopotamia, writing was a sacred practice for the Egyptians. Simply to name something or someone and preserve that name in writing was an act of mystical power. So, from the start, they recorded the events, ideas and beliefs they held dearest; and continued to do so for the 3,000 years that their civilization flourished.

In one sense, this was a profound blessing while I was writing this book because I knew that, in this chapter, I would not need to speculate, or try to deduce from archaeological fragments and records just what the people were up to. In another sense, I also knew that any attempt to explain the core activities and beliefs of this staggeringly complex, self-recorded people would be to play with fire. At least 200 years of intense scholarship has added thousands of works of description and analysis to the bibliography of these wondrous people. All the more important, then, I decided, to stick to the themes central to my search: why the Egyptians mummified their dead and what they believed happened after they died.

The Nile – the longest river in the world – is fed from Central Africa. Every year monsoons swirl in from the Indian Ocean unleashing torrents of water which flow northwards, first through the Sudan then on across Egypt, bisecting the desert all the way to the river's delta and eventually into the Mediterranean. Until the new Aswan Dam was built in 1971, this torrent of rainwater caused the Nile to burst its banks each year around July. The water flooded all over the valley floor which in places was twenty miles wide. The valley then remained inundated for two to three months, and when the waters finally receded they left behind them a thick coat of extremely fertile black alluvial silt.

In very ancient times, the people of the Nile valley hunted the many species of wild animals which lived in the floodplain, fished the rich waters and gathered wild plants in the valley. When they learnt how to tame cattle, they grazed them in the lush pastures along the river. But it was the coming of agriculture which released the enormous potential of the valley. With its hot climate and the annual gift of renewed fertility, the valley was a natural bread-basket which, outside of the flood season, could be farmed almost all the year round. Wheat and barley were the staple crops and the people continued to rear cattle for meat and milk. Thanks to the fecundity of the land, the population grew rapidly and learned to construct dykes and ditches for irrigation and to collect silt for fertilizer. The annual flood, however, was not always consistent, and in years when the flood waters did not rise to normal heights there could be famine.

Like the peoples of the oases of the Taklamakan, the Egyptians did not bury their dead in the fertile black soils of the floodplain; they took them to the sterile red soils of the surrounding desert. There, in the ancient pre-dynastic days before 3000 BC, they wrapped their dead in goatskins and reed mats, then laid them to rest on their sides – their legs drawn up in the foetal position – facing east, towards the rising sun. The hot dry sands rapidly desiccated the bodies in the shallow graves, creating natural mummies. Some of these have survived to the present day. So, while the black soils of the floodplains nourished the living, the red soils of the desert preserved the dead.

A few days after we arrived in Egypt, Joann decided to take us to Dendera to the famous temple of the goddess Hathor, partly built by Cleopatra VII. There, she said, we could see one of the few depictions of the mythic origins of mummification. I was really keen to get on to this, but Joann was adamant that there was no point in diving in at the deep end. To understand better, we would have to go back to the beginning. It was a two-hour drive to Dendera, so I settled back to listen as we jostled down the busy road through the verdant fields and waterways of the Nile valley.

LAND OF IMMORTALITY

According to the ancient Egyptians, before the world began there was only water and darkness – barren, sterile waters, the waters of chaos. There are several variants of their creation stories but, in essence, the primordial act was the appearance of a mound of black earth in the waters. On the mound a bud grew, eventually opening just as the lotus flower opens each morning.

With the opening of the lotus flower the mound was transformed into the 'Island of Flames'. From it emerged the new-born sun-god, Re, greatest of all the gods. Having created himself, he set about creating all the other gods. In one version of the myth, he took his penis in his hands and ejaculated on to the land. From his sperm sprung Shu, god of the air, and Tefnut, goddess of moisture, thus generating the basic elements within which life could be sustained. Shu and Tefnut then coupled to produce Geb, the earth god, and Nut, goddess of the sky. This couple then mated, producing four offspring: two brothers who married their two sisters. Osiris, the god of order, married his sister Isis, and Seth, the god of disorder, married his sister Nephthys. This set the stage for the first great divine battles, and these, in their turn, led to the need for mummification.

Osiris was a wise and just ruler and, having taught his subjects the arts of agriculture, architecture and many other fine things, the people thrived and a golden age prevailed. But only briefly. Osiris's younger brother Seth was obsessively jealous of Osiris's success and constantly plotted against him. Osiris, a god of pure goodness, who found it impossible to see evil in others, ignored Seth's machinations, but this only incensed Seth more. In a fit of rage, he turned himself into a furious bull and trampled Osiris to death. Not content with killing him, he hacked the body to bits and scattered the pieces all over Egypt. Osiris's soul, left without a body to reside in, departed from the world of the living and descended into the darkness of the underworld. As the first living being ever to die, it was fitting that he should take command of the land below the setting sun, the Kingdom of the West. And, as Osiris had no son and heir, Seth was immediately able to seize power and usurp the throne.

Distraught with grief, Isis — who was already a powerful goddess in her own right, with extraordinary powers of magic, healing and divination — scoured the land, collecting up the scattered remains of her husband-brother and pieced him back together. Then she called upon the jackal-god Anubis to help re-form her husband. Anubis set about embalming Osiris's body — the first time this had ever happened — and his work was so successful that, thereafter, he was seen as a special god for the dead.

Once Anubis had re-formed Osiris, Isis used all her magical powers to conjure him back to life. As he started to stir, Isis turned herself into a kite and hovered over his body. He revived for just long enough to impregnate the Isis-kite with his sperm.

Isis then sped away to a secret refuge in the Nile delta where she gave birth to Horus. There, she reared the boy-god with the help of the cow-goddess Hathor who acted as Horus's wet nurse. When the child was old enough, Isis brought him before the council of the gods and demanded that her son receive his birthright, the kingdom of Egypt. At first, the gods disagreed and refused to let a mere boy take over from the super-powerful Seth. But eventually Isis entrapped her wicked brother-in-law. Disguising herself as the beautiful widowed wife of a cowherd, she came to petition King Seth. She explained that her husband had died shortly after she had borne him a son. The boy went to claim his cattle, but a stranger came and seized the cattle. When the boy protested, the stranger threatened to beat him. Seth, lecherous as ever, heard the beautiful woman's tale and pronounced, 'How can a stranger seize the cattle when the son is still alive?' Isis, delighted, turned herself into a kite, flew into a nearby tree, and laughingly declared to all the gods, who had to agree: 'Seth, you have judged yourself.' So, Re ordered that the kingdom of the living be returned to its rightful ruler, Horus.

Seth, however, was not about to give up the throne without a fight. Decades of combat ensued with the mighty Seth ever escaping the rage of Horus. Isis used all her powers to protect her son, but could not bring herself to actually destroy her brother-in-law Seth. Re, tiring of the endless turmoil and chaos generated by the divine feuds, eventually sent a messenger to Osiris to hear his judgement of the dispute. After a perilous journey to the underworld and back, the messenger returned with Osiris's reply. Predictably, Osiris had pronounced in favour of his son and against his brother Seth. He was also furious that, throughout all the preceding years of civil war, justice had not been done for his son. Re, incensed by Osiris's criticism, sent the messenger back to the realm of the dead with a haughty reply. This time, Osiris exploded with anger and replied: 'Here in the land of the dead there are many powerful demons. Should I send them up to the land of the living, to return to me with the stolen hearts of evil doers? I am much stronger than you; sooner or later even the gods must come to sleep in my Beautiful West.'

With this threat, the conflict was finally resolved and Re ordered Seth to be bound and brought to him. Seth finally accepted the judgement of the gods and abdicated. As compensation, Re invited Seth to join him in the heavens, to become the god of storms, raining down thunder and lightning on the people below, and to defend him on his nightly journeys through the underworld.

Horus took up the throne and, thereafter, was succeeded by human pharaohs who, on accession to the throne, added the title 'the living Horus' to their own names. Thus, Horus became the divine prototype of all the kings of Egypt and, customarily portrayed with a falcon-head, is found depicted in many of the pharaohs' tombs.

IN SEARCH OF THE IMMORTALS

This epic myth essentially links the original creation of the world with the establishment of kingship in Egypt, and establishes the divine mandate of the pharaohs. Representing Horus, they are always on the side of order, conquerors of chaos. But the myths are more ambiguous about the relationship between life and death. In Seth's killing of Osiris, we witness the first original death and see death's victory snatched away by Isis who magically restores life and potency to Osiris. Death is also cheated by Anubis's mummification techniques and Isis's magic. At the end of the cycle, we hear of a threat so powerful from Osiris, the master of the land of the dead, that even Re, the sun-god, gives in to death's demands. But Osiris was not acting in an evil way. On the contrary, he was demanding the restoration of harmony in the world of the living. His ultimatum – to unleash the monsters of the underworld in the land of the living – was given merely because he wanted to re-establish orderly relations between the cycles of life and death. As the first dead being, it was, in a sense, his duty to create this balance.

The model the gods chose to re-establish this balance was based upon the two cyclical movements of their sun-god, Re. Each morning he is 'born' in the east, then travels 'alive' across the sky bestowing life-giving rays on the recipients below. In the evening he 'dies' – disappears – only to be 'reborn' the next morning. At the same time, during the course of the year, he travels north and south from the equinoxes to the solstices and back again. During the Egyptian year this results in a nine-month period of growth and 'life' for the dry land, followed by a brief period of 'death' when the land is flooded. The land is then magically 'reborn', rising out of the waters of chaos, in a renewed state of fertility. The task facing Re and Osiris was to discover how the human cycles of birth, life, death and rebirth would fit into the divine cosmic masterplan.

Having now mastered the broader picture, I knew I needed to flesh out the minutiae of their vision. Joann, as usual, not only knew the answers but also took us to the relevant sites to show how the Egyptians had expressed their ideas. Many of their tombs illustrate intimate details of what the ancient Egyptians conceived themselves to be.

At birth, according to them, all humans have a body, *sah*, and in the centre of the body lies the heart, *ib*. The heart was held to be the seat of consciousness and feeling. People also all have a soul called the *ka*. This soul is the life force, the essence of being. In addition, people have a *ba* which is often translated as spirit or personality. The *ba* is, perhaps, the divine qualities, the qualities of immortality. Besides these, all people have names, *ren*, and shadows, *shuwt*. These two last features, the name and the shadow, provide metaphysical protection for the human being. At death, the *ka* remains within the body in a dormant state of suspended animation. The purpose of mummification, therefore, is to retain the perfection of the host's body as home to the *ka*. The aim of the final funerary rituals, performed within the tomb, is to bring the deceased's *ka* fully back to life. Thereafter, the *ka* will be nurtured by the offerings placed in the tomb and by the depictions of food production and daily life on the coffin and tomb walls.

The *ba* manifests itself as a human-headed bird which at death leaves the body and is free to roam in the world of the living during the day time. At night, however, it returns to the body of the dead for succour and can also travel through the heavens in the company of the gods.

The role of the *ba* in achieving immortality for its host body was critical. It was the *ba* which had to travel through the underworld and survive a series of trials before it could be reunited with the *ka*. If the *ba* was successful, then its fusion with the *ka* created an *akh*, the ultimate state of being, a 'being of light', which would endure for eternity. Reaching this transcendent state was, the ancient Egyptians believed, the ultimate goal of all human beings.

But achievement of this state of eternal grace was dependent, first and foremost, on the successful preservation of the body by mummification.

IN SEARCH OF THE IMMORTALS

The oldest mummies in Egypt are natural. The bodies were simply placed in the sand wrapped in animal skins and reed mats, then covered with sand. A few grave goods were included to help the deceased on their otherworld journey. This practice lasted thousands of years, and no doubt the people soon realized that the bodies of their ancestors were preserved underground by the salty desert sands.

Gradually, though, as the people became more sedentary, relying more on farming and less on roving herds of cattle, a social differentiation appeared in their mortuary practices. While the poor continued to bury their dead in the sand, the rich began to build little mud-brick houses with underground chambers for their dead. These tombs had roofs made with wooden poles, covered by branches and consolidated with mud – building techniques, incidentally, which were extraordinarily similar to those used by the peoples of the Taklamakan. Imposing as they doubtless were, these simple tombs placed the bodies at a remove from the desiccating sands and the bodies did not last as well. They also made life easier for grave-robbers, who could simply tunnel in under the roof to pillage anything of any value inside. Grave-robbing, it seems, is among the most ancient of professions, at least in Egypt.

After the country was unified around 3100 BC, there was a great outpouring of artistic and technical innovation. This included some rethinking about how best to protect the ancestors. Gradually, rich people's tombs were hidden further away from the settlement sites, deep inside the limestone bedrock of the hills in the desert. In the first dynasty, possibly even earlier, attempts were also made to deliberately preserve the bodily outline of the dead by wrapping them tightly in linen bandages soaked in resin which would harden when dry. In the fourth dynasty, the embalmers started to remove the internal organs. Later, they experimented by stuffing the abdominal cavities with linen and aromatic materials, and used natron, a naturally occurring salt compound of sodium carbonate and sodium chloride, as a desiccant and sterilizing agent.

Over the millennia which followed, Egyptian mummification techniques varied as embalmers strove to perfect their art. From the fourth to the twenty-first dynasty, for example, the viscera were removed, purified then placed near to the body in the tomb. In the twenty-first dynasty, the embalmers started to replace the viscera inside the abdominal canopy in packages. In later periods, even more effort was made to retain the likeness of the dead person, by making incisions and inserting stuffing to fill out areas such as the cheeks, stomach, buttocks and thighs, which were prone to shrinkage. But the underlying principles guiding the mummifiers and the ritual timetable they adhered to seemed to change very little over the millennia.

The actual mummification was carried out by a series of ritual specialists, the embalmers. Although they were crucial in ensuring a safe entry for the dead into the afterlife, some of the embalmers were treated very ambiguously in the land of the living. Just as many societies consider butchers to be dangerous, polluting beings, so certain embalmers were treated as unclean.

The whole embalming process was carried out over a period of seventy days. On the first day, the body was washed thoroughly and the brain removed and discarded. Then an embalmer, known as the 'ripper-out' or the 'slitter', took an obsidian knife, made a cut down the left side of the person's abdomen and removed the stomach, intestines, lungs and liver. Only the heart was left in place. The 'ripper-out' – held to be unclean – was then ritually chased away from the corpse. The removed perishable organs were thoroughly washed out, dried with natron, treated with aromatic oils and resins, and either placed in special jars or to one side, to be returned to the body. Natron was then heaped all over the eviscerated body and left to desiccate for forty days.

The next step was to wash the interior of the body cavity, scent it with cinnamon and spices, and fill it with a temporary stuffing which included natron and sometimes juniper berries. From time to time, the embalmers replaced the interior stuffing with fresh materials. Finally they coated the mummified body with cedar and juniper oils and scented resins, then wrapped it tightly with linen bandages coated in resin. As they wrapped the body, they inserted special amulets and charms in the bandages to give it extra protection. While this was taking place, the priests read relevant passages from *The Book of the Dead*, encouraging the deceased to come back to life. In the case of pharaohs, their fingers and toes were capped with golden thimbles. When this was complete the priests would chant:

> Your fingers are gold and your nails are electrum! You are touched, in truth, by the emanation of Re, the divine body of Osiris! Your legs will carry you to the eternal abode and your hands will carry you as far as the place of infinite duration, for you are regenerated by gold and revived by electrum. Your fingers will glitter in the abode of Osiris, in the embalming workshop of Horus himself . . .

Once all the preparations were completed, the body was returned to its family who took it westwards, towards the setting sun and its underground tomb.

While the rituals varied little over time, the places the ancient Egyptians chose to bury their dead did. Starting out as mere pits in the sand, then developing into simple bench-shaped houses, the next form were rock-cut tombs, hewed into the solid rock in nearby hills or mountains. Although the tombs were always conceived of as homes for the dead, this move deeper underground brought the physical placing of the dead more into line with their metaphysical beliefs: that is, the actual bodies were now placed in the underworld. Then, by the third dynasty, around 2600 BC, King Djoser hit upon the idea of building a massive monument over his tomb, a stepped pyramid. His pyramid, at Saqqara, is the oldest stone monument in the world. But why build a pyramid in the first place?

Joann and I put this question to Dr Zahi Hawass, current Director of the Pyramids at Giza and Saqqara. We were sitting in his office in the shadow of the Great Pyramid. A sandstorm was blowing outside. He was flanked on either side by two *eminences grises*: Egyptologists – a quietly-spoken American pyramid expert, Dr Mark Lehner, and a fellow American sporting a blazer and red-and-white polka-dot bow-tie. Minions scurried in and out of the room whenever Dr Hawass rang his bell, which he did frequently. This persisted throughout our discussion. The Director and his dignitaries looked at us quizzically, rather in the way I suspect a pharaoh's Grand Vizier would have looked down at inquisitive but naïve foreign emissaries in ancient times.

The pyramids, Dr Zahi Hawass patiently explained, are, in essence, representations of the primordial mound which rose up from the waters of chaos at the beginning of creation. Recall that the mound contained an egg, the embryo of the sun-god Re. As he burst forth from the mound and ascended to heaven, so too would the pharaoh ascend from his mortal tomb to be carried up the sunbeams on the pyramid to be reunited with his divine creator and ancestor, Re. The shape of the pyramid, Dr Hawass pointed out, mimicked the rays of the sun travelling down from heaven. Originally the tops of the pyramids were capped with gold so that each morning, as the sun rose, the first thing to be lit up was the golden tip of the pyramid, blazing its welcome to the reborn god. In addition to their celestial, spiritual roles, the pyramids also performed an essential secular function. Contrary to popular belief, they were not built by millions of slaves but by specialized craftsmen. Each year during the flood season, when it was impossible to work on the land, the pharaoh would summon labourers from throughout the land to build his great funerary monument. Dr Hawass considers that these massive undertakings drew the entire nation together, giving it a central focus, a goal. Recent excavations have uncovered the living quarters, medical centres, bakeries and even the graves of the workers who built the pyramids, and it is clear that they were well treated and well nourished. Their skeletons inevitably reveal that many suffered back problems, but who wouldn't when hauling millions of blocks of stones around, each weighing several tons? The Great Pyramid is made from 3,200,000 blocks of limestone, with an average weight of 2.5 tons. Napoleon Bonaparte, coming upon the great pyramids for the first time in 1798, calculated that if the stones of the three pyramids were dismantled they would form a wall three metres high and a metre thick which would encircle the whole of France.

But not all pyramids were built on this epic scale. Dotted around the site at Giza there are several much smaller, less imposing pyramids. Twenty miles away at the site of the oldest pyramid, Saqqara, there are pyramids of all sizes. Some of them were evidently poorly constructed and are now falling down. At the site of the construction workers' cemetery, Dr Hawass has uncovered many tiny pyramid tombs built from mud brick, where the workers have imitated their masters on a tiny scale. So, impressive though the great pyramids are, it was not the size that counted for the ancient Egyptians, but the cosmological concepts embedded in them.

As Dr Hawass's fascinating discourse drew to a close, I enquired if the royal tomb in the Great Pyramid was still accessible. Dr Hawass tinkled his bell vigorously, and an obsequious young man entered the room. For our benefit Dr Hawass spoke to him in English, ordering him to fetch the key to the doorway into the Great Pyramid and escort us inside. After that, he suggested, we should visit the Sphinx, where we would be permitted to walk right up to the monument. Our audience over, we made a graceful withdrawal, showering thanks and compliments upon the generosity of today's Grand Vizier of the Pyramids.

The sandstorm had subsided sufficiently for us to dash to our minibus and drive round to the 'entrance' of the Great Pyramid. Four steps above ground level, there was an iron grid across a narrow stone doorway. A security guard let us pass through while our guide found the switch and turned on the lights. At first, we walked easily along the narrow tunnel, down some stairs, then past the first of the portcullises, points where massive granite blocks had been dropped down internal shafts to block the passage and keep out looters. The tunnel then became much lower, so we had to walk in a semi-squat. Eventually it opened out into a small chamber with a long, low shaft running off it, uphill. The roof of this tunnel was only about a metre high, so we had to scramble upwards over low steps for a long time until we came to a large empty chamber – the pharaoh's burial chamber.

The walls, floor and ceiling were all pitch black. At the back of the chamber stood a massive black sarcophagus, lid off and empty. On the walls of the room I could just make out some small vents that apparently went right from the heart of the pyramid to its upper surface; vents through which rays of sunlight could travel down, creating paths for the king's *ba* to use and gain access to his mummified body with his *ka* inside; paths which would allow his *akh* to ascend straight up to the sun or the heavens. Doubtless once full to the brim with magnificent treasures, by the time the Great Pyramid was traced and cleared in the nineteenth century, nothing except the sarcophagus had escaped millennia of looting.

It was surprisingly warm in there, but then we were standing in the centre of several million tons of solid rock, in a man-made cave at the heart of a man-made mountain. Natural limestone caves are much cooler, but, unlike the pyramids which are above ground, they are really inside the earth. Rock takes a long time to warm up but, once it does, it retains its heat. This pyramid had had 4,500 years under the baking Egyptian sun to warm up. My guess is that the temperature was about 20C. I made a mental note that the embalmers must have been really skilled to get bodies to endure at this temperature.

Back outside, the wind had dropped sufficiently for us to get around without choking on the flying sand, so we took up Dr Hawass's kind offer to take a close-up look at the Sphinx. Restoration work on the great lion-man, whose reputation had reached the hearts and minds of people from Morocco to Siberia by 500 BC, had just finished. The Sphinx looked magnificent. Behind it, the great pyramids pointed to heaven through the murky, dust-filled air.

Some thousand years after the pyramids were built, around 1500 BC, royal funerary customs changed once again. Despite elaborate security systems, grave-robbers had persisted in looting the royal pyramid tombs. So gradually the pharaohs opted to be buried in tombs cut deep into the bedrock of the Valley of the Kings, in the hills to the west of what was then Thebes, today Luxor. That this change should have occurred is important. It shows that although the kings and priests had successfully incorporated the pyramid-tomb concept into their cosmological schema, pyramids were not vital to them. The pyramid generated an artificial underworld home for the body, soul and spirit. Later pharaohs, aware of the threat of tomb-robbers, thought their chances of achieving immortality would be better if their bodies were placed in secret guarded tombs cut into natural rock. After all, a pyramid is a gigantic advertisement for the presence of a dead king with a sizeable treasure-trove in attendance.

LAND OF IMMORTALITY

Another important development was that pharaohs began to have the interiors of their tombs elaborately decorated. From then on, the walls of the tombs were graphically illustrated with many aspects of the underworld journey that the sun made nightly, as well as the afterlife journeys that the dead would have to undertake.

So we made our way across the verdant west-bank floodplain to the starkly barren Theban hills – hills of the west, place of the setting sun and eternal resting place of such kings as Tutankhamen and Ramsses VI. All lie beneath the pyramid-shaped mountain above, in the Valley of the Kings.

Only one royal tomb is known to have survived undisturbed until the twentieth century AD – the tomb of the boy-king Tutankhamen. He died very suddenly, long before an elaborate tomb could be completed for him. His tomb, therefore, is very small and only the burial chamber is decorated. Nonetheless, anybody who has seen its contents cannot help but be totally overawed by this apparently 'meagre' collection. The images of his funerary mask, his three coffins and his fabulous jewellery and regalia are so well known that there is no need for me to describe them here. Suffice to say that seeing them close up in the Cairo museum is a deeply moving experience. The objects are so superbly designed and crafted, so breathtakingly beautiful, that it is scarcely possible to believe that they were made 3,300 years ago.

Not everything in the tomb was a work of art, however. It also contained things that Tutankhamen might need in the afterlife – food, utensils, a wine cellar, chariots and even model boats. His little tomb, simple though it is, has an elusive magical charm.

One image particularly touched me. It depicts Tutankhamen's successor, Ay, performing the ceremony of 'Opening the Mouth' on his predecessor. This was the climactic point of the last rites, performed at the door of the tomb to bring the mummy 'back to life' before the tomb was sealed. It was performed for Tutankhamen in 1327 BC. Most of the population would have turned out to see his funeral cortège make its way to the Valley of the Kings. His gorgeous coffins would have been surrounded by professional mourners tearing at their hair and smearing dust over their tear-stained faces. Senior courtiers and servants would have borne his funerary goods to the tomb and a special dance would have been performed outside the entrance to the tomb. Here, the mummified body would have been stood upright as the priests began the ceremony of 'Opening the Mouth'.

In this ceremony, not just the mouth, but the eyes, nose, ears and all the senses were revived by the magical chants and spells of the priests – and the one who held the mummy would have worn a jackal-headed mask in honour of Anubis, god of mummification. The final gesture would have been to bring an ox leg and touch it to the lips of the dead king. This, the ancient Egyptians believed, installed the power of the animal in the reborn *ka* of the king. Restoring the power of speech was considered absolutely essential for the dead person, because one of the major defences for the *ba* as it wandered in the underworld was to be able to name any opponents it might encounter.

After the ceremony was complete, the mummy and all the funerary goods would have been taken into the tomb, the priests sweeping away their footsteps as they withdrew. Having left the deceased copious instructions in *The Book of the Dead* on how to undertake the perilous journey through the land of the dead, the tomb would then have been sealed.

Right next to Tutankhamen's tomb lies the far grander underworld home of Ramesses VI. As we walked down the steady incline from the entrance to the tomb, Joann explained that it had been open since antiquity. Robbed of all its contents, except for the massive granite sarcophagus, it has been a tourist attraction for thousands of years.

The entrance hallway is spectacular. Dazzling images adorn a wide clear shaft. At the bottom, the shaft opens out into a large rectangular room which has superbly decorated walls and ceiling, and a semi-circular roof. Across the centre of this vault stretches a double image of the sky goddess Nut, her heads painted on the western side of the tomb, her great long bodies stretching the entire length of the roof, and ending in the black triangles of her pubic hair at the easternmost end of the vault. One of her bodies, her night body, is adorned with stars and, at regular intervals along both bodies, the sun is shown twelve times, representing the twelve hours of the day and the night. All around her are scenes depicting the golden barque of Re, carrying the sun-god and his attendants across a black background.

The ancient Egyptians believed that each evening when the sun set it was swallowed by Nut and spent the next twelve hours travelling through her body, the underworld. When it finally emerged from her vulva each morning at dawn its rebirth was marked by redness in the sky – the goddess's blood of childbirth.

During this process, the sun-god Re manifested himself as a ram-headed figure called 'Flesh of Re'. His passage was not easy. Just as Osiris had warned, the underworld was populated by many demons and the monstrous snake Apophis who attacked him as he passed through each of the twelve hour-gates of the night. Every night he had to do battle with them but, sure as night leads to day, he defeated his enemies and finally made it to the place of rebirth to return once again to the land of the living.

The underworld, as already mentioned, was also the land of the dead, who lay dormant in the darkness until the moment Re passed them in the night. His radiant light awakened them and brought them back to life. Their *ba*, which took the form of human-headed birds, could choose to join him on his nocturnal journey and, as long as all went well, they too could be reborn into the world of the living with the rising sun. But the *ba* in the underworld had a solemn role to perform. Like the sun, they too had to chart a course through its labyrinthine tunnels, past the many demons, snakes and monsters which tried to entrap them, sometimes with nets. Their ultimate search was for Osiris himself.

I stood staring at Ramesses' great granite sarcophagus and gradually began to see that I was contemplating a set of concentric universes. At the outermost lies the great cavernous body of Nut, the sky goddess. The sun travels over her body in the daytime and through the caverns of her underworld body at night. The centre of this universe is the land of the living. Inside the land of the living there is a large man-made cavern – the royal tomb – where the sun, in metaphorical terms, takes the same route from east to west across the vaulted ceiling. At the heart of the tomb is the sarcophagus itself, another smaller cavern. At the heart of this lies the mummified body. Its rib cage is also a tiny cavern and at its centre lies the only organ the Egyptians would permit to remain in place, the human heart, seat of all knowledge, wisdom and feeling. Now I was beginning to understand.

Sharing these thoughts with Joann, she mused that it was all rather like a set of Russian dolls: open one and inside there is another and another. But in the Egyptian case, a series of protective but inanimate 'shells' each contain a much more vital force within its bounds. Within the shell of the universe lies the land of the living; within the shell of the underworld lies the coffin; within this lies the body, and at the centre of the body lies the heart – the seat of eternal life. As the dead person passes from the realm of the living to the realm of the dead he moves physically and spiritually to the encapsulated night-time zone of the underworld.

But once the revitalized body and the *ka* and *ba* are established in the tomb, the *ba* is free to make occasional visits to the land of the living. The main mission of this epic journey, however, is the search for Osiris, seated on his throne in the hall of judgement, known as the 'Hall of Two Truths'.

〰

LAND OF IMMORTALITY

The underworld, which the ancient Egyptians called the *Duat*, was very similar to the land of the living. A river ran through its centre, with plains on either side flanked by mountains. Like the land above, there were lakes, islands and deserts. The only natural feature which differed from the land above was a narrow gorge where they believed the sun-god entered the underworld every evening and where the souls of their dead passed through at the end of their lives. But there were also supernatural dimensions to the underworld which would terrify the newly-arrived souls.

There were lakes of fire and a mound where a head would rear up as the dead soul approached, and there were many demons with weird names like 'backward facer from the Abyss'. The trick, which would neutralize their power, was to pronounce their name. *The Book of the Dead* provided all this information, and there were also maps and spells to chant when confronting a specific peril. The book's formula for banishing a serpent goes like this: 'Be gone! Go and drown yourself in the lake of the Abyss, where your father commanded that you should perish! I am Re, before whom men tremble. Be gone, rebel, lest you feel his knives of light!'

Once the *ba* had successfully navigated its way through gates guarded by knife-wielding demons and the like, it finally arrived at the sixth (midnight) hour of the underworld and entered the Hall of Judgement where Osiris was accompanied by a panel of forty-two gods. The *ba* had to address them all by name and answer questions about the conduct of the dead person while he or she lived. At the same time, the heart of the deceased was placed on the scales of judgement and weighed against the two feathers of Ma'at, goddess of Truth, Divine Order and Justice. As the scales were checked by the jackal-god Anubis and Thoth, god of knowledge, the *ba* recited the 'negative confession', listing a number of crimes, such as theft, treason, boastfulness, that the supplicant had *not* committed. At the end of the negative confession, the *ba* declared, 'Nothing evil shall come into being against me . . . in the hall of justice because I know the names of all the gods who are in it.'

If, despite the negative confession, the scales showed the heart to be heavy with sin, then the fate was instant. The heart was thrown to Amut, the 'Devourer of the Condemned Dead', a monster with the head of a dog or crocodile, the forelegs of a lion and the hindquarters of a hippopotamus. Without the heart, the deceased died a final death – never again to be reunited with its body and *ka*, and that human being ceased to exist.

If the soul was found to be light and pure, free of sin, lighter than the feathers, then the *ba* was permitted to return to the body and fused with the *ka*, forming the perfect immortal human-divine soul, the *akh*.

After that, the destiny of the divine soul varied in Egyptian thought. In the early dynasties it was said that the soul would rise up into the sky and join the circum-polar constellations; in other texts, the *akh* of the dead pharaoh was thought to join Re and to travel with him on his endless cycles of day and night, light and dark. On his way to join Re, he had to be ferried over a celestial lake to the land of the gods where he would be greeted as one of them. Thereafter, he would sail on Re's heavenly barque and, according to one version, act as the sun-god's secretary. A third and later variant on this theme of immortal destiny held that the unified soul joined Osiris, who was not only god of the underworld but also the god of fertility and resurrection – the one who ensured that when seeds were placed in his dark soil each year they would return to life and the plants would thrive. This ultimate power of growth promised rebirth for the dead soul, too. A spell from the *Coffin Texts* invokes this power:

> Whether I live or I die, I am Osiris,
> I enter in and reappear through you,
> I decay in you, I grow in you . . .
> I cover the earth,

LAND OF IMMORTALITY

Whether I live or die I am barley,
I am not destroyed.

So it was that the Egyptians believed they would attain immortality.

The extraordinary richness and precision of the Egyptian vision of creation, life, growth, death, rebirth and immortality, merits careful evaluation. As the only fully articulate mummy-making culture in the world they have provided us with precise reasons why they felt the preservation of the body was an integral part of the process of achieving immortality.

Texts make it clear that if the living do not remember and repeat the names of the dead, then the latter will have little chance of achieving immortality. The magical power of words once again – to name something or someone is to give them life. In a sense, they are right. We do live beyond death in the memories of the living. It is only when those memories have gone that we cease to be. That we persist in writing books about Tutankhamen and Cleopatra thousands of years after they died is, in the Egyptian sense, the proof of the pudding. They live on in our minds and so have achieved immortality.

Whether their individual beings still exist as discrete entities some-where out there in the universe is as yet unknowable. But the paths they expected to take were clearly laid out for them – and for us – to contemplate. As I began to get a sense of how the entire afterlife journey unfolded for the ancient Egyptians I was struck once again by its similarity to the classic sequence of the Near Death Experience.

The actual Out of Body Experience sequence, where the victim seems to leave his or her body and see it from above, is not easily discernible in the Egyptian vision of death, but it is worth bearing in mind that the *ba* is represented as a bird-person which is free to leave the body and fly up and down between the lands of the living and the dead, returning to the body from time to time. The Egyptian *ba*-soul is able to travel out of the body, just as the NDE person's does. Even more striking, the main underworld journey the *ba* undertakes conforms with experiences described by NDE people. The Egyptian soul travels to the underworld, meets divine beings, experiences life-recall and receives the judgement of the gods. But as the Egyptian soul belongs to a person who is dead – rather than on the brink of death – the option of returning to a living body is obviously not a possibility.

Studies of NDEs throughout history have revealed that the actual imagery of the experience is culturally specific. A Buddhist, for example, may see images of lotus flowers, golden light, perhaps even the Buddha himself; St Paul was shown both the glory of heaven and the torment of the damned in hellfire. Yet the underlying structure of these visions – including the Egyptian vision of the afterlife – seems to conform to a universal pattern.

What is certainly clear is that over the millennia of Egyptian civilization, much thought and vast resources were put into contemplating death, the afterlife and its ramifications for the living. And the system that evolved was highly intricate and polished.

Like other cultures mentioned in this book, the ancient Egyptians practised human sacrifice. In the early days, a king would go to his grave with wives and servants, all executed so they could tend to him in the afterlife. But by about 3100 BC, the Egyptians desisted from human sacrifice and settled for burying their dead with statues of their kin, servants and so on instead.

A moral element, familiar to most Christians and Muslims, also entered the Egyptian afterlife equation. As mentioned earlier, they believed people would live forever if they were judged to have led pure lives. They did not take this idea to the extremes of the Judaeo-Christian tradition, which posited that a sinner would be punished for eternity. They settled for instant total annihilation. Nor did they follow the oriental path of reincarnation where an eternal soul is constantly reborn in a new body. Rather they chose a more subtle approach where the unified spirit, at one with divinity, participates in the constant drama and delight of rebirth.

What surprises me is that the ancient Egyptians did not opt for the notion of physical resurrection, the core concept of Christian dogma. Given that they went to such trouble to preserve their dead, it seems very strange that they held out no hope of re-animating their bodies.

In a way, it strikes me as even stranger still that Christianity, which embraces the key notion of resurrection, does not advocate the preservation of the body in anticipation of the eventual re-animation – re-awakening. Ironically, throughout history, Christians have been the greatest persecutors of mummy-making peoples and the greatest destroyers of the world's mummy legacy. In 394 AD, Rome officially adopted Christianity and, as Egypt was a part of its Empire, mass conversion to Coptic Christianity sounded the death-knell for the culture of ancient Egypt bringing about an end to their traditional religion and 3,000-year-old mummification practices.

A thousand years later a macabre taste developed in Europe for using ancient Egyptian mummies for medicinal purposes. Thousands of bodies were exported, then ground up and sold as a universal panacea. It was not until Napoleon Bonaparte invaded in 1798 that Europeans began to take a more enlightened interest in ancient Egypt. Bonaparte had had the foresight to take a team of historians, astronomers, mathematicians, engineers, naturalists, artists and printers on his expedition and they spent two years studying everything they encountered. Their results were published in the *Description of Egypt*, a massive tome which announced to the world the glories of this ancient world. Ever since then, successive generations have dedicated their lives to the study of these people.

But throughout this period, scholars tended to concentrate on the internal dynamics of ancient Egyptian society, searching deeper and deeper for the origins of their ideas and practices within Egypt itself. Consequently, there has been a tendency to ignore – or dismiss – arguments which suggest that some of these concepts may have originated elsewhere. Similarly, until relatively recently, little attention has been paid to the ways that Egyptian ideas and beliefs were disseminated throughout the ancient world. This tendency to look at 'cultures in a vacuum' is typical of much of this century's scholarship, but a new generation of scholars – Joann among them – is now questioning the orthodox view which posits that all the glory of ancient Egypt was somehow self-generated. Their starting point is that the Egyptian civilization developed within the much broader cultural framework of all the peoples of North Africa, the Mediterranean and the Middle East. Their assumption is that Egypt both exported and imported technologies and ideas from its neighbours.

At its zenith the Egyptian empire stretched from the Lebanon in the north to Nubia (modern Sudan) in the south, and from the deserts of Arabia to Libya in the west. It maintained relations with all the neighbouring nations of the ancient world; and as new powers, such as Greece and Rome arose, they were attracted to Egypt like bees to honey. Egypt's relations with its neighbours were sometimes friendly, sometimes not. The great funerary temple of Medinet Habu built by Ramesses III around 1180 BC is covered in images of him doing battle with his neighbours and, inevitably, defeating them. In his time, the main threat came from the displaced 'Peoples of the Sea' to the north, and from the Berber-speaking peoples living to the west in the desert and along the coast of North Africa. The Egyptians' blanket term for them was 'Libyans'. After victory in battle, the Egyptians employed a unique form of body count – they cut off the right hands and the penises of the slain and presented them to the king. All this is graphically illustrated on the walls of Ramesses III's temple. Over time, however, relations with the Libyans improved and some were allowed to settle in northern Egypt. Eventually, there were even pharaohs of Libyan descent.

After Alexander the Great conquered Egypt in 332 BC, he founded a Greek dynasty, the Ptolemies, who ruled the land for a further 300 years. Cleopatra VII, a Ptolemy, was Egypt's last great ruler. The Romans annexed the country but Egyptian influences spread like wildfire to Rome. One Roman nobleman, Gaius Cestius, even built himself a pyramid tomb which still stands in Rome today. Egyptian deities made their way into the Greek and Roman pantheons. The cult of Isis was a strong rival to early Christianity, and inscriptions to Isis have been found as far afield as a Roman site in London. As with Cleopatra and Mark Anthony, the Greeks and Romans who settled in Egypt quickly adopted Egyptian religious beliefs and many of them were mummified.

Not all Egyptian practices were adopted, however. Herodotus, writing in the fifth century BC, noted that the Egyptians 'did everything differently from everyone else'. While, for example, the Greeks cremated their dead, the Egyptians did all they could to retain a semblance of life. By Herodotus's times, Egypt was already famed as 'the land of the mummies'.

- Elsewhere in North Africa it is not yet clear whether mummification was a common practice. In 1959, however, an Italian archaeologist excavated a rock shelter in Libya and found the body of a child wrapped in animal hide. Two radio-carbon tests gave very different results. One dated the body to around 3200 BC; the other nearly 2,000 years earlier. The child had definitely been eviscerated and deliberately mummified. There is scant other evidence of mummification from

IN SEARCH OF THE IMMORTALS

North Africa but there has been very little detailed archaeological research into the pre-Islamic period there. One tantalizing clue has been found in Egypt, however.

In 1881, a sensational discovery was reported to Gaston Maspero, Director of the Egyptian Antiquities Service. A cache of mummies – eight pharaohs, their queens and notables – had been found in a secret hiding place near the Valley of the Kings. Around 1050 BC, the high priests and royal retainers – apparently alarmed by a sudden upsurge in grave-robbing – had gathered up all the royal bodies they could find and hidden them. After he saw the mummies, Maspero wrote: 'When I see and touch the bodies of so many illustrious kings we never imagined could be more than names to us . . . I still find it hard to believe that I am not dreaming.'

The cache was moved to Cairo where all the mummies were photo-graphed, catalogued and either displayed or put into storage. Public and scholarly attention naturally focused on the royal remains, but several other mummies were also found in the cache. One of them, labelled 'Unknown Man E' when he was photographed, was well preserved but wrapped in animal skins – the only known mummy, buried in a rock-cut tomb, to have been found wrapped in animal hides. The fact that he was hidden in the royal cache suggests that he was an important dignitary, perhaps a foreign noble or emissary who died while in Egypt; and the most plausible explanation for the unique way in which he was dressed for the afterlife is that the embalmers knew that *his* people would wrap their dead in animal skins.

In 1927, an amateur archaeologist named Warren Dawson made a detailed examination of one of the mummies in London and pro-nounced that the method of mummification was similar to that used in Egypt in the twenty-first dynasty. The mummy, however, proved not to be Egyptian – it came from the Canary Islands, 2,000 miles to the west of Egypt, and had been laid to rest wrapped in goat skins.

Early in 1998, I happened to mention this to Victor Mair, who had introduced me to the mummies of the Taklamakan. His reply came as something of a shock. He told me that his friend Thor Heyerdahl lives in the Canaries and – guess what? – he had found pyramids out there . . .

Chapter 5

Canary Islands

last mummy-makers of the old world

I never noticed him when I was a student but, tucked away in a seminar room in the department of Biological Anthropology at Cambridge University, there is a mummy. He stands upright in a glass case and seems to be extremely well preserved. He comes from the Canary Islands, from an extinct people known as the 'Guanches', the last mummy-makers of the Old World. One afternoon in October 1998, my assistant Pippa Dennis and I drove up to Cambridge to see him.

I liked him right away. One of very few remaining preserved Guanches, he is dry and leathery, and stands naked in his case with his hands crossed demurely over his private parts. He is very wrinkly, but does not have the emaciated look of many Egyptian mummies. Fluffy, curly hair, with a few flecks of grey, covers the top and back of his head. His finger- and toe-nails have been carefully bound to him with thin leather thongs. He has a very neat incision across the top of his abdomen where the embalmers have opened him up to remove his internal organs, then carefully sewn him up again with fine stitches. There is something noticeably odd about his face, though. There are few signs of damage to the skin, but the face looks flattened, distorted, askew.

IN SEARCH OF THE IMMORTALS

Peering out from his glass case at the ape skulls and half-curious undergraduates, he seemed to be okay where he was. The back of the case is wooden, the other three sides glass, covered by a cloth which prevents direct sunlight falling on him. There is no special climate or light control, but he doesn't seem to mind. Like hundreds of mummies around the world, he is just another oddment with a chequered history assigned to a local museum collection. In his case it is the Duckworth Collection at Cambridge University, which curates along with him various curios such as hair from the Negritos of the Andaman Islands, collected by the anthropologist Radcliffe-Brown in the early years of the twentieth century.

In a way the Guanche mummy is lucky to be intact and still with us. At the end of the nineteenth century social Darwinist anthropologists, bent on discovering the secrets of racial evolution, set great stead by craniometry. Believing that skull size and shape indicated racial affiliation and intelligence, they often stripped 'inconvenient' soft tissue from mummified bodies to measure the bones more precisely. In many cases they simply threw away what they removed.

The Royal College of Surgeons is said to have had eight Guanche mummies at the beginning of the twentieth century, but all but one were used for medical research and then destroyed by bombs during the Second World War. The remaining mummy at the Royal College of Surgeons was given to the Museum of Mankind – a subsidiary of the British Museum – about sixty years ago. This museum was closed in 1998 and its entire collection moved to the British Museum. When we asked the curator in charge of the mummy if we could see it, he was not aware of its existence. We had its catalogue number and gave it to him. Some time later he shamefacedly told us that the mummy had been lost. It had been in the collection in the 1960s, but could not be found.

Considering the British Museum justifies its tenure of objects, such as the Elgin Marbles, on the grounds that it offers superior conservation and protection to priceless antiquities, this is a pretty appalling state of affairs. The curators of the museum may not be aware that, as far as I can establish, there are only about twenty surviving Guanche mummies worldwide. These priceless human relics are the last remaining evidence of the youngest and least well documented mummy-making tradition in the Old World, a tradition of at least 1,000 years' duration, and a tradition which is, in many respects, as complex as that of ancient Egypt. To have lost one of the last twenty Guanche mummies is extremely negligent. Let's hope that every effort will now be devoted to finding the missing body. Like many Native North Americans, Australian Aborigines and other peoples who have discovered that the tombs of their ancestors have been pillaged by rapacious Europeans over the last centuries, I would consider this search to be a matter of respect. These are the remains of human beings, not pot-sherds or rusty spears. As revered ancestors, they should be treated with dignity. Mummies are part of our human legacy: gifts from the past to us and future generations. We are only just beginning to grasp the phenomenal wealth of information stored in them and this point, as we shall see, is graphically illustrated by the case of the Cambridge Guanche mummy.

The use of mummies for medicine, as freaks at peep-shows or simply as fashionable display objects was popular throughout Europe from the late Middle Ages onwards. The Spanish − conquerors first of the mummy-makers of the Canaries then later of the mummy-makers of the New World − added a religious dimension to the dispersion and destruction of the mummies. According to Catholic ideology, preserving and revering the dead was a form of idolatry. This provided the Spanish with the pretext they needed to indulge in a wholesale trade in ancient remains which was so devastating that, today, almost no Inca mummies exist in South America and only a pitiful handful of Guanche mummies remain.

Until we had the Cambridge Guanche dated in 1998, nobody knew when he had lived. He had been acquired in 1762 by a British naval officer, a Captain Young, who was visiting the Canaries. Young doubtless had the body stored in the very damp hold of the ship for the voyage home and the body may well have been handled roughly on the journey from his cave tomb to the British ship or during the journey back. Certainly some examiners thought that the damage to his face could have occurred during his post-mortem travels. There are also various nicks of missing skin on his body which may have been caused by rodents. This would not have happened in the Canaries where there are no indigenous mammals, but could have occurred aboard ship.

After various shenanigans in Ireland and England, the mummy was eventually presented to Trinity College, Cambridge, where it resided in the Wren library, a fine building overlooking the river Cam and the University 'Backs'. Somehow this genial mummy seems appropriate company for the eccentric dons of the college, such as Sir James Frazer, author of *The Golden Bough*, an epic Edwardian tome on the ancestral myths and rites of ancient Europe.

In the 1920s, the mummy was transferred to the Faculty of Archaeology and Anthropology at the University. It also underwent its first serious 'scientific' examination by W.R. Dawson, a successful London businessman with a penchant for archaeology. He provided the first detailed description of the body and also compared it with Egyptian mummies of the twenty-first dynasty, which date to about 1000 BC. Dawson's findings, however, need to be treated with caution. He was not a professional archaeologist and was a great believer in diffusionism – the idea that if you come across two or more similar objects in disparate parts of the world they must somehow be culturally related. In his paper comparing the Guanche and Egyptian mummies with a mummy from the Torres Straits, just north of Australia, he found similar techniques at work, and concluded that there must therefore have been links between

THE LAST MUMMY-MAKERS . . .

Egypt, the Canaries and Australia. This all seems a little far-fetched to me but nonetheless his work sparked an idea in my head that there might be connections between Egypt and the Canaries. By this stage, I had been working for many months on the mummy-making cultures of the world and was becoming more and more convinced that these cultures had communicated with each other a great deal more than is generally acknowledged. Links between one end of the Mediterranean and the other, 2,000 or more years ago, now seemed less far-fetched than I had at first imagined.

In 1968, an up-and-coming mummy expert, Don Brothwell, got permission from Cambridge to give the Guanche a state-of-the-art make-over. He X-rayed the mummy from all angles, but could not get good plates of the mummy's skull. He could see that the mummy had extensive face injuries, but was not sure if they had been inflicted before or after death, or had been the actual cause of death. In the 1960s considerably more 'intervention' was permitted in such biological investigations than is now allowed and Don was given permission to cut open the body in the abdominal region to see what was inside. He made a U-shaped incision about ten centimetres across, cut through two ribs and lifted up the flap of skin. Inside he found that the abdominal cavity was packed with what appeared to be earth mixed with pine-needles and possibly human entrails.

After clearing the packing from one side of the cavity, he pushed upwards and found the heart, very desiccated, and both lungs. He left the heart in place, but removed one of the lungs. He did not check the lower end of the abdominal cavity very thoroughly, nor did he replace the 'stuffing' he had removed. Closing the flap back down, he glued it carefully into place. He then made a slit in the right shoulder to remove some bone. Finally, he removed the mummy's right hand at the wrist. He wanted to rehydrate this to see if he could recover its fingerprints.

IN SEARCH OF THE IMMORTALS

He had a cast made of the hand before he started the rehydration process, which lasted for several months. The process was relatively successful and Don got his fingerprints. The hand, however, could not be dehydrated again, so the Cambridge Guanche now has a prosthetic right hand.

Don found anthracosis in the lung he removed, a disease associated with over-exposure to smoke from fires. This, he reasoned, was evidently the result of living in smoky caves, as most of the Guanches did. The mummy's abdomen was stuffed with mud-like material which also contained ground-up fragments of pine bark. In the area of the buttocks and thighs, the mummy had also been opened up and had 'packing' inserted to try to retain the original shape of this area of the body. X-rays seemed to indicate that the brain had been removed from the skull. The mummy was generally in good condition, the frame of a man in his thirties or forties with no other obvious medical problems. In the paper Don wrote about the investigation, he confirmed Dawson's observations that the cut-marks on the body were in similar positions to those found on twenty-first dynasty Egyptian mummies.

The mummy was then returned to Cambridge where it stood, relatively unmolested, until March 1999, when it was transferred to the Duckworth Collection, currently under the curation of Dr Robert Foley.

As my interest in the Guanches grew, Pippa and I decided to visit Don Brothwell to hear his personal views on how or who had mummified the Cambridge Guanche. Don admitted that he was baffled. Superficially, all the signs pointed towards Egypt, yet Egypt and the Canaries are over 2,000 miles apart and there is a discrepancy of at least 1,000 years between the earliest known Guanche mummies and the Egyptian mummies of the twenty-first dynasty. I wondered if advances in investigative techniques during the last thirty years might help unravel the enigma. Don's eyes lit up. Yes, he said, there is a very good chance that they would. Meantime, he added, there were people we should go to talk to in the Canaries – people who could help us find out more about the Guanches on the ground. Ah, me, aeroplane time again...

To spy out the land and make the initial contacts, Pippa went first. By the time I joined her a week later, she was looking really perplexed. Everyone on the islands seemed to have different views, everyone seemed to disagree with everyone else, and the evidence on the ground was frustratingly thin and fragmented. The only thing that most experts agreed on was that it was laughable to posit Egyptian connections with the pre-history of the Canaries. Any similarity in mummification techniques, they all insisted, was pure coincidence.

There were two good reasons for such scepticism. First, there are no archaeological remains from any time indicating an Egyptian presence on the islands. Second, there is no evidence of artificial mummification among the mummies which have survived and remained on the islands. My first priority, therefore, was to go and see the islands' leading expert on the mummies, Dr Conrado Rodriguez Martin.

The Museo de la Natureza y el Hombre is housed in the old city hospital in Santa Cruz, capital city of Tenerife. A beautiful Spanish colonial building in the old part of the city, Conrado's office and laboratory have lovely high ceilings and huge windows, so the rooms are full of light and air. Conrado's English is good, Pippa's Spanish is fluent and mine is okay, so the conversation spun away in both languages, each of us switching when we did not know a particular word. Conrado's eyes sparkled – and he smiled almost all the time, especially when we got going on the mummies.

Yes, he knew that the Cambridge mummy was artificially mummified, and, yes, there were lots of descriptions by the early Spanish chroniclers of the mummification process. They also said that the Guanches, like the

Egyptians, had specialist embalmers. Half-revered, half-outcasts, there were male embalmers for the men and female embalmers for the women. Not all Guanches were mummified, only members of important families. Studies of Guanche bones had revealed that some members of the population suffered periodic food shortages while others did not. This may have been due to variable climatic conditions in different parts of the islands or it may be evidence of social differentiation. There was also evidence of violence. The Guanches, it seems, were especially enamoured of that most biblical of weapons, the slingshot. Many of their tombs contained perfectly rounded stone balls, four to five centimetres in diameter and weighing 300 – 400 grams.

Conrado called his assistant and asked her to fetch a particular skull for us. It had a big dent right in the middle of the forehead, about three centimetres across and a centimetre deep. We could have rolled a slingshot ball into the dent and it would have fitted perfectly. Technically, it was a depressed fracture of the skull. 'It killed him for sure,' Conrado said. 'In some parts of the island as many as thirty per cent of the skulls we have found have these depressed fractures. Not all lethal, but all pretty painful.' Conrado would know. As well as being the world's leading expert on Guanche mummies, he is a practising orthopaedic surgeon. Bells were beginning to ring in my head about the Cambridge mummy's injuries.

Conrado took us to see the museum. Beautiful brand-new displays – well illustrated with photos and reproductions of artefacts – outline the archaeology of all of the Canary Islands. We found ourselves staring at strange spiral rock carvings, simple stone grindstones, photographs of cave mazes and the early chroniclers' sketches of the Guanches. Then we came to the mummy room.

Four beautifully displayed bodies were in climate-controlled cases, subtly lit so that they were just visible but not being damaged by the light. All the complete mummies were wrapped in goat-skin shrouds, so not all their bodies were visible. But it was immediately clear to me that none of them was anywhere near as well preserved as the Cambridge Guanche. I questioned Conrado more closely about their current condition. He agreed that, in most cases, the bodies were in too poor a condition to determine whether they had been artificially mummified. So it was not the case that they had not been deliberately preserved, it just could not be proved that they had. I asked about mummies on the other islands and he confirmed that they were in worse condition than his mummies in Tenerife. Even though the goat-skin wrappings had survived, most of the mummies on Gran Canaria were almost entirely skeletal. So the jury was still out on the archaeological evidence of some form of connection between Guanche and Egyptian mummification techniques.

Our next meeting was with Rafael Gonzalez Anton, Director of Archaeology at the museum. I asked him first about Guanche material culture. In essence, they were cave dwellers who lived mostly by grazing goats and some cattle on the slopes of the mountains. They grew grain in the valley floors which they ground up with stone grindstones to make a sort of cake. Considering they were island people, they used surprisingly few maritime resources, fish and seafood playing a relatively minor part in their diet. They did not weave cloth from cotton or wool, but were very skilled at making clothes and funeral shrouds from goat skins. The leather for these was worked until it was soft and supple, patterns were incised into it and it was sewn with great delicacy using bone needles. They had no iron, but used obsidian knives which are razor sharp. Like the ancient Egyptians, they also used these knives in the mummification process, to make incisions. They were good potters, sometimes decorating their pots with images of the sun. One unusual feature of their pottery was that they incorporated little lugs with holes in them around the necks of some of their pots – presumably milk containers – so that they could pass a leather thong through them and hang the pot clear of the ground.

Some tell-tale points were emerging. Metallurgic skills were very widespread by the time the Guanches' ancestors must have left the mainland, so the lack of metals among their artefacts presumably resulted from there being no ore on the islands. This absence, right up until the arrival of the Spanish, strongly suggested that the islanders had remained pretty isolated from the mainland throughout this period. Iron, bronze, even copper goods have such obvious advantages to farming peoples that I have no doubt that they would have been the most important trade items, if trade links existed. A more enigmatic point was that their overall orientation seemed to have been towards a life of farming and herding inland, with surprisingly little interest in coastal areas and maritime resources. This suggests that the people who migrated from the mainland to the islands were not coastal people, but hill-farmers and herders.

Rafael told us that, on the whole, he was pretty sure that the Guanches were Berbers who had migrated from North Africa to the islands some time around 500 BC. But he was not sure that they were the first people to visit the islands. Recent evidence, he claimed, suggested that these were the Phoenicians, the famed navigators of the Mediterranean. Originating in the Lebanon, by 500 BC the Phoenicians had set up bases at Carthage (in what is now Libya) and at various points along the North African coast as far as Lixus, in what is now northern Morocco. They were, of course, great traders and navigators and certainly maintained trade relations with ancient Egypt. One of their admirals, Hannon, is known to have sailed down the coast of Africa as far as Guinea around 500 BC. He stopped off in the Canaries without doubt and may well have spotted fine stands of pine there, greatly coveted by boat-builders of the time. He may also have noted the abundance of tuna fish in the waters round the coasts of the islands. Tuna, converted into a paste called *Garum*, was a highly prized foodstuff throughout the Mediterranean in those days.

THE LAST MUMMY-MAKERS . . .

So Rafael's views were that the original colonists were either Phoenicians, or possibly North African Berbers, transported there by the Phoenicians to set up *Garum* factories. He admitted that there is, as yet, scant evidence to support this view, but he had recently revealed to the public a mysterious stone which supported his claims. The Zanata stone is roughly the shape of a tuna fish and contains a tiny inscription, apparently in the ancient Libico-Berber script, which may be read as *Zanata*, the name of a Phoenician goddess.

I was to find out later that this 'discovery' is highly contentious. But by the time Rafael had finished elucidating his colonization theories my head was spinning. We had made some progress. The Phoenicians were trading partners with the Egyptians and could hardly have failed to notice the great pyramids of Giza, tombs of the mummified pharaohs. Yet quite how all this esoteric knowledge could have got transplanted to the Canaries was far from clear.

Whenever I get to a new location, my strongest urge is to get out, look around, and gauge the feel of the place. The Canaries, because of their fine climate and easy access to Europe are, of course, famed as centres of mass tourism. On Tenerife, however, tourism is mostly confined to the southern-most tip of the island. Santa Cruz is on the northeast corner, a bustling port and commercial and administrative centre. Motorways almost encircle the island, linking the tourist centres to the airport and other towns which ring the coast.

The island is dominated by a massive volcanic mountain, the peak of which rises to nearly 3700 metres above the ocean. On really clear days it is even visible from the shore of the African mainland, 120 kilometres away. I already knew that it was a very special place, a place of pilgrimage for the Guanches, and it presented a temptation I simply could not resist. As soon as we were through at the museum, Pippa and

IN SEARCH OF THE IMMORTALS

I jumped into our hire car and headed for the hills.

Thirty minutes down the coastal motorway to the south, we swung off and started to climb up into the mountains, keeping a sharp look-out for caves and marking them on the map every time we spotted one. In the next few days, however, we learnt not to bother – there were hundreds of them. The Canary Islands are literally riddled with caves of all sizes and shapes; and Tenerife is home to the longest and deepest volcanic tube in the world, aptly named 'The Gateway to Atlantis'.

The climb to Teide's volcanic crater winds up steep outer slopes covered in pine forest. The road is in good condition, but mostly consists of a never-ending set of bends. By the time we made it to the crater's lip, the sun was low on the horizon, casting huge shadows across a seemingly lunar landscape. Enormous barren lava fields, all dark brown and jagged-edged, spread out as far as we could see. With hardly a plant in sight, the lava fields were periodically broken by massive outcrops of rocks, arches, pillars and, of course, caves – caves everywhere. We drove on to the centre of the crater as the sun began to set. Massive lava pillars stood vertically up out of the ground like some giant tectonic Stonehenge. With the sun burning them red, awesome was the only word for it. Towering above them, like a giant natural pyramid, is Teide.

When I get to places like this, I always try to imagine what it must have been like before the roads were put in – before all the signposts, car parks, hotels and other garbage that Westerners feel are essential for today's survival in the wilderness. How would it have felt to be a lone Guanche herder, picking his way through the lava fields to this magical natural temple? There was absolutely no doubt in my mind: he would have felt raw primeval power at this holy place under the volcano.

A few weeks later, we returned to the Teide crater with Joann Fletcher and Maria Morales, an archaeologist from the Tenerife museum. Joann asked Maria what she thought the Guanches would have made of the place. According to the early Spanish chronicles, Maria replied, the Guanches would come up here on a sort of pilgrimage and hide prized objects in the rocks as offerings; and they would bury their most important dead in the caves. They believed that a very powerful devil or demon lived in the volcano. One chronicler even implied that the Guanches thought of this place as 'hell' and contrasted it with the pleasant valley of La Laguna, just outside what is now Santa Cruz, which they called 'paradise'.

All Spanish chronicles have to be treated with caution. Many of the chroniclers were priests who tended to superimpose Christian concepts on aboriginal cosmological ideas all over the world (especially, as we will see in Part Two, in South America), so I am not at all sure that the Guanches believed that the devil resided in Teide. It did make sense, however, that great supernatural power would be attributed to a volcano. But if this power was negative, why bury your most revered dead within it? My mind strayed back to ancient Egypt where as we have seen the people believed that the underworld, where the souls of the dead resided during the night, was also home to monsters and giant snakes with which the sun-god Re had to battle every night so that he, the sun, and the souls of the dead could be reborn each morning. In Egyptian thought, then, placing the mummified bodies of the dead in the murky, dangerous underworld was *de rigueur*. Was this mere coincidence or yet another tantalizing link between the two cultures?

Joann then asked Maria what was known about Guanche religious beliefs. Maria replied that the Guanches worshipped the sun, the moon and the stars. Furthermore, she explained, they held special fertility rites at peak-top mountain sites where they could be as close to the sun as possible.

Pippa and I had visited several of these sites on both Tenerife and Gran Canaria a few weeks earlier. They are very beautiful, but rather baffling. The Guanches evidently chose spots high in the mountains, open places with spectacular views. There they engraved – or enlarged – channels in the rocks, punctuated with deeper circular holes at intervals along the sloping rock face. From the top of these miniature watercourses, the Guanches apparently poured quantities of goats' milk which flowed down the channels, filling the holes. A full hole would then overflow and the milk would continue to cascade down the channels in the rock. Pippa and I tried pouring water down these channels. It was fun, but did not seem to signify much. However, when we went out with Maria, she took us – and some milk – to a different site called La Masca.

La Masca is situated far out along a needle-like ridge. In places the path is only a metre or so wide, with sheer drops on either side. At the end of the trail, there are the channels with holes that we had seen elsewhere, but this time decorated with two very distinct symbols. One is a sun symbol, etched deep into a flat rock. It is a circle with a centre point and 'spokes' radiating out to the edge. It could represent a wheel, but the Guanches did not have wheels or carts, so it is almost certainly a sun with radiating sun-rays. It is only about forty centimetres across and, as the rock is very dappled, not very obvious. But when Maria started to pour milk over it, the entire symbol seemed to come to life. The white liquid ran along the spokes then all round the edge of the 'rim', lighting up the image. The milk then ran down an overflow channel into a large pool below. Joann commented that she could see how the people must have been repaying the sun and the earth for nourishing them, their children and herds, and requesting that the fertility should endure. Then she added that libations of milk were also offered to the goddess Isis in ancient Egypt. As described in the previous chapter, Isis not only instigated the very first process of mummification, she was also the universal mother, healer and nurturer.

THE LAST MUMMY-MAKERS . . .

A little further along the cliff from the sun symbol, a figure is carved deep into the face of a vertical piece of rock. It is a sort of oval shape, about fifty centimetres long, with a deep dot in the centre. Maria introduced us to it, confidently pronouncing that it was a fish. Joann took one look at it then, almost casually, asked Maria if she was sure it was a fish. 'To me,' she said, 'it looks exactly like an eye, carved in just the way the Egyptians did it. See how it has a long fairly flat top, the upper lid, and a much more rounded lower line, with the pupil right in the middle. And look where it is looking . . . ' The 'eye', indeed, was looking straight down the valley to a cleft in the hills where we could just see the sea. Besides being the all-seeing symbol of wisdom for ancient Egyptians, the eye was closely associated with the goddess Hathor, goddess of fertility. We were all impressed.

So, it was beginning to look as if the sun-worshipping mummy-making Guanches had rather a lot in common with the ancient Egyptians, rather more than coincidence could account for. But we had not yet looked at the most astonishing piece of evidence to be seen on the islands – a piece now in the care of the most famous marine explorer of the century, Thor Heyerdahl.

Thor shot to international fame when he managed to sail his balsa-wood raft, the *Kon Tiki*, from South America to Melanesia in the 1950s. Then in the 1960s he managed, at the second attempt, to sail from Egypt all the way to Barbados in a papyrus boat, the *Ra*. His aim was to demonstrate that ancient mariners, possibly the Egyptians themselves, could have crossed the Atlantic, taking with them their ideas about pyramid building and sun worship. There are, of course, hundreds of pyramids in Mexico and in many other parts of Central and South America and, as we will see in Part Two, most Native American cultures also revered the sun.

IN SEARCH OF THE IMMORTALS

〰〰
〰〰

On his way to the New World, Thor stopped off in the Canaries and seems to have liked the place. He now has a house there and spends much of his time in Tenerife. A few years ago a friend sent him a cutting from a local newspaper, a report that the local council was about to demolish a mysterious pyramid-like structure to make way for a new road scheme. Thor rushed to the site and was astonished to find himself looking at a complex of walls, enclosures, plazas and small stepped pyramids. They were built from the local lava, but the stones of the outer walls and corners appeared to have been shaped into neat blocks.

Thor immediately contacted his friend Fred Olsen, owner of the Olsen shipping line, who agreed to purchase the land and fund Thor to restore the pyramid complex. This work is now largely complete. In the course of the restoration, the workers came across a small cave-mouth in the bottom corner of the largest pyramid. Thor got his resident archaeologist to partially excavate the site, and found both contemporary and colonial rubbish in the cave, and also pre-colonial Guanche remains – pottery fragments, bone needles, even a slingshot stone, identical to the ones Rafael had shown us in the museum. This cave, therefore, had certainly been used by the Guanches but it is not yet clear whether it was a habitation or funerary cave.

Thor's actions inevitably attracted a lot of attention in the press, and local academic reaction was, in general, hostile. The first response from the archaeologists, including Rafael, was to announce that the so-called pyramids were not ancient at all. There were no references to them, they claimed, in the chronicles and they had in fact been built by Spanish farmers clearing the stony land for agriculture.

Personally, I detected an element of being 'caught with your pants down' in the vitriolic denunciation of Thor. Even if the pyramids do eventually turn out to have been built after the Spanish conquest, they are, architecturally, a most intriguing aspect of the Canary Islands' heritage and definitely worth preserving. I suspect that those responsible for authorizing their destruction realized they had acted improperly and felt that by attacking Thor they could cover up their own short-sightedness. Further, it transpired that until a few years ago there were in fact two pyramid complexes on Tenerife: the one found by Thor is in the town of Guimar, the other near the town of Icod de Los Vinos on the other side of the island. The latter was demolished to make way for a road scheme some years ago.

Thor very kindly showed us around the site, then sat down for a chat about his views on the Egyptian connection. In essence, he believes that mariners used papyrus boats to navigate all around the Mediterranean and, from at least the days of ancient Egypt, went even further afield. When he sailed *Ra* into Lixus on the north coast of Morocco in the 1960s, local fishermen, he told us, were still using papyrus boats for offshore fishing. The distance from Lixus to the Canaries is a relatively short sail along the coast in fairly safe waters. He did not believe, he added, that the Guanches had just drifted over to the Canaries, but thought that at some point in time there had been an organized migration there. You do not, he said, just put seed-grain, goats, cattle and farm equipment into the back of a flimsy canoe and set off for the great blue unknown. He is sure that the Guanches made a planned landing on the islands, most likely in papyrus boats.

He also thinks that the original colonists were pyramid-builders and sun-worshippers. To support this argument, he reminded me that in Egypt itself pyramids come in all shapes and sizes; that some are very small, like the ones on the Canaries. The oldest are stepped, probably because this was the simplest method of construction. And Egypt and the Canaries are not the only places in the Mediterranean basin where pyramids exist: there are small, often circular stepped pyramids in many parts of North Africa and Thor has recently found others in Sardinia.

IN SEARCH OF THE IMMORTALS

〰〰

His most recent discovery – which he was due to excavate in the spring of 1999 – is in Sicily, where he has found pyramidal structures at the base of Mount Etna.

My head began to whirl. I had visited Sicily a few years previously and made a special trip to look at Mount Etna. Like Teide, it is a great pyramid-shaped volcano. Now Thor had discovered miniature man-made versions of itself at its feet. All these structures, according to Thor, are aligned with the sun. His pyramids at Guimar, for example, have been checked by astronomers from the local university who found them to be perfectly aligned to the sun at the summer solstice.

As a parting shot, Thor suggested that we should visit another pyramid on the island of La Palma. We couldn't miss it, he said. It was only a few minutes' drive north of the airport and clearly visible from the main road. This one had not been restored by anyone, so it would give us the chance to see one in the raw.

That suggestion, though, would have to wait a while. Our next destination was Gran Canaria where we were due to meet Mike Eddy, an English archaeologist who had spent eleven years in the Canaries. He had made a detailed study of one valley, the Guayadeque, where people still live in caves today. I, for one, was getting desperate to get up into the caves, to make a personal visit to a Guanche home.

Mike is a great bear of a man. His passport photograph makes him look exactly like an Azerbaijani mafioso hit-man, which isn't at all fair. He is nothing like that in the flesh, but there is certainly plenty of him. As we stood on the floor of the Guayadeque valley, looking up at the caves, he explained that the funerary caves were on the shady western side of the valley and the habitation caves on the sunny eastern side.

I looked at the row of caves on the sunny side. There must have been at least twenty of them. Yes, Mike explained, this was an entire cave village, and there were five more of them further up the valley. In its heyday the population of the valley might have been as many as 600 people. Then, quite casually, Mike said, 'Okay, let's go.' Joann paused, looking up at several hundred feet of boulder-strewn slopes, mostly covered in very large prickly cacti. Then, shrugging her shoulders, she stepped in behind Mike and off we went.

It was quite a climb, but not as difficult and dangerous as it had looked from below. Scrambling up the last slope, we climbed into the first cave. It was little more than a large hole, with a couple of recesses, but the floor was interesting. It was littered with hundreds of bones, some of them certainly human. Sometimes, Mike explained, when a habitation cave on the edge of the cave village was abandoned, it might be used to inter the dead to save the trouble of carrying the corpse all the way down to the valley floor, then up the really precipitous slope to the burial caves on the other side. Moving on, we came to a near-vertical rock with a big overhanging cavern above it, which we had seen from the valley floor. Actually getting into it, however, was not going to be easy.

Working our way round the base of the cave, we eventually found a place where a sapling was growing hard up against the steep rock face. It provided just enough support to allow me to scramble up onto the ledge above. Leaning down, I helped Joann up with a hefty pull. Mike followed without much trouble. Turning round, we stared into the cave-mouth, noting a large central area that still had traces of layers of straw that the Guanches had put down as floor covering. In the floor of the central front chamber there was a large hole – the grain store. All round its lip, we could see a fine rim of smooth clay. Mike explained that this was the remains of a clay 'seal' which had held the cover of the grain store in place and confirmed for the owner that no one had been pilfering the grain.

IN SEARCH OF THE IMMORTALS

We were, Mike added, standing towards the back of the original cave. Roof falls had brought down what must once have been a larger main chamber. Yet, even bearing this in mind, we were still amazed at the complexity of the 'house'. A whole series of smaller chambers branched off from the main chamber, making a labyrinth of rooms, some interconnected. Most of the rooms had niches cut into the walls as shelving. I suppose we are all indoctrinated with the idea that cave-dwellers were, by definition, primeval simpletons, but here was a superb residence for a large family, totally dry and brilliantly insulated with a near-constant temperature year-round, and some of the most spectacular views imaginable. And central to those views were the funerary caves on the other side of the valley, the eternal homes of their mummified ancestors.

Mike said there were a dozen or so more large habitation caves in this village, and at the far end there was an *atalaya*, a look-out post on a flat rock where a watchman would have a clear view down the valley. This highlighted a half-formed idea in my mind. Like the fortified hill-villages of Medieval Europe, the Guanches, it seemed, had deliberately chosen these sites because they were easy to defend. We had just seen for ourselves how difficult it was to get up to the village from the valley floor. Given that every time they needed water they would have had to make that trip, they could have built houses on or near the valley floor, but up on the hill they were less vulnerable and safer from raids and skirmishes. That the look-out post was at the lower end of the village made it clear that if trouble was going to come, it would come inland from the coast, not downhill from the upper ends of the valley, or from the volcano at the heart of the island.

This caused me to wonder if part of the pattern of warfare practised by the Guanches consisted of inter-island raiding. From Tenerife you can see Gran Canaria, Gomera and La Palma, and it is known that at the time of the Spanish conquest the Guanches had boats which they used to move between the islands. Although nowadays we tend to lump all peoples of the Canaries under the blanket-term 'Guanches', they were, in fact, organized into much smaller units. There were nine 'kings' on Tenerife alone, and each island had its own leaders, dialect and at least some distinct cultural and artistic traditions. The Spanish conquest took almost a century to complete, from 1402 to 1498, and during that period the Spanish made and broke alliances with the various Guanche factions, even persuading some of the Guanches to go into battle with them against other 'enemy' Guanches. So the Guanches faced human foes alongside the ever-present threat posed by the active volcanoes on the islands. These threats, it seemed, must have had a bearing on why the Guanches wanted to preserve their dead, but the exact relevance of this to the puzzle was not yet precisely clear.

As we sat sipping local red wine in the cave-bar of the inhabited cave-village further up the valley that evening, we started to discuss the two Canarian combat systems – wrestling and stick-fighting – which are said to be a direct legacy of the Guanches and still practised today. *Lucha Canaria* is a hugely popular form of wrestling. I watched it on TV one night and there was no doubt in my mind that it conforms to the style known as Greco-Roman wrestling. The holds used, the rules of engagement and the methods of throwing and scoring points all place it within this category. The problem, however, with it being 'a direct legacy of the Guanches' is that this type of wrestling is both more ancient and more widespread than its name implies. Wrestling is probably the most ancient form of physical recreation in the world. Both the ancient Egyptians and the Babylonians had organized wrestling systems by 3000 BC and the actual origin of the sport was probably much, much earlier than that. Direct legacy or not, it was not a surprise to find that the Guanches wrestled. More promising as a direct legacy, though, is the Guanche system of stick-fighting, *Juego del Palo*.

To see this we went to the capital of Gran Canaria, Las Palmas, to meet up with a team of stick-fighters at the university. They gave a brilliant performance of the art. They used two types of weapons – a long, heavy staff, about two metres long and six or seven centimetres thick, and a much shorter, lighter stick, a little over a metre long and only a couple of centimetres thick. They wielded the staff with both hands, making slashing strikes and jabs with the butts at either end of the weapon, constantly wielding and parrying, and sliding their hands up and down the staff. They wielded the lighter stick with one hand, leaving the other free to parry and shield the stick-fighter from his opponent. Although the movements were clearly codified, the bouts they showed us were entirely improvised, each opponent free to unleash whatever set of moves came to him. No contact is permitted during these bouts, but the combatants freeze momentarily if they manage to penetrate their opponent's guard. They were good, these guys, fast, agile and crafty. The crack of stick on stick echoed round the little garden. Joann watched intently, listening to Mike's translation of the instructor's narration of the history of the art. She was quiet for a few more minutes, studying the movements and postures of the fighters, especially those little frozen moments when a strike managed to get through his opponent's defence. Then she simply pronounced, 'This is exactly like the stick fighting you see on the walls of the temple of Ramesses III, at Medinet Habu, not far from the Valley of the Kings. It's identical.'

So, we could add martial skills to our growing list of cultural and religious parallels between Egypt and the Canaries. 'Coincidence' was being edged out of the picture by 'connections'.

There was just one more thing I wanted to do before we left the Canaries – visit the unmolested pyramid that Thor had talked about on La Palma.

One of the difficulties in interpreting the pyramids in Guimar is that they are so complex. There are all sorts of walls running in many directions and at least two pyramid-like structures. The land they are built on slopes steeply towards the sea and one of the presumably desired effects of the construction is that they create relatively flat patches of land on many different levels. They are also surrounded by terracing which, given that the Guanches did not build terraces, was certainly built after the conquest. So it is not easy to differentiate what is known to be agricultural terracing from what may be Guanche pyramids. I hoped that the situation would be less complicated at the pyramid on La Palma.

It was. We saw it from the road. A single stepped pyramid standing on a rise overlooking the sea. Perhaps fifteen metres high, it has seven steps from its base to its flat top. The base, which is not quite square, is roughly twenty metres wide and twenty-five metres long; the platform on the top about seven metres by ten. A very well cut stairway runs up one corner of the structure to the platform on top. It was built with the same volcanic lava as Thor's pyramids on Tenerife, with apparently shaped stones forming the outer walls, infilled with smaller stones. It is a dark brown-black colour, a monument which stands out starkly against the sea when viewed from the landward side.

Looking at it more closely, I was intrigued to see that, even though it is a four-sided stepped structure, hardly any of the angles are true right-angles. The verticals all slope slightly inwards, as all true pyramids should; most of the horizontals are slightly skewed, angles of maybe eighty to one hundred degrees rather than the expected right angles. The whole structure also tips very slightly downhill towards the sea.

Like the Guimar pyramids, it is set among abandoned agricultural terracing and a network of walls butt up to and surround it. Yet gaps have been left in these walls allowing direct access to the monument from at least as far away as the road where we parked, maybe 400 metres away. Perhaps most revealing of all, just a few metres below the lowest end of the pyramid the land suddenly gives way and there is a sheer drop of about thirty metres to land just above the shoreline. Now if this building is simply supposed to be the result of colonists wishing to clear the land for farming, then why on earth didn't they just tip the stones over the precipice rather than going to all the trouble of piling them up into a carefully planned massive structure? And why would good Catholic Spaniards (or Genoese) want to build pyramids in the first place? It was, as Joann put it, an enigma.

We stood on the top, trying out various ideas. Could it have been a watch-tower? It was placed in a prominent position, but there were higher slopes just a few hundred metres to the south obscuring the view in that direction. Could they have grown crops on it? No, it was definitely much too dry and there was no sign of any attempt to place soil on the rocks. Could it have been used for drying crops? That was a possibility but, if so, surely there would have been similar – and documented – 'drying pyramids' elsewhere in Spain or Southern Europe. It was really baffling. Joann made some basic points clear, though. Here was a monument, intentionally constructed, one of three known monuments on the Canary Islands. Like the other two it had been deliberately placed between the sea and the giant volcanic mountain behind it. It was very conspicuous, a monumental statement saying 'I am here, notice me.'

Since I first saw it I have thought long about this pyramid and my mind keeps returning to one basic point. By the fifteenth century, the Spanish, like all Europeans, knew plenty about building monuments. Their masons knew how to cut stone and build vertical walls using mortar to consolidate the stonework. Their building traditions, both for religious and military structures, had evolved over centuries, but definitely did not include pyramids in their repertoire. In fact, I would suggest that as they were pretty conservative Catholics, they might well have considered pyramids heretical. But there is also something deeper, something which says that these structures are not conceptually or practically related to late medieval Europeans. They were built by a people who had a vision, an intention, but who were not well schooled in geometry, masonry and the use of mortar. They are more like acts of faith, devotion, than the product of craftsmen. I cannot believe these are the works of European minds or hands. Yet somebody built them.

So, almost reluctantly, I had to add pyramid-building to our list of links between the Guanche and Egyptians.

Back in England, preparations were underway for Don Brothwell to re-examine the Cambridge Guanche mummy thirty years after he had last looked at it. His main aim was to put it through a CT scanner at Addenbrookes Hospital. CT scanners, essentially a much more sensitive form of X-ray, are ingenious devices. They can detect soft tissue as well as bone, and generate images of the skeleton and the interior of the body in 'slices', as if you are cutting it into slithers a few millimetres apart. When this information is fed into a computer, it can reproduce the body in 3D graphic form. The CT scanner cannot tell you exactly what you are seeing inside the body, but it can tell you the density of the material it is scanning. Liver, for example, is of a different density to intestines and, of course, a very different density to bone.

Don invited Joann to attend along with her friend Joyce Filer, an ex-student of Don's, who is now Special Assistant for Human and Animal Remains in the Department of Egyptian Antiquities at the British Museum. Joyce had recently CT-scanned about twenty of the BM's Egyptian mummies. On this occasion, however, the CT scanner would be operated by an Addenbrookes consultant, Dr Nagui Hamoun, who is, most appropriately, an Egyptian Coptic Christian and direct descendant of ancient Egyptians.

Early on the morning of Sunday 7 March 1999, Don, Pippa and I called at the Department of Biological Anthropology to pick up the mummy. I can confess to a real tingle of exhilaration as I carried him to my car and laid him gently in the back. He was wrapped in bubble-wrap and not very heavy. As I drove out of the departmental car park, I uttered a silent prayer that we would not be stopped by the police on the way to the hospital. Even though he was wrapped up, it was transparently obvious that I had a 'stiff' in the back of my car!

At Addenbrookes, everyone changed into surgical gowns and donned face masks and rubber gloves. The room went quiet as we took off the bubble wrap – only Don, Pippa and I had seen the body before. Joann and Joyce were immediately entranced. Best friends, they both adore mummies and this one was obviously an exceptionally fine specimen. As Don showed them around the mummy's exterior they constantly remarked on his similarities to Egyptian mummies. Although the Guanches had used thin leather thongs while the Egyptians used cotton thread, the way in which the strings bound the finger- and toe-nails to the body were very similar. Likewise, although the stitching on the Guanche mummy was both finer and neater than Egyptian counterparts, the abdominal incision had been sewn up – something the Egyptians had started to do in the twenty-first dynasty.

The incision for removing his viscera had been made high on the front and to the right of his abdomen. Typically, the Egyptian incision would have been at the side on the left, but Tutankhamen had been opened up in the same place as the Guanche. The slit marks on the back, buttocks and thighs were also very much in the same positions as those found on twenty-first-dynasty mummies. Joann, whose greatest passions in life are ancient hair and tattoos, got out her torch and magnifying glass and examined his hair. Her immediate reaction was that it had been styled and treated after death in almost exactly the way that the ancient Egyptians styled their mummies' hair. She actually squeaked with delight when she found a louse egg-case which demonstrated that the Guanches, like the ancient Egyptians, had kept their hair clean. Apparently, nits prefer clean to dirty hair. She then detected typical male-pattern baldness and an attempt by his embalmers to cover up his bald patch. He had a few grey hairs, so he was clearly a mature male.

Overall, the superficial examination revealed extraordinary similarities between the Guanche and later Egyptian mummification techniques and post-mortem care. The Egyptologists were clearly impressed. Now it was over to the CT scanner. This started at the top of the mummy's skull and worked downwards. After just a few 'slices' we knew his brain was still in place. This was rarely the case in Egypt. They usually made a little hole at the back of the nose to enter the skull cavity, and then fished the brain out through the nasal passage. Once the machine had finished scanning the head, Dr Hamoun set up the 3D reconstruction of the skull on his office computer.

About half an hour later there were sharp intakes of breath from the experts as the 3D model turned from the back of the mummy's skull to his face. It was a mass of smashed bones. A fragment of the jaw-bone had been struck so hard, it was now over his eye socket. Dr Hamoun calculated that the entire face had been displaced by twenty-five degrees to the left. The consensus was that he had been hit by an extremely heavy club or staff on the right side of his face, and that the blow had killed him instantly. As he fell to the ground, he had also struck the left side of his head on something hard like a rock, or had possibly received a second blow. The two blows sent fractures ricocheting round his face and cranial bones. One of the radiologists present said the fracture reminded her of pre-seatbelt injuries when people's heads went through car windscreens. Only the mummy's injuries were even worse than those.

So now we knew the cause of death. Standing there, I could hear the crack of the heavy staves that the stick-fighters wielded.

Back at the scanner, the machine was imaging the chest, moving steadily downwards. As we already knew his heart was there and the lung which Don had left inside. His liver was there too and below it the 'packing' which Don had left on the right-hand side of the body. The interesting thing about the stuffing was that it was much the same density as soft tissue, prompting the Egyptologists to wonder if his organs had been removed, purified, packed in earth, then replaced in his abdomen, as the Egyptians had done from the twenty-first dynasty onwards.

Further down the scanner revealed that his bladder and rectum were still in place. Below them, where we had seen the slits on his buttocks and thighs, we could see that the holes had been filled with a granular material, possibly ground-up pumice or volcanic lava. This, once again, conformed to the ways in which later Egyptian mummies were packed out by their embalmers, to make them as life-like as possible.

When the scanning was completed, we took the mummy back to the room where we had unpacked him and had a final look. As we went through the ancient ritual of wrapping the mummy, I quizzed the experts on whether, in the light of the day's work, they now thought that Guanche and Egyptian mummification techniques were related. The consensus was that the techniques were uncannily similar. I added that, having now spent several years studying mummy cultures worldwide, I had not encountered any other mummy-makers whose techniques so closely resembled Egyptian techniques.

There had to be a link, and the obvious place to look for it was North Africa.

THE LAST MUMMY-MAKERS . . .

Our first port of call was Lixus, the place where Thor Heyerdahl had seen papyrus fishing boats in the 1960s. Now called Larache, it is a very ancient port. Originally settled by the Berbers, it became the Phoenicians' main base outside the Mediterranean; the base from where Rafael Gonzales believes the Phoenicians set out to colonize the Canaries.

The old city stood on a hill about five kilometres inland from the coast. The ruins there are mostly Roman but our guide, archaeologist Mohammed Habibi, stated categorically that Egyptian influences were clear during its phase under the Phoenicians. Archaeologists had even found a small statue of a sphinx there. More importantly, around 30 BC the daughter of Anthony and Cleopatra was married to King Juba II, the Berber king of the province of Mauritania. Although Cleopatra's dynasty, the Ptolemies, were of Greek origin, she was a fervent advocate of ancient Egyptian culture and religion, and certainly educated her daughter in the Egyptian tradition. So there can be no doubt that, by the turn of the millennium, Egyptian ideas and beliefs were mingling in the areas that the Guanches hailed from.

But the archaeological evidence for the first colonization of the Canaries suggests that the Guanches probably arrived there as much as 500 years earlier than the days of Juba II and Cleopatra. We pressed on inland, in search of older sites.

Next day brought us to a little village called El Gour outside the town of Meknes. We were in the company of a charming young Moroccan archaeologist, Josef Bokbot. He was interested in our project for two reasons — first, he had actually worked in the Canary Islands for some time and knew the sites well; second, he is a Berber.

The first site we visited was an enormous circular tomb, the burial site of an important but unknown Berber leader who lived around 800 BC. The tomb was a circular stepped pyramid, its outer walls superbly crafted with smooth dressed stonework, and originally it had had three steps, each about two metres high. While the base wall was vertical, the walls of each of the higher steps all tilted inwards a little, which is why it qualifies as a pyramid. This structure was originally paired with a ritual platform (now destroyed) about 300 metres away. The two structures were perfectly aligned with the sun at the summer solstice. We seemed to be getting somewhere.

A day's drive took us across the High Atlas mountains to the end of the metal road. As night fell, we switched vehicles into Land Rovers and set off into the Sahara, speeding over the smooth sand at 80 k.p.h. and raising great plumes of dust until we reached the border village of Merzouga. Here, a French couple have built a beautiful little hotel. All our rooms had stairways leading to a small dome, then out on to flat roofs, all surrounded by low mud-baked walls. By a sort of social osmosis, we all ended up on the roof, sipping whisky, gazing at the star-filled skies and listening to the breathtaking silence of the desert night.

In the morning, the sun rose over majestic sand dunes just a few hundred metres from the hotel. Soon we were speeding once again across the sand, this time heading straight out into the desert. Two hours later the vehicles pulled up at the foot of a low rise in pure desert – stony, rocky, no vegetation at all. Dotted around the hills were several mounds of stones, inconspicuous from a distance. Josef led us to one of them, revealing a low entrance on one side. We had to crawl, but it was quite easy to get in. Inside, there was a central space with several little chambers off it. The ceiling was made from huge flat slabs of rock. Mike's first reaction was that the layout was very like a smaller version of a Guanche cave. This chamber, or chapel as Josef called it, had a very special function. According to Berber tradition, if an individual had a problem – say a man had lost his camels or a woman was worried because her husband was late returning from a camel caravan – they would come here, sleep the night and the solution to their problems would be revealed in a dream.

Taking us back outside, Josef led us round the side of the circular structure. It had been excavated in the 1950s and the top removed. In the centre of the structure was the large tomb of a very important Berber chief. It was about 2,800 years old. On the other side of the wall of this inner tomb was the dreaming chamber – the chapel. So, according to tradition, by spending the night right next to a revered ancestor the problems of the living could be resolved.

This set bells ringing in everyone's heads. Mike said that the Guanches also liked to commune with their ancestors and visited the burial caves to do so. More strikingly, though, Mike reminded us of a site he had taken us to called Galdar on the north coast of Gran Canaria island. Here, there were both circular houses and large tombs built almost identically to the tombs we were now standing by in the Sahara. The largest of the Galdar tombs had been excavated in the 1930s, just before the outbreak of the Spanish Civil War. Subsequently, the excavation report had been lost and no one knew exactly what the archaeologists had uncovered. The tomb consisted of a very large central burial chamber with several smaller chambers clustered round it. There also seemed to be some sort of entrance into the smaller, outer chambers. Seeing the dream-tombs here at Taouz, Mike was amazed at their similarity to Galdar and thought that they could provide an explanation for the mysterious entrance and outer chambers there. They, too, might have been dream chambers.

For my part, I was trying to remember a passage from Herodotus where he describes the customs of the Libyan tribes living to the west of Egypt. Of the Nassamones he wrote:

In the matter of oaths, their practice is to swear by those of their countrymen who had the best reputation for integrity and valour, laying their hands upon their tombs: and for purposes of divination they go to sleep, after praying, on the graves of their forebears, and they take as significant any dreams they may have.

IN SEARCH OF THE IMMORTALS
∿∿

In 450 BC, the Nassamones lived at least a thousand miles east of where we now stood, about halfway to Egypt.

Joann, too, was immediately alert to the idea of dreaming near to, but not in direct contact with, ancestral powers. She reminded us of the temple of Hathor at Dendera. There, in the sanatorium next to the main temple, there is a whole set of small low chambers. People with problems or illnesses slept and dreamt in these chambers, and next day they took their dreams to the priests of the temple for interpretation and instruction on how best to proceed. Divine dreaming – dreaming alongside ancestors to resolve problems – seems to have been a pan-North African idea.

A common underlying pattern was emerging: veneration of the dead was essential to the living because the dead could help the living through life. Placing the dead in a cave or dark chamber within a hill or mountain (real or man-made), was the ideal way to preserve them and ensure their continued support and protection. The spirits of the dead were associated with night-time and dreaming, the time when the sun is absent, travelling through the underworld and life is in suspension. Fertility – through notions of rebirth and regeneration – was also bound up in this system: just as the sun was reborn each day, so the birth of new generations of children and animals was ensured with the aid of the ancestors.

Josef took us out of the tomb and up to a flat rock a few metres away. It was covered in rock-carvings of cattle – the symbol of Hathor, cow-goddess, goddess of fertility – who we know is even more ancient than Egyptian civilization. Such carvings exist throughout the Sahara and many of them are very ancient. For the peoples of North Africa, before the rise of the Nile civilization, cattle were their life-blood, the source of their fertility. No surprise, then, that the Berbers at the westernmost edge of the Sahara should have placed images of fertility right next to the tombs of their most revered ancestors.

∿∿

THE LAST MUMMY-MAKERS . . .

My confidence that Guanche culture shared common roots with all the peoples of North Africa was growing steadily, but there was another outstanding element in their culture which I wanted to see and consider. The Guanche were people who, for very good reasons, liked to live in caves as well as interring their beloved dead in them. Evidence from Galdar and other places on the Canary Islands show that they were perfectly capable of building houses, but preferred caves. There are quite a few known habitation-cave sites in Morocco and caves are still used there today for animal husbandry. But, as far as we could tell, there were no known sites of entire cave villages and cemeteries like the ones in the Canaries. Enquiries with Moroccan archaeologists drew a blank.

Established experts on the archaeology of this part of North Africa are almost non-existent in European universities, but Pippa tracked down an amateur archaeologist, Mike Millburn, whose great passion is the archaeology of the Sahara. I had met him several years before when I was preparing to film the Tuareg (who are also Berbers) in Niger. We had had a genial lunch and agreed to keep in touch. So when Pippa told him she was working with me, he decided to offer up a snippet of information he had been keeping to himself for many years. In the 1870s, he explained to Pippa, a British botanist, Joseph Hooker, had gone on a plant-collecting expedition to Morocco and kept a journal, which is now in the British Museum. In this, he mentioned passing a dry watercourse in the limestone hills to the west of Marrakesh near the village of Tarselt. There he had seen a large set of caves high up in the cliffs which showed signs of human habitation. Unable to reach them, he had simply passed on. Mike Millburn had not had the chance to follow up this lead, but he gave Pippa the book reference and wished us luck.

I sent Pippa out in advance to see if she could find Tarselt and the caves. After a great deal of fruitless driving around, she eventually found a village called Tarseat which had a dry river-bed running through it and limestone cliffs on each side. By the time she got there, it was four in the afternoon, and only then did she discover that there were no French speakers in the village – all the villagers were Berbers. Needless to say, when she was reduced to sign-language – gesturing up the valley and making big round circles with her arms – they had no idea what she was talking about. Realizing this was not going to work, she set off up the valley. After about half an hour's walk she came to a fork in the river-bed. With darkness not long off, she knew she would have to choose one way or the other. She chose to go right, walked on for another hour, but saw no caves. Turning back, she made it back to her car just as it was getting dark. Next day she had to fly back to England. She had not found the caves, but felt she was getting close.

Thinking it worth a shot, Mike, Joann, Pippa and I set off, taking a Berber-speaking driver with us. At the village he soon established that there were some caves up the valley which the shepherds still used to give shade to their flocks on hot summer days. We hired a couple of donkeys and a guide, and set off. As we reached the fork in the river-bed, we all breathed a sigh of relief when our guide turned left. After about ten minutes, we could see depressions in the limestone cliff-face which gradually increased in size.

Climbing up to the top of the scree which lines the valley, I made my way along the base of the cliffs. Sure enough, a few minutes later I was standing outside a cave. Its roof looked fire-blackened, but I knew from other cave experiences that limestone can excrete tar-like substances which look very like soot, so no point in jumping to conclusions. A few metres further on, however, we came to some larger caves where Mike and Joann found fragments of pottery in the scree below the cave mouth. And, as I climbed into the fifth cave, a smooth stone caught my eye. I pulled it out from under a boulder. It was a heavy grindstone, broken but absolutely identical to the grindstones the Guanches had made in the Canaries. There was now no doubt about it. These were habitation caves. Shepherds would never carry heavy grindstones all the way up this barren valley. People must have lived here. The pottery, too, had one peculiarity: little lugs with holes pierced in them so that a cord could be passed through and the pot hung up, just like the ones the Guanches had made.

Further up the valley, Joann disappeared, then reappeared at a cave 'window' high up on the cliff-face and called for us to join her. A narrow path had been etched into the cliff, leading to a small platform and a narrow tunnel into the rock face. A few metres inside, the tunnel opened out into a really spacious chamber, linked to another which had the two 'windows' we had seen from below. Off this main chamber there were many more rooms, some with little alcoves and shelves. We were amazed. It was just like the caves we had visited in the Guayadeque valley in Gran Canaria.

Gazing around the valley, we could easily see that there had once been at least two cave villages. Furthermore, there were caves on both sides of the valley. The pottery fragments and grindstone were all lying on the sunny side of the valley, leading Mike to speculate that perhaps the Canarian pattern was repeating itself, with funerary caves situated on the shady side, habitation caves in the sun. Even more tantalizing, we could see some caves high on the cliff-face which appeared to have been sealed up with mud bricks. These could only be reached safely by using abseiling gear from above and we were not equipped for that. Our guide rose to the occasion, offering to take us further up the valley to a point where we could climb up on to the top of the hillside. From there, apparently, we would be able to see all the way to the Atlantic coast, about a hundred miles from the Canary Islands. But time had run out for us, so reluctantly we made our way back to the village and our car, then to the hotel in Marrakesh, then, next day, to England.

IN SEARCH OF THE IMMORTALS

For me, finding Hooker's caves had provided the missing link: concrete evidence that it was cave-dwelling Berbers who had set out to cross the waters to the Canaries and set up their own little world there. A world which had drawn its inspiration and organization from an ancient pan-North African culture, a culture which found its most wondrous and elaborate expression in the pyramids, sun worship, fertility cults and mummification techniques of the ancient Egyptians. Cut off from the mainland, the Guanches had continued to express this ancient culture for a millennium after the fall of ancient Egypt. Only then did history in the grotesque form of the cannon and swords of their Spanish destroyers – catch up with them.

The crushing of the Guanches taught the Spanish vital lessons in the subjugation and systematic genocide of non-European peoples, lessons they would put to brutal use just a century or so later when a young marine adventurer, Christopher Columbus, set out from Tenerife in the Canary Islands on his way to the New World.

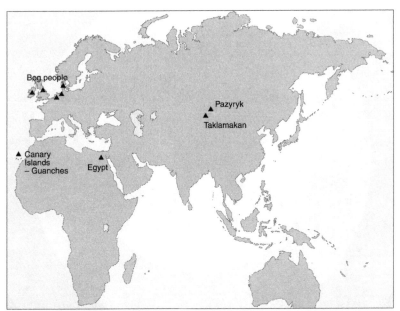

Mummy Sites in the Old World

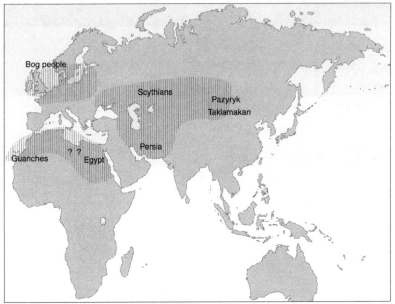

Extent of Mummy-making Cultures in the Old World

Part Two
The New World

Chapter 6

Between the Old World
and the new

Most people who are interested in mummies assume that the greatest mummy-making tradition in the world was that of ancient Egypt. In some ways this is true – the ancient Egyptians did dedicate more time and effort to the glorification and preservation of their dead than any other culture. But the Egyptian mummification tradition was nowhere near as prolonged or diverse as that of South America, where people started to preserve their dead more than 4,000 years earlier.

In various parts of the continent, the native South Americans continued to do this until the arrival of the Spanish in the fifteenth century AD, a time-span of more than 8,000 years. The South American traditions, therefore, are the most extensive and variable in the world. They are also relatively unknown to the world at large because, unlike those of ancient Egypt which have been the subjects of intensive study for nearly 200 years, until recently the mummies of South America have hardly been studied at all.

When I set out for Peru in 1998 to investigate these ancient peoples, I had literally never heard of some of the most important mummifying cultures I would come across there. Furthermore, the process of discovery is far from complete. In 1997 a major cache of mummies was discovered high in the Andes and when I was there a year later a rumour was going around that Inca mummies had been found. If this does prove to be true, these will be the first mummies from that period to have escaped the wrath of the Spanish, who systematically destroyed any they found. Given that the work of several distinguished experts is now focused on the mummifying cultures of the ancient New World, I have little doubt that major finds will continue to come to light in this area over the next few years.

Could there be any links between the mummy-makers of the New and Old Worlds? At first glance, the answer appears to be no, unless you adhere to theories such as those of Graham Hancock and Erich Von Daniken who posit in their writings unseen races of supermen or aliens cruising the world thousands of years ago, sowing the seeds of global civilization. On a less fanciful level, we cannot totally dismiss the possibility of real links between Europe or North Africa and the Americas, or between the Americas and Asia. Thor Heyerdal's extraordinary voyages in the *Kontiki* and the *Ra* have demonstrated that such journeys could have taken place. The great Sinologist Joseph Needham has also reported voyages by Chinese navigators whom he believes reached the Americas in the fifth and seventh centuries AD. However as yet there is no sound archaeological evidence to back these claims up.

Superficially then, it seems unlikely that the idea of mummy-making was transmitted directly from the Old to the New World or vice versa. Yet there are clearly some striking parallels between Old and New World practices and beliefs. In a way this is not surprising, as mummy-making arose in response to a set of universally shared human experiences: the trauma surrounding death. We all face the same problems when somebody dies. There is a body to dispose of, and a rent to repair in our social and psychological fabric. That people should find similar answers to similar problems on different continents is understandable. And if those people also live in ecological conditions which have much the same effect on cadavers – the Sahara, the Taklamakan and the Atacama deserts, for example – then the scene is set for parallel but unrelated mummy-making cultures to develop. But there are deeper, older links between the peoples of the Old and New Worlds that need to be explored. For these, we need to go back to the original peopling of the Americas.

For decades it has been accepted that people first entered the Americas via the Bering Straits during the last Ice Age, when sea-levels were low enough to permit them to walk across from Asia to Alaska. Coming from Asia, it has always been assumed that the people making the crossing were of Mongoloid ethnic stock, but recently the ethnic identity of the first Americans has been questioned. The discovery of 'Kennewick Man' in 1994 brought the biggest challenge to the conventional view, as well as a political storm. 'Kennewick Man' is a 9,000-year-old skeleton found on the banks of the Columbia river in Washington state, USA. The archaeologists who found, measured, photographed and X-rayed him concluded that he was Caucasoid not Mongoloid. A cast was made of his skull and a forensic expert was asked to reconstruct his face. He did look decidedly European.

When the local Native Americans got to hear of this, they demanded the immediate return of their ancestor's bones and the right to bury him with full tribal honours. This was a neat way to dispose of a potentially thorny problem: if the original Americans were ethnically Caucasoid, European-looking people, then Native American claims to ownership of land, sub-soil deposits and so on, could be severely jeopardized. The legal custodians of the bones of Kennewick Man were the Army Corps of Engineers, responsible for all river banks in Washington state, and they found themselves caught between angry Native Americans demanding the return of their ancestor and scientists who were saying that he could not possibly be their ancestor. To avoid antagonizing the Native Americans, the Engineer Corps declined to let the scientists continue their investigations, but did not return the bones to the claimants. At the time of writing this book, the stalemate persists.

Meanwhile, other scientists have been pioneering new methods for determining how and when populations moved around the globe by studying the genetic composition of existing groups. Once again Native North Americans have proved to be an anomaly. Early in 1998 researchers at Emory University, Atlanta, reported that a genetic marker common in most Native Americans is absent in Asian populations, although it is found among Europeans, especially Finns and Italians.

Experts have not yet offered any historical or archaeological explanation for the presence of these 'European' traits in Native Americans' pre-history and genetic make-up, but my guess is that these 'markers' did not come across the Atlantic. Having discovered the very mixed ethnicity of the ancient peoples of Central and Northern Asia in my research for the earlier chapters of this book, it makes sense to me that some of the first Americans were also of mixed ethnic stock, their genes carrying both Mongoloid and Caucasoid markers.

Along with this physical evidence of links between the peoples of the New and Old Worlds, there is also a fundamental cultural link: shamanism. We have seen how this ancient belief system has roots which go back to the cave cults of Western Europe and how — before the rise of the 'world religions' — it was widespread throughout Asia. It is almost certain, too, that this was the belief system which sustained the first Americans as they made their way into the New World. The ethnographic record shows that even today there are amazing similarities between the belief systems of the people of Siberia and those of North and South America. Anyone who has seen or heard shamanic rituals performed by these peoples cannot fail to notice how closely related they are. And when shaman experts, such as Michael Harner, peel away the differences in language and local cultural symbolism, the underlying content of the two shamanic visions are almost identical, even though the people have been physically separated for thousands of years.

Many thousands of years after the arrival of the original Americans, great civilizations emerged in the Americas. Their religious systems elaborated the shamanic vision, and evolved complex but culture-specific cosmologies. The cosmology of the Aztecs, for example, owes much to — but is distinct from — the visions of their precursors, peoples such as the Maya and Toltecs.

At the same time that the Aztecs were perfecting their practice of mass human sacrifice as the cornerstone of their religious and political systems, the Incas had linked the human and supernatural worlds through the person of their emperor. They believed that he was born of the sun and that on death his soul would become divine while his body lived on in mummified form. But elaborate as these state religions became, they are all underpinned by a perception of the world which is in essence shamanic.

Outside of the areas controlled by these pre-Hispanic states — throughout the vast Amazon basin, on the plains to the north and south of the rainforests, even as far as Tierra del Fuego — native South American perception was shaped by the visions of their shamans. In some areas this still holds true today and I am sure that the first great mummy-makers shared the same basic vision.

Because none of the mummy-making cultures of South America was literate, the search for their inner intentions must, once again, rely upon the archaeological record, and an interpretation of the imagery and symbolism they left behind with their dead. But the New World differs from the Old in that there are still people living there whose world-views may not differ greatly from the outlooks of the mummy-making peoples who preceded them thousands of years ago.

The Maku – a people I spent two years with – live deep in the rainforests of the northwest Amazon. They are hunters, fishermen and gatherers of wild forest foods. For the past few generations they have also made rudimentary gardens but their orientation is very much towards living with the resources that nature provides in the forest. When I lived with them, they had had little contact with the outside world and the way they saw the world was essentially shamanic. I was the first outsider to learn to speak their language and live, hunt and travel with them. Although it took time and patience, I eventually gained a feel for how the world looked through their eyes. For most of the time they treat the world in much the same way as we do. They go about the business of sustaining and reproducing them-selves and their society in entirely rational ways. But at special moments – moments of need or crisis – the way they see and interact with the world is very different from the Western perspective. The boundaries between culture and nature, dream and wakefulness, mind and spirit, seem to blur and fuse in ways which are disquieting for the Western mind.

In Maku eyes the worlds of people, nature and the supernatural are all highly interconnected. These people are superb hunters with incredibly sharp eyes and ears. Yet almost daily they would catch a strange distant rumble, sigh or crackle in the forest, on the very edge of ordinary perception. 'Baktup', they say, meaning ghost or bad spirit. They – especially the women – catch glimpses of them, too, and talk about them round the hearth in the evening, trying to guess who or what they have seen. One rainy season, when game was scarce and the fish hard to find in the swollen streams, my adopted mother-in-law announced that the village was 'rotted' – bewitched. All of us men had to go out, hunt hard and bring back meat for the pot so that the village could return from rotten to alive and grow again.

BETWEEN THE OLD WORLD . . .

Every Maku man knows charms and spells to recite over a sick person. Aided by smoke from a cigar, these 'spells' call upon the cooling powers of sweet fruits, breast milk, vegetables and herbs to take away fevers. Some of the men also know the great long chants which link the living to the world of the ancestors, the 'Birth Children'. These live above rocks which form a dome (the sky) and the sun, moon and stars cross under this dome. The ancestors reveal themselves during the spectacular sunsets which are so common in Amazonia, and the Maku believe that the redness of the clouds at dusk is caused by the ancestors showing their red-ochre face-paint to the living mortals below.

The Maku do not believe that they – or we – are the first to inhabit the earth. Before us there were at least three preceding creations, each one destroyed by a cataclysmic fire which consumed the face of the earth. The people before us were the 'Sugar Cane People'. After the fire bore them away the great creator, 'Bone Son', came down from his world at the very top of the cosmos and surveyed the scorched earth. Determined to start it all over again, he set off on a series of epic journeys. Sometimes accompanied by his little brother (the two brothers are sun and moon), he survives eternal night, opens a Pandora-like box and creates day. A mighty flood drowns the world and Bone Son loses his younger brother. As the flood subsides, he finds a crab playing a pan-pipe made from his little brother's finger bones. After killing the crab, he takes the bones, mixes them with clay, moulds them, blows spells and brings his brother back into being. He has discovered how to make people.

In another set of mythic adventures, the brothers set out to overcome the monstrous jaguars and giant harpy eagles which terrorize the land at the time. In these tales, they constantly turn themselves into other creatures. One minute they become lizards, wriggling underground to escape the ring of fire that Old Jaguar has set round them; the next, they become stinging ants, then small tame birds in a basket. At a drinking party, they entice two beautiful girls to take them (as birds) out of the cage and into a nearby clearing. There they suddenly revert to human form, make love to the girls, and transform themselves back into the little birds. The girls then carry them back into the house, giggling.

The two heroes survive countless crises – drought, floods, fires, cannibalism, poisonings, even thunderbolts – and, eventually, having made the world a safe enough place for humans, they create the 'Birth Children', our ancestors. The Birth Children then set off on an epic journey upstream from their birthplace – the Amazon, 'Breast Milk River'. They survive a series of ordeals, avoid a host of malevolent spirits who try to entrap them, and eventually establish the social order that we live in today. They accept that many types of bad spirits also inhabit the world they live in, and learn the ways of those spirits: give them names, places to live, and learn how to avoid the harm they intend. These places still exist today, the houses of the spirits of the forest.

In Maku eyes, the power of the super-heroic creator-figure Bone Son overcomes chaos and creates order in the natural world. He tames earthquake, eclipse, flood and fire, and establishes the orderly cycles of day and night, wet and dry seasons, and ultimately life and death. Humans, relatively frail beings, can live within these parameters. He does not eliminate all supernatural events and beings, but brings them within the grasp and tolerance of human perception. To do this, he learns how to transform himself and others.

The power to transform, to shift from human to animal or supernatural form, lies at the heart of Maku mythology and plays a part in their ordinary life too. Shamans are attributed, not just by the Maku but throughout South America, with the ability to turn themselves into jaguars. In animal form, they may hunt and kill people. In spirit form, they hunt and kill souls, causing sickness and death. When thunder rumbles, the Maku say that it is the roar of jaguar-shamans and they fear sickness.

Once, just before dusk, when I was walking back alone to my host Chai's house, a jaguar suddenly stepped out on to the path just a few metres in front of me. I looked at it and it looked at me – both of us frozen to the spot. Then it sprung on to the trunk of a tree beside the path, still staring at me. The sudden move caused me to react automatically. I raised my rifle and fired, at the same time going down on to one knee in a defensive posture. The jaguar jumped off the tree and ran straight at me, but, changing its mind, veered off into the forest when it was about two metres from me. I fired a couple more shots, but only grazed it. Arriving back at Chai's house I was very shaky indeed, and told everyone what had happened. At first there was shocked silence, then Chai said: 'Don't worry, How, that was just an animal, nothing to worry about, it was just an animal-jaguar. You'll be okay.'

During the course of the evening all the men of the village came to reassure me that it was just an animal. Next day we went to check, found its claw marks and a puff of fur that I had grazed off with my bullet. That was positive proof that it was a mere animal and I had nothing to worry about. This is a world where things are not always what they seem to be, where images may carry spiritual charges, making them symbols. It is the world of the unconscious, of the dream and of the spirits.

At some rituals, the Maku drink a sacred potion called *cahpi*. They make it by pounding and boiling the stems of a wild vine. It is extremely bitter and my first action after taking it was to vomit profusely. This is expected and desired as it purges the body of food and purifies the soul. As the active ingredients set in, sound, colour and shape seem to blend, transform, intermingle. The men chant their 'sky high song' and are symbolically carried away by the chant and the drug to the land of the Birth Children, the homes of the ancestors high above the sun, moon and stars. On the way there, myriad strange visions swirl before their eyes, and people experience the transformation of plants into animals, animals into humans, and animals into spirits and the like. The drug has been used throughout Amazonia for thousands of years. Derived from the wild vine *Banisteriopsis cahpi* in Peru, it is also known as *ayahuasca*.

Living within this complex network of symbols keeps the Maku sensitive to the minutiae of the world around them. But there are also guiding principles which underpin their world-view. At the very base of these is the notion of growth. Everything grows and moves forward in time. If it does not, then decay results and rot sets in. Nurturing this spiritual and physical growth is the basic aim of life.

It took nearly eighteen months before Chai and his relatives began to explain the underlying principles of the system. By that time Chai had become a firm friend as well as my main instructor. In his late thirties, he was a popular man who liked to live life to the full. He was a skilled hunter, great drinker, good chanter and a womanizer – one of the few Maku I knew who had two wives. He had married two sisters and lived with their mother and a third sister who was married to someone else. The third daughter's children, however, bore an uncanny resemblance to Chai. Although not an active shaman, Chai was well versed in spell-blowing, chanting and the performance of the sacred rites of initiation. He knew all the basic Maku myths, but if in doubt consulted his mother-in-law whose knowledge of the myths was phenomenal.

Once I had fathomed the elements of their mythology, Chai and his family taught me more about the secret principles which underpinned their beliefs. For them, the world is composed of two fundamental forces – the hot force and the cool force. Too much of either and you are in trouble. Meat is quintessentially hot, inedible in its raw state; sweet fruits are cool and therefore safe to eat. Cooking renders meat edible and is, therefore, in essence, a cooling act. So if you eat meat (a dangerously hot force), you must 'cool' it first by cooking and only then eat it with 'cool' vegetables or bread. After you hunt (a hot activity), you should take a cool dip in the stream. Excess heat causes illness, which must be treated with cool forces. The system is uncannily like the ancient Chinese philosophy of *yin* and *yang*.

These hot and cool forces are also the basic elements of human composition. When we are born, all humans are enveloped in an aura called *baktup*. This is a hot, negative force – and the same word is used to mean shadow, ghost, bad spirit, darkness and blindness. As we go through life, the 'ghost force' gradually shrinks until it is tiny and finally ends up on our wrists. We are also born with a cool, positive force, *howugn*, which means both the physical heart and the soul. At birth this is very small and resides in our chest. As we age, it becomes more and more powerful, steadily enveloping the body in a cool, protective aura which shamans can see. So the life cycle is itself a gradual transition from a state dominated by the hot negative force of the ghost to a state where the cool positive force of the soul prevails.

When we die, the Maku believe that the ghost escapes from the inert body, rather as a parasite might abandon a dead host. It then slips off into the forest and hangs around the campsite, making noises and trying to frighten people. The living are not greatly in fear. Sometimes an older person will talk to it, soothe it, and tell it to go away and stop bothering people. In the days after death, the people also hold ritual conversations with the deceased. They call it 'talking afar'. They tell the deceased how far away they are now on the great journey to join the ancestors; they talk of what they must be seeing and give news of the living back at home. (Because they move around a great deal themselves in life, this 'talking afar' is not confined to dead people. When I finally left Chai and his family to return to Europe, Chai said they would all 'talk afar' to me over the next few days, to comfort me on my way, to get themselves used to my absence.)

IN SEARCH OF THE IMMORTALS

As the people grieve, wash the body and prepare it for burial, its soul begins its journey to the afterlife. At death, the large strong soul of the living person immediately shrinks, as Chai put it, 'to the size of a piece of pig's shit'. Soon Bone Son, the creator, comes to it, places it gently in a little gourd and gives it a draft of flower pollen to snort up its nostrils. This causes the soul to 'ascend-grow' and rise up to the land of the ancestors above the sky. There it will remain for eternity – the Maku have no notions of reincarnation or resurrection.

Within these cycles of growth and decay, the Maku notice that all living things pass through periods of hardness and softness. In periods of rapid growth, plants, animals and people are essentially soft. Flowers, new growth and young leaves are perceptibly softer than mature trunks and stems. They make similar observations about people. They call newborn babies and infants 'soft game animals', explaining that their souls are as yet so small and weak that they have not yet achieved human status. Adolescent boys are called 'soft-bodied ones', pubescent girls 'soft breasts-coming-out ones'. So at times of maximum growth people are in a state of softness. Although the Maku do not stress this, there is also the inference that once grown and formed we move into a 'harder' state of being.

At death, they point out that the body undergoes rigor mortis and hardens. This is important for the Maku as they see a parallel with the way that soft flowers become hard seeds. Life becomes suspended in a hard state, and for plant-life to begin again the seed must soften and open. This is one of the reasons why Bone Son comes to the soul of the dead person, which has shrunk and become hard like the dead body. By giving the soul a snort of pollen (soft plant sperm), Bone Son brings the soul back to life by softening it. This allows it to grow once again and ascend to the world of the ancestors.

The main ritual cycle that the Maku enact centres around the initiation of adolescent boys into manhood. In this ritual the men play large sacred trumpets which summon the ancestors to come and 'harden' the boys (the 'soft-bodied ones'). During the rituals, people exchange and consume large amounts of wild fruits and nuts which are both symbolically and literally 'hard' plant-life in a state of suspended animation. Making these foods fit for human consumption entails either cooking them or leaving them to soak in water for several days. Both methods transform hard, inedible fruits or nuts into soft, growth-giving human food. So, overall, the Maku see the process of softening as fostering life and growth while hardening signals the cessation of growth which will eventually lead to death.

The Maku world is a world which has fallen before; a world restored to life by a mythic hero who only partially overcame the forces of nature and super-nature in his quest to make it fit for humans to inhabit; a world where people have their place in the order of things, but do not dominate it; a world where people may both suffer and derive strength from forces greater than themselves.

It was with these memories and ideas in mind that I set out to investigate the oldest mummy-making tradition the world has ever known.

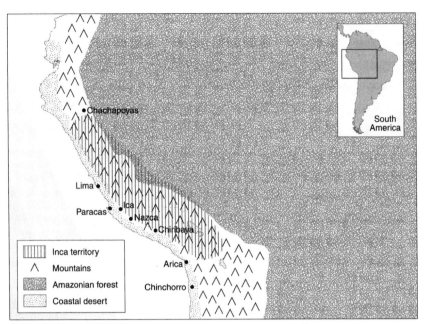

Mummy Sites in the New World

Chapter 7

Coastal Chile and Peru
the first
mummy-makers

People first reached South America somewhere between 14,000 and 20,000 years ago. The early archaeology of the continent is very patchy, but it is generally held that these First People were hunter-gatherers who spread slowly down the Andes chain, reaching Patagonia 12 – 13,000 years ago. People on the move tend to stick close to water sources, partly because they need it themselves, partly because animals must come regularly to water to drink. As they foraged their way down the 'spine' of South America, they must have noticed that the rivers run out of the mountains both westwards and eastwards.

Descending to the east, the slopes of the mountains are covered in dense forest. Taking that route, the people would have found themselves in tropical rainforest. As yet, we do not yet know if or when this happened – the soils of Amazonia are so acidic that they rapidly dissolve almost all traces left by humans. Travelling to the west, however, the First People came across a very different landscape. The western slopes of the Andes are extraordinarily barren. As you descend, you find yourself in one of the driest deserts in the world, the Atacama. But where the rivers cut across the desert, there are narrow strips of lush greenery lining the river valleys. In many places these valleys are only a few kilometres long, linking the foothills of the mountains to the Pacific coast. Some of the First People took this route around 10,000 years ago.

Away from the verdant river mouths, the Pacific coast is utterly elemental: sky, earth, water and wind — nothing else. The yellows, oranges, pinks and browns of the desert cut into the brilliant blue sky. Only the white of the breakers blurs the line between the grey and yellow sands and the turquoise ocean. There are craggy cliffs and rocks jutting out of the spume, not a plant to be seen anywhere, nothing to soften the edges. It is apparently a landscape both barren and desolate, and awesomely beautiful. It is also deceptive.

The sea birds — thousand upon thousand and so many different species — betray the sense of desolation. There are pelicans and cormorants, gulls of every shape, size and hue, lovely delicate terns and small waders darting in and out of the surf. The *raison d'etre* for this cacophony of winged beauty is simple: the ocean teems with life. The Humboldt Current pushes cool waters from the Antarctic up close to the west coast of South America, creating perfect conditions for the growth of plankton, an ideal fish fodder. Bigger fish eat the little plankton-eaters and are, in turn, the prey of sea birds and marine mammals: large colonies of sea-lions bask on the rocks off the coast or cruise effortlessly around offshore. Marine plant-life is also abundant, providing nourishment for both animals and humans. The cool waters cause a ridge of high air-pressure from sea-level to about 1,500 metres above. This band of cool air reduces moisture in the atmosphere, causing a total absence of rainfall in normal conditions. The shoreline temperature is a pleasant 21 — 25C throughout most of the year.

Was this a sort of earthly paradise which the First People had trekked to? A stunningly beautiful landscape, constant fine weather, abundant and varied food and a good water supply — surely it would have been a good place to settle down.

THE FIRST MUMMY-MAKERS

Settle they certainly did. They became sedentary. When evidence of the first human presence on the Pacific coast came to light early this century, archaeologists assumed that these people were nomads, drifting along the coast or perhaps seasonally migrating between the mountains and the sea. But recent finds have established for sure that the First People soon decided to stay put. One piece of evidence for this is the presence of graveyards which contain many bodies: nomadic hunter-gatherers do not usually transport their dead to a specific spot for burial, they dispose of the corpse wherever the person dies. The most startling discoveries in these graveyards were the oldest and most elaborate mummified human bodies ever found.

The earliest mummies unearthed on the Pacific coast of what is now southern Peru and northern Chile date back to 8000 BC. Most had been placed flat on their backs in shallow graves, in the 'extended' position. They had mummified naturally. The Atacama desert, like the Taklamakan and the Sahara, is an excellent medium for the preservation of human soft tissue.

As with the people who had mummified their dead in other deserts, we can safely assume that the First People had learnt fairly quickly that the bodies of their dead remained intact in their desert graves. In Egypt we have seen how this discovery gradually led to the elaboration of techniques for artificially mummifying the dead. In the Atacama, however, the introduction of artificial mummification was much more dramatic. Around 6000 BC these ancient people began not only to preserve their dead but actively re-make them.

In his excellent book, *Beyond Death: The Chinchorro Mummies of Ancient Chile*, physical anthropologist Bernardo Arriaza describes his first close encounter with these ancient human works of art. It happened on 20 October 1983, just another ordinary day at the Archaeology Museum in Arica, Chile, where he worked, until a phone-call came from a construction company in the city centre: workmen who had been digging a trench for new water pipes had uncovered an ancient cemetery, partly exposing several bodies. As much of

IN SEARCH OF THE IMMORTALS

Arica is built over cemeteries housing skeletons and natural mummies, Arriaza and his colleagues were not unduly surprised and set out for what they expected to be a routine visit.

> As we arrived, the scene was mesmerising: a profile of the trench revealed several mummies lying on their backs, lined up in a row, as if they were travelling together through eternity when their trip was unexpectedly interrupted. The mummies' black shiny faces glistened against the brown sandy soil of the bluff. Their peaceful expressions contrasted with the astonished faces of the gathering crowd... The ancient mummies we saw this time proved to be completely different from those we were accustomed to seeing. They were thousands of years older. These bodies had received extremely complex treatments of artificial mummification and were not naturally desiccated as are most mummies from Arica. Only a few people in the world knew about these artificially prepared mummies, called Chinchorros.

During the following months, archaeologists Vivien Standen and Guillermo Focacci unearthed a total of ninety-six mummies from this site, and sixty of them had undergone complex mummification. It was the task of Arriaza and his colleague Marvin Allison to try to figure out exactly who these mummies were.

These were not, however, the first mummies of this type to be discovered. In 1917 a German archaeologist, Max Uhle, unearthed several of them – some on a beach called Chinchorro, which in local Spanish means both 'raft' and 'fishing net'. Nowadays, the culture which created them is known by that name. Uhle did not realize how old the mummies were – and while their discovery aroused some academic curiosity at the time, this had all but evaporated until the spectacular finds in 1983.

THE FIRST MUMMY-MAKERS

The Chinchorro mummies were very fragile. Some had been damaged by the construction workers, others were virtually disintegrating when found. Sad though this was for posterity, it gave the team a great chance to find out just how they had been mummified, and an opportunity to establish more about these ancient people. They soon discovered that the Chinchorro way of death was totally unique, embodying a series of techniques found nowhere else in the world before or since.

From around 5000 BC, when a Chinchorro died, someone took the body and 'unmade' it. Using stone knives, this person decapitated then skinned the entire body, taking particular care with the skin of the head. The skin was then set aside for re-use, perhaps preserved in salt water to keep it soft and pliable. The soft tissue was then removed – internal organs and flesh. In some cases, the skull was split open and the brains and eyes removed. In other cases, it seems that the brain was scooped out through the *foramen magnum* – the hole at the base of the skull where the spine attaches to the brain. The hands and feet – too tricky to skin – were cut off and dried whole. The next step was to dry out the remaining body 'frame'. Traces of scorch-marks on the bones suggest that either hot coals, ashes or heated sand were applied to the defleshed skeleton to clean, dry and perhaps 'harden' it.

Once the body was 'clean' – purified – the process of rebuilding it began. Using sticks about 1.5 centimetres thick, one stick was placed along the whole length of the spine, and left to protrude at the top in order to hold the skull in place. This spine-stick was then tightly bound to the backbone with reed cords. Next, two long sticks were attached, one to each ankle, and run up the line of the legs, through the pelvis, up into the rib-cage to the top of the neck where they met, sticking out through the *foramen magnum*, and helped to hold the head on.

In some cases, the mummy-makers filed away the tops of the elbow, shoulder and knee bones to ensure that they would fit snugly, then bound all the major joints tightly together with reed cords. The same cords bound the legs to the long sticks. Some mummy-makers used a bundle of twigs or reeds to bind and reinforce the arms, fixing the bundle at one wrist, then feeding it up the arm, through the chest, across the shoulders, through the clavicles, and all the way down the other arm. This was all wrapped and bound tightly in place. Now the body was 'framed'.

Meantime, the mummy-makers took the empty skull and filled it with grass, ashes, soil or animal hair, or a mixture of these. Once full, they took the two halves of the skull and the lower jaw and bound them tightly together. They then applied a thick white paste to the face bones to fill the face out. The next step, in many cases, was to place the skinned face back on the skull, fixing it in place with a glue made from ashes. A scalp with short black human hair was then attached to the skull using more ash glue and sea-lion skin to hold it in place. After the head had been rebuilt, the mummy-makers added a thick layer of black paint on top of the face skin, so that they could sculpt the owner's face, moulding a nose, eyes and a mouth. The mouth was constructed in a rounded shape as if it had been left open.

Having secured the body frame, the mummy-makers then filled and covered it with white ash paste, remoulding the shape of the trunk and limbs. At this time they also, as appropriate, moulded breasts and genitalia. Following this, they put patches of the corpse's skin back on to the 'body'. In some cases, they also added sea-lion skin patches. The next step was to replace the head on the body, and then, using brushes made from bunches of dried grass, paint the corpse black. The paint was made from manganese sand collected from the beach and ground up with mortars and pestles. The end-result was a dull black mummy, so the final task was to polish it up to a bright sheen, using either a smooth piece of wood or a water-polished pebble.

THE FIRST MUMMY-MAKERS

〰

The completed mummies remained obviously human, but very stylized in appearance. The bodies — stuffed, coated and painted — have a rigidity which reminds me more of a corn-dolly than a human. The faces are elegant, almost serene, but lack individuality. The features are flattened and look like carefully designed masks. These are not images of how the person looked in life, but images of how the Chinchorro thought people should look after life.

Given the extraordinary effort and technical skill the Chinchorro put into the creation of their mummies, it is unlikely that these simple forms were 'the best they could do', but how they *wanted* them to be. The images suggest to me that the Chinchorro deliberately transformed their dead from an individual state of being to an idealized state, fit for the society of the dead.

Bernardo Arriaza pointed out that these mummies are works of art, perhaps even religious icons. Like statues of Christ, the saints, the Buddha or Hindu deities, they are idealized representations of human forms who have achieved a different state of being from puny mortals. They are both physically and artistically purified.

When someone from a small group of people dies, the sense of grief and loss is intense. At the same time, the living are left with a decaying corpse, which is a potential health hazard. Rotting corpses can cause and transmit disease. The physical details of the decomposition process are exceedingly unpleasant. The Chinchorro answer to this problem was to remove all that would decay and replace it with pure, clean materials which did not rot. The materials they chose for this process mostly came from the sea or shoreline.

There is one other small detail of the mummy-making process that may give us a clue about Chinchorro beliefs. If, when the skin of the deceased was returned to the remade body, it did not fit properly or if there were bits missing, the people — as mentioned above — used patches of sea-lion skin. Many peoples around the world feel a special affinity with a particular species of animals: some native North Americans, for example, feel especially close to bears. Like humans, bears are omnivores, live in stable family groups and know a great deal about plants. Having observed that bears understood the medicinal properties of some plants and used these to treat themselves for sickness and injuries, the native North Americans did likewise. In Western culture, large marine animals, such as walruses and manatees, gave rise to legends of mermaids who were thought to be fish-people.

The Chinchorro certainly preyed on sea-lions – the largest marine mammals in their neighbourhood – and doubtless also swam with them and shared the same food sources. Perhaps they even learnt from them where new food sources could be found; and when changes in the weather could be expected. To use their skin in the sacred task of remaking their dead loved ones seems, to me, to confer a special status on sea-lions. Perhaps, rather like our mermaids, they were the Chinchorro's 'Water People'.

The final – and perhaps the most crucial – observation that experts have made about the Chinchorro mummies is that when they were newly completed they were strong, rigid entities: strong enough to stand upright, or at least to be leaned at an angle, perhaps against a small pile of sand. They also noted that some of the mummies had several layers of paint on them and must, therefore, have been repainted from time to time. This strongly suggests that on completion they were not merely laid to rest underground for eternity. They were either kept above ground or occasionally disinterred, presumably on special occasions. So the dead either symbolically remained with the living or were returned to the living from time to time, just as the Maku summon their ancestors with their sacred trumpets to ensure that their boys grow into manhood and society keeps moving forward.

THE FIRST MUMMY-MAKERS

∿∿
∿∿

The mummies themselves give us some idea of their creators and their world-views, but do not tell us why the Chinchorro mummified their dead in the first place. To search for more clues, we need to go back thousands of years to the world in which the Chinchorro lived.

Living by the river mouths along the Pacific coast, the Chinchorro enjoyed an abundant and constant food supply which was evidently relatively easy to obtain without needing to be a nomadic people. They built small houses – some round, some rectangular – by piling up a low wall of large pebbles and embedding sticks in them to support a roof of reed mats or perhaps sea-lion hide. Some of these may have been only half covered because in a climate where it hardly ever rains the purpose of the roof is to provide shade. Although these structures may seem flimsy to us, hundreds of thousands of poor people still live along this coast in houses made of cardboard, plastic sheets or reeds.

The little cluster of Chinchorro houses would have been home to twenty to forty people – three to seven families – a typical size for most hunter-gathering peoples. Near the houses, huge mounds of seashells testify that the Chinchorro lived mainly on sea food, with sea plants, marine mammals and some land animals as supplements. The skulls of many of the men show a deformation in the bone structure of the ear known as auditory exostosis. This is caused by repeated exposure to cold water, so it seems that the men spent much time diving, collecting shellfish and other molluscs. Certainly, this condition would have given them earache and a loss of hearing that could eventually have led to deafness.

Bags for collecting shellfish are commonly found near Chinchorro graves, as are fishhooks, made from seashells and thorns. They also used spears both for fishing and for killing mammals. Along with the skills required to catch fish and game, the Chinchorro were experts in skinning, dissecting and cleaning their prey. Like all other hunter-gatherers they would have had detailed anatomical knowledge of the fish and animals they caught.

They also had fire, which they may well have used both for cooking and preserving meat and fish. When a small group of hunters kills a large game animal – a tapir or deer for the Maku, a sea-lion for the Chinchorro – they face a delicious dilemma: too much meat. The first thing that the Maku do is to share the kill between all the families of the group. Each family then builds a simple wooden rack about eighty centimetres above the ground, lights a small fire underneath it, and places all the surplus meat on it. The fire smoke-roasts the meat, and, as long as it is kept burning slowly, the meat on the rack will remain good for a month or more. Everybody eats well for a long time – including friends and relatives from neighbouring groups who are invited over to eat, drink manioc beer, dance and have fun. I think the Chinchorro would have acted in much the same way when they killed a big animal, especially as we know they had flutes and rattles to make music with.

On some occasions it may not have been necessary for them to kill their prey. When I visited their coastline in 1998 the weather had been unsettled for several months. Walking along a beautiful deserted beach I suddenly caught the unmistakeable stench of rotting flesh. Several dead sea-lions lay along the high water mark. They had probably died because of changes in marine ecology brought about by recent weather changes. The Chinchorro, too, would have been presented with such gifts from the sea and doubtless learned to determine whether a carcass was still edible.

So the Chinchorro, who were obviously expert anatomists and skilled at dissecting and preserving their prey, would have been able to use all this specialized knowledge when it came to preserving their dead.

Well equipped, knowledgeable hunter-gatherers, they probably did not need to put long hours into the task of keeping everyone fed, and had plenty of time therefore to dedicate to other matters. Conventional wisdom finds this odd because it is often assumed that hunter-gatherers had to dedicate their entire lives to subsistence survival. But detailed ethnographic and archaeological investigations have proved the opposite to be the case.

In a seminal paper, 'The Original Affluent Society', Marshall Sahlins, a brilliant anthropologist, demonstrated that even if you lived by hunting and gathering in some of the most harsh environments on the planet — the Kalahari desert or central Australia — you did not have to work hard to survive. Subsistence needs could be met by men in about thirty hours of 'work' a week, with women spending a little more time on both gathering and food preparation. So there has always been time to think about and do other things. If, then, you were lucky enough to occupy an environment as rich in natural resources as the Chinchorro's coastal world, subsistence would not have been a problem. And, given the universal tendency to keep busy and occupied even during leisure time, I would expect the Chinchorro to have developed some special skills or talents. But why did they choose to put so much time and effort into venerating and preserving the dead? Could the answer be that, from time to time, their own lives came under sudden threat?

Although, as I have mentioned before, the weather for most of the time in the area of the Chinchorro homeland is stable, every twenty-five to forty years a warm current from off the coast of Ecuador works its way south, displacing the cold Humboldt Current as far south as Chinchorro territory. Because this occurs around Christmas time, this phenomenon is now named *El Niño*, after Christ. These currents cause torrential rain to fall in the desert, and the resultant floods can be devastating, as was the case in 1998 when whole villages and towns were laid waste in the Atacama. Accompanying these drastic weather changes, violent storms and tidal waves smash into the coast, events which must have been as devastating for the Chinchorro as they are for people today. This area is also a seismically-active part of the world, where earthquakes and volcanic eruptions violently disrupt the tranquillity of the coast. The Andes, a little inland, are known as a 'young' mountain chain, where sudden natural upsets, such as earthquakes or heavy rain, instantly cause huge landslides, floods and rock falls.

So the Chinchorro havens of peace and tranquillity could suddenly have been transformed into a seething, chaotic hell by forces which they doubtless assumed to be supernatural. The Chinchorro, in fact, experienced the kind of global calamities which the Maku evoke so dramatically in their mythology. In the face of such potent manifestations of the wrath of the gods, who did the Chinchorro turn to for guidance and protection?

Here, it is useful to take a look at some other native South American visions of death and the powers of creation and destruction. Like my Maku friends, the Aztecs also believed that the present human creation was not the first, but the fourth cycle of creation – the previous three having been destroyed by earthquake, flood and fire. They reported that shortly before the arrival of the conquistadors a fiery ball had crossed the firmament (presumably a comet), presaging the imminent destruction of the present cycle of creation. They believed that the only way to placate the gods – and to ensure that the sun rose and set in a blaze of red each day – was to feed them human hearts and blood, a theme we will return to in later chapters. The Aztecs' ancient predecessors, the Maya, also believed that the world moved through cycles of creation and destruction. Their astronomer priests calculated that the present cycle will come to an end in the year 2013 AD. The Incas also feared that their world was about to end. This is not surprising when we consider the devastating impact which natural disasters bring about in this region. In 1604, 1868, 1877 and

THE FIRST MUMMY-MAKERS

~~
~~

1987, for example, earthquakes devastated coastal cities built on ancient Chinchorro settlement sites. In the 1868 and 1877 disruptions, tidal waves destroyed the city of Arica in the Chinchorro heartland. The waves were so huge that several ships ended up in the centre of the city. The archaeological record points to the regular recurrence of these disasters throughout pre-Hispanic times, and it is known that these events made their mark in mythology. An ancient historical document, known as the Hoarochiri Manuscript, states:

> In ancient times the sun died. Because of his death it was night for five days. Rocks banged against each other. Mortars and grinding stones began to eat people. Buck llamas started to drive men.

The manuscript goes on to describe a classic flood scenario where only the peaks of the high mountains remained out of the water. We have already seen how people revere mountains all over the world as the homes of gods or powerful spirits. For today's people living along the Pacific coast, they are still treated as sanctuaries, havens where people flee in the face of ferocious storms and tidal waves.

The Chinchorro certainly went through these traumas and took steps to circumvent their impact. In particular, they sited many of their cemeteries on high ground, out of reach of tidal waves. Their foresight in doing so is the principal reason why their sacred heritage, their mummified dead, has survived for so many millennia. This decision to bury their dead in places where they may not have actually lived, but where they would be safe from the elements, shows once more how much the Chinchorro loved and revered their dead. It is as if they believed that we mortals, who must endure 'the slings and arrows of outrageous fortune' in life, have a duty to ensure eternal peace and tranquillity for our forebears in the afterlife.

IN SEARCH OF THE IMMORTALS

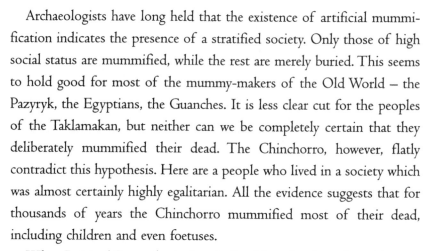

Archaeologists have long held that the existence of artificial mummi-fication indicates the presence of a stratified society. Only those of high social status are mummified, while the rest are merely buried. This seems to hold good for most of the mummy-makers of the Old World – the Pazyryk, the Egyptians, the Guanches. It is less clear cut for the peoples of the Taklamakan, but neither can we be completely certain that they deliberately mummified their dead. The Chinchorro, however, flatly contradict this hypothesis. Here are a people who lived in a society which was almost certainly highly egalitarian. All the evidence suggests that for thousands of years the Chinchorro mummified most of their dead, including children and even foetuses.

When I visited Bernardo Arriaza in Las Vegas he showed me his copy of a mummified Chinchorro foetus. A charming, doll-like object with a serene face and open mouth, the tiny mummy was a work of love and affection, and it was hard to believe that it contained an unborn child. If my seven-year-old daughter had seen it, I am sure she would have wanted to pick it up and cuddle it. Bernardo then went on to explain that the oldest known Chinchorro mummies are mostly children.

We know that Chinchorro society was extraordinarily stable for thousands of years, and there are few signs that it either expanded or contracted over time. In most hunter-gatherer societies, couples produce children every two or three years but many do not survive infancy. Maku women do not like to talk about children they have 'lost', because they say it makes them cry. But during the two years I spent with them, I learnt that most women had lost about half the children they had borne. We might think that this would harden them, make them resigned to child death, but that certainly was not the case.

One couple, my adopted aunt and uncle, had a little girl of about five who was so emaciated she could hardly walk. She spent most of the day in her parents' hammock, moaning. Every morning her father would gently pick her up, carry her down to the stream and wash her. Her mother would then coax her to drink a little warm broth. Her father explained to me that her body had been invaded by a bad spirit. Whenever her groaning intensified, he would take her in his arms and quietly chant spells to soothe her.

The crisis came several months later when we were all on a hunting trip deep in the forest. Her father had carried her for several hours to the camp and, that evening after dark, she began first to cough then to pant, her breath coming in shallow gasps. I was the only one with a blanket so we wrapped the child and her mother in it. Her father and uncle, both senior and knowledgeable men, rolled a large cigar and sat next to her hammock, chanting. Sometimes the spells came out with great force, trying to drive out the bad spirit, then the brothers would lapse almost into whispers as they uttered the secret magical formulae which would cool and restore her. They chanted all night. Nobody cried out, everyone was incredibly calm as if concentrating on defeating death. We kept the fires going all night against the chill damp air. As the first light began to filter through the smoky clearing, the little girl stirred and looked into her father's eyes. She did not smile, but we all knew the worst had passed.

Had she died, there would have been great grieving and sadness, and the death rituals would have been performed to send her calmly on her way to the land of the Birth People, and to start healing the great hole her absence would have created in this tiny group. People such as the Maku or the Chinchorro, who spend almost all their lives together, are intensely close-knit and – as mentioned before – the loss of a person is felt intensely. Perhaps the reason why the Chinchorro decided to preserve their dead was to keep the loved one with them and ease this terrible sense of loss.

There is, however, another important aspect to death among hunting people which modern urbanized people tend to forget.

IN SEARCH OF THE IMMORTALS

Hunters are professional killers who deal with death almost on a daily basis. The taking of an animal's life sustains and perpetuates their own lives. In almost all cultures, including our own, death is followed by the ritual sharing of food and drink at the wake. This is usually interpreted as a reaffirmation of life, a return to normality. But at its roots – among hunting peoples – it may also be an affirmation of the positive role that death plays in the flow of life. If we combine this notion with the ideas which people, such as the Maku and Chinchorro, hold about the course of events beyond life, then death begins to lose its sting.

My Maku friends told me, face-to-face, about their afterlife journeys. Much as we would love to do the same with the Chinchorro, the only way we can 'talk' to them is through the 'messages' they left behind in the sands of the Atacama. One point particularly intrigues me: hardly any material objects have been found in Chinchorro mummies' graves, unlike many Old World peoples who sent their loved ones into the next world fully equipped for a long journey. A few fishhooks and net-bags have been found, but no sign of food, cooking implements or anything else that a living Chinchorro might need for a journey. So, perhaps, the Chinchorro did not want their dead to travel – to go away. If not, where did they think the souls of the dead went?

A simple answer – given the fishhooks and net-bags, along with their use of sea-lion skins in mortuary rituals – would be that they believed their dead were going on a very short journey, perhaps down to the sea, to join the souls of the Water People, their kindred animals the sea-lions. It is also worth bearing in mind that the path of the setting sun, used by so many other ancient peoples as the direction to take after death, lies westwards over the Pacific ocean. Or perhaps they believed that their dead took flight to the nearby mountain tops, their refuge in life from the natural disasters discussed above. Certainly, as we shall see

THE FIRST MUMMY-MAKERS

in following chapters, mountain tops were immensely important to successive generations of mummy-makers in this part of South America. Perhaps the Chinchorro sowed the seeds of this idea.

I believe, however, that a different explanation fits the facts at our disposal. It is to do with how these ancient peoples – not just the Chinchorro but all the ancient peoples of the Americas and many others who lived in the Old World at the same time – perceived reality, a perception which is so obvious to those who live it that it is very hard for them to explain. In essence, the message is that ordinary waking consciousness is not the only mode of consciousness available to us. We think that by taking psychoactive drugs, dreaming, going into a trance or having Near Death Experiences, we experience *altered* states of consciousness. And we attribute these strange experiences to internal alterations in our brain chemistry. Native South Americans and many others, however, disagree. They believe that in these states we gain access to different dimensions of reality, enter different planes of existence. Physicists might call them parallel universes. In trying to teach young people, or outsiders such as myself, about these metaphysical dimensions, they often use the metaphor of a journey to these other worlds, but they do not mean it literally. The common characteristic of all these non-material planes of existence is that they lie outside the constraints of normal, linear time and space. In dreams or trance, under the influence of drugs or at the point of death, the sun does not need to rise, nano-seconds may last for eternity. In Near Death Experiences, people live out these extraordinary expansions and contractions of time and space. It is clear to me that, looking through the eyes of people such as the Chinchorro and the Maku, the world of the dead and the ancestors is just another dimension to the timeless, spaceless alter-universe. The ancestors do not get older nor are they near or far in kilometres or light years. They just are.

IN SEARCH OF THE IMMORTALS

It was the genius of the Chinchorro to give their ancestors a physical form, a manifestation in the world of the living of this parallel, mystical plane of existence. There was no need for a journey, they were not going anywhere, they were remaining with their loved ones; providing a gateway to the metaphysical world, a world that offered protection and comfort in times of crisis and acted as concrete evidence of continuity of life after death and throughout succeeding generations.

That Chinchorro society thrived under this protective mantle of preserved ancestors for more than 3,000 years shows that at one level they got it right. What they achieved was a balance of life-and-death forces which generated stability for hundreds of generations.

When change came, as it always seems to, it took an interesting form for the Chinchorro. Around 3000 BC, after making black mummies for more than 2,000 years, the Chinchorro started painting the bodies of most of their mummies red. They ceased removing all the soft tissue from the dead, although they still eviscerated them, packed the bodily cavities and created clay masks over their faces. At this stage, the mummies were given much longer hair pieces and were sometimes dressed in loin cloths for males and grass skirts for females. Two mummies have been found from this epoch which were not painted at all, merely covered in mud, perhaps signalling that this era, too, was coming to an end. The red-mummy period lasted until about 1700 BC. Beyond that, the Chinchorro continued to bury their dead wrapped in reed mats, laid out flat on their backs but without any modification to the corpse at all. At the same time, several new practices appeared among the living: they began to wear beads, braid their hair and to modify the shapes of their skulls by binding their children's heads to flat boards. The heads of the dead were then often elaborately wrapped in turban-like cloths.

As Chinchorro society continued to change – not least with the blossoming of new, fine basket-weaving techniques and horticulture – the ancient mummy-making traditions first waned then disappeared. We do not know for sure why the Chinchorro gave up their unique art, but it seems likely that these cultural changes and external influences brought about the demise of their own unique way of preserving their dead.

It would be wrong, however, to assume that the Chinchorro had been living in isolation for all those millennia. From as early as 7000 BC, there is evidence of a shared technology and of trade in animals, plants and birds between the highlands and the coast. Highland sites – some of them at 1,500 metres above sea-level and dating to 7000 BC, possibly older – have been found to contain the remains of fish and shellfish. Perhaps even more surprising, a few objects have been found on the coast which originated in the tropical forests of the Amazon, on the far side of the Andes. We do not know if individuals made the epic trek from Amazonia to the coast or vice versa. More likely, desired goods, such as parrot feathers, passed from hand to hand down the same kind of long-distance trade networks we have already encountered running across pre-historic Eurasia.

Although the Chinchorro may have been at the far end of these networks, one thing is for sure: they were not alone. And where goods travel from hand to hand, ideas surely pass from mind to mind. Bernardo Arriaza has mused that the peoples of the coast and highlands might even have intermarried. All the evidence so far uncovered points to the very public nature of Chinchorro mortuary practices, so it seems almost certain that the Chinchorro's highland neighbours would have known about these rites, even if they did not choose to adopt them themselves.

As we shall see in the following chapters, the archaeological record is still tantalizingly patchy in South America and we cannot, therefore, say for sure that there was a direct continuity from the Chinchorro tradition to the later mummy-makers of the region. But I believe that the Chinchorro mummy-makers set the stage for the continued veneration and preservation of the dead right up until the arrival of the Spanish in South America. People die, traditions disappear, but in my experience ideas have a habit of lingering.

Chapter 8

Coastal Peru
valleys of
the dead

El Niño hit Peru with devastating effect in 1997–8. The warm current sent bank after bank of rain clouds inland over the coastal desert. When they hit the mountains, they dropped their payloads of torrential rain for weeks. The wet season normally ends around Christmas but that year it just kept on raining, all through January and February and well into March, when I arrived.

Chaos reigned. Flood waters hurtled down the slopes of the Andes and across the desert, destroying entire villages and killing hundreds of people. Bridges vanished, roads, railways, power and communication lines were cut everywhere. Planes caught in sudden storms were hurled into mountainsides. Landslides ripped up anything in their way, not just on the coastal plane but throughout the Andes. People drowned or were buried alive. Dams burst and floodwater choked the sewage and drainage systems of many towns, contaminating domestic water supplies. Irrigation and flood-control systems were pulverized. Apocalypse gripped the country by the throat.

Seeing at first-hand the devastation *El Niño* brings was at once sobering and instructive. The 1998 *El Niño* was severe but far from the worst to hit Peru over the millennia.

IN SEARCH OF THE IMMORTALS

As if the peril from the sea is not enough, there is also peril from deep within the land. As I mentioned in the previous chapter, geologically the Andes chain is a young unstable region. It sits upon a piece of the earth's crust abutting the Nazca Plate, which is gradually sinking, and its movement is sometimes violent, causing earthquakes. In 1970, an earthquake in northern Peru killed 70,000 people and destroyed the homes of thousands more. Earthquakes also trigger tidal waves like the ones which devastated the Arica area in the late nineteenth century.

All the people who have ever lived in Peru have had to come to terms with these overwhelming natural forces; they must have moulded the way they perceived life, death and the world of the supernatural.

I arrived in Lima at the end of March 1998 with my assistant, Tara. We went first to the house of Sonia Guillen, Peru's leading mummy expert. Quiet and charming with piercing black eyes, she spoke with a clarity and precision which exuded authority without the macho self-importance so typical of male Latin-American 'eminences'. Just six months earlier she had taken charge of a spectacular and mysterious cache of mummies discovered high in the Andes. They are known as the Chachapoyas, 'The Cloud People'.

We were hoping to head north into the mountains to visit them right away, but *El Niño* was still wreaking havoc with transport and communications. To get to the mummies at that time would have entailed a local flight followed by a sixteen-hour journey by four-wheel-drive vehicle just to reach the town of Chachapoyas, several hours from the village where the mummies were being cleaned and stored. There was no guarantee that even the four-wheel-drive would be able to get through, as many bridges were still down. This was a real blow as I had set my heart on the trek up into the mountains to visit the holy lake where the mummies had been found.

Over lunch with Sonia and her tour-agent friend, Miryam, we gathered that the weather was at last beginning to improve, so if we waited for another week or so then our chances of making it to the mummies in the mountains would be a lot better. Then Sonia turned to me and said, 'You know, Howard, there are a lot more mummies here besides the new ones we found up there last year . . . '

We sat back and listened with increasing amazement as Sonia reeled off place after place and culture after culture where there were mummies to be seen and studied all over Peru. She told us about a valley near the town of Ilo where she has a museum and research centre. She still does not know exactly how many cemeteries there are there, maybe 200 – 300, each with hundreds of mummies in them. She explained that her team find new mummies there every day. There was Nazca and Ica, and a cemetery at Chauchilla where it is possible to see maybe a hundred mummies still in their tombs. She explained that the last three are not far from the Paracas peninsular, home to the oldest mummies in the region which are about 2,500 years old. The Paracas people also have human trophy heads, she added.

By the end of this verbal tour of Peru's mummydoms, Tara and I were staring wide-eyed at each other. Then Miryam took over. She has been organizing special tours for people interested in the archaeology of Peru for twenty years and, she explained a little coyly, a friend of hers is in charge of all Peru's regional archaeological sites.

'Let's look at the map, Howard,' she said. 'As you can see, most of the sites Sonia is talking about are along the Pan-American Highway, down the coast to the south of here. They are not very far apart and you can see a lot of them quite quickly. You can even visit the Nazca Lines and have a plane ride over them if you want. It's quite fun and not very expensive. There was a lot of flood damage down there, but the road is now clear in most parts so you should be able to get around okay.'

As we started taking notes, marking the map, discussing distances, where to stay, which special places to see, the penny slowly began to drop. These two charming ladies had got all this figured out long before the mad *Ingles* had arrived. They knew how little I knew and how much I needed to learn to do justice to Peru's amazing mummy heritage, and they knew the best ways for me to do it. A warm glow spread through me as I realized we were in safe, very capable hands.

'I suppose the best way to do this is to pick up a hire car and head off down the Pan-American Highway, then,' I said. Miryam's eyes twinkled. 'I have already made the reservation,' she replied.

Eight-hundred kilometres to the south of Lima and nearly 4,000 years ago the Chinchorro had *not* suddenly disappeared from the archaeological record. People continued to live and die in the coastal oases of the Atacama, but around 1700 BC they changed the way they treated their dead. They no longer dismembered them but laid them gently on their sides in the graves, knees drawn up to their chins in the 'flexed' position. Although I am sure they remained aware that the bodies of their dead would stay intact, they no longer took any special steps to ensure that this would happen. Bodies mummified naturally in the salty desert sands, and the world's oldest, most complex mummifying tradition just came to an end. But the picture is not as simple as this.

Even though Chinchorro society was extraordinarily stable for thousands of years the archaeological record shows that there was a steady increase in contacts between them and the people living inland, in the Andes. Trade networks, as mentioned in the previous chapter, had evidently grown up during this period, allowing goods to pass from hand to hand between the coast and Amazonia. Indeed, ancient trails still exist which link the coastal oases where the Chinchorro lived to settlements high in the mountains. So it is very likely that the Chinchorro made treks up into the mountains to trade, and that this put them in contact – directly or indirectly – with a wide spectrum of peoples, ways of life and cultures. And while life in the coastal oases seems to have been stable, major changes were taking place in other areas, especially from about 3000 BC to around 2000 BC.

Most important among these changes was the development of horticulture, with the domestication of maize, cotton, squash, beans and potatoes. The first signs of cultivation among the Chinchorro seems to have coincided with the end of their ancient mummification practices, and I believe that the two events were related. The transition from hunting, fishing and gathering to farming has been studied in many parts of the world and several basic changes in economic and social organization are very widespread. In general, growing crops involves working longer on more routine tasks (sowing, weeding, watering, harvesting, and so on) throughout the year than hunter-gatherers are used to.

My Maku friends, who are at this cultural crossroads right now, make a clear linguistic distinction between the pleasant and challenging experiences involved in going out to forage in the forest and the tedium of 'work' – clearing and planting gardens, making houses and so on. They remain inefficient farmers because they do not like the 'work' it entails.

It is pretty clear that the Chinchorro, living by foraging from the twin environments of the seashore and the coastal oases, enjoyed plenty of 'leisure time', and that much of this was dedicated to the dead and their incredibly elaborate mortuary rites. The loss of leisure time when they started farming may well have meant that they simply did not have time to look after their dead in the traditional way. And it was not just farming which was eating into their leisure time. When they started cultivating cotton, they learnt to weave; and, with the introduction of working with clay, they began to make pots.

The coming of farming also tends to lead to a reshaping not just of work patterns but of the structure of society as a whole. Unlike hunter-gathering, where nature provides a constant flow of fresh foods, crops provide little or no food until they are ripe, when they produce an enormous surplus. This surplus must be stored and redistributed to the people who produced it over the months between harvests. In most parts of the world, notably in the cradles of the great 'civilizations' of both the New and Old Worlds, this led rapidly to the stratification of society. Chiefs, priests – or a combination of the two – took control of the food and made themselves responsible for its redistribution. If genuine surpluses existed, then two things could happen. Those who controlled the distribution of food could cease taking an active part in its production and divert some of it to feed specialists who were dedicating their time to activities which were deemed desirable did not produce anything edible. These people were then free to become full-time weavers, potters, builders or metalworkers. This process was certainly under-way in other parts of Peru around 2000 BC, and no doubt the Chinchorro got to hear about it, see it and were sucked into it.

Not that this all happened overnight – the changes were doubtless gradual, probably spread out over centuries. And there are some intriguing pointers as to how these changes came about in the graves of the Chinchorro's successors, the Quiani. Whereas the Chinchorro placed their dead in group tombs, the Quiani made individual ones. They also placed many more goods in the tombs and started to include food items among their offerings for the dead. Both these factors suggest a shift away from the collective, where the group of mummy ancestors were safeguarding the band as a whole and perhaps protecting communally-held territory. With the coming of farming, the emphasis shifted to the individual who doubtless wanted his or her ancestors to protect individual property, both in the form of material goods and individual plots of farmed land.

Two other curious features marked the closing years of the Chinchorro and their transition into the Quiani. First, the Chinchorro started to bind the heads of their children at an early age, causing the skull to deform in

Chinchorro mummies from the Arica area of Chile, the oldest artificially mummified bodies so far discovered. After the bodies had been defleshed, the Chinchorro moulded stylised faces and body parts over the bones and skin *(Enrico Ferorelli / Colorific)*

After the Chinchorro had defleshed their dead they strengthened the skeletons by binding sticks to the principal limbs and the backbone *(Enrico Ferorelli / Colorific)*

Many Chinchorro children, infants and even foetuses were mummified. They also sometimes carved little wooden figurines to place in the graves *(Enrico Ferorelli / Colorific)*

The Chinchorro buried their dead in communal cemeteries, leading archaeologists to conclude that they were sedentary rather than nomadic hunter-gatherers and fishermen *(Enrico Ferorelli / Colorific)*

he Algarrobal valley in Southern Peru is typical of the many fertile river valleys which
t through the desert, linking the Andes with the Pacific. Home to the Chiribaya people
out 1000 years ago, the river mouths had been colonised by the Chinchorro thousands
years earlier *(Joann Fletcher)*

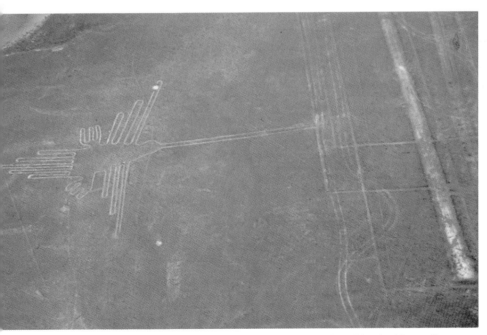

erial view of the hummingbird, one of the many animals depicted in the Nazca lines.
ummingbirds were thought to be messengers of the gods, capable of flying between the
avens and earth *(Hutchison)*

The macabre looted cemetery of Chauchilla, near Nazca in Peru, contains dozens of well preserved bodies peering out of their open graves *(K.Rodgers / Hutchison)*

Mummies found near the Sipan valley on the northern coast of Peru. Not as well preserved as the ones to the south, they have been found with spectacular caches of gold and ceramic grave goods *(Eric Pasquier / Sygma)*

A superbly preserved four-pointed hat from the Chiribaya culture of the Algarrobal valley, southern Peru *(Joann Fletcher)*

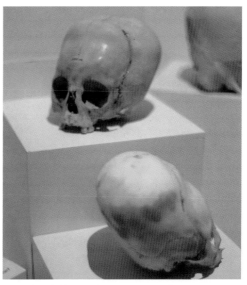

Cranial deformation was popular amongst the people of the Peruvian coast from about 1000 BC for at least 2000 years. These Chiribaya skulls may well have been adorned with long hats which accentuate even more dramatically the elongation of their heads *(Joann Fletcher)*

The monkey motif on this Paracas funerary cloth looks repetitive at first glance, but closer inspection reveals continual transformations on the colouration of both the adult and infant monkeys *(R.Frerck / Robert Harding)*

Anthropomorphic designs with spectacular colouration were often deployed by the Paracas weavers *(H.R.Dörig / Hutchison)*

The mummy bundles from the Paracas peninsula in coastal Peru were often superbly adorned with specially made funerary clothing and gold, stone and seashell jewellery *(Robert Harding)*

(from Vision of Peru, Violet Clifton, Duckworth, 1947)

A sixteenth-century engraving depicts the mummified body of an Inca emperor being borne through the streets on a ritual occasion. The Incas were deeply dedicated to the care of their dead, a custom which shocked and revolted their Spanish conquerors

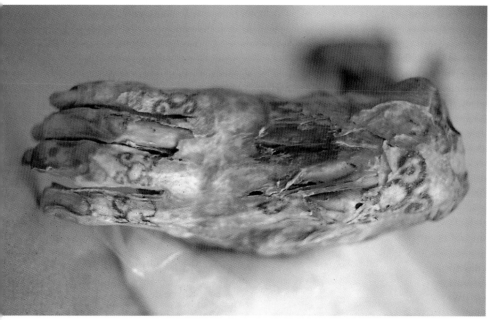

The Chiribaya sometimes tattooed their fingers, thumbs, backs of their hands, arms, legs and backs with motifs which were either animal or abstract designs *(Joann Fletcher)*

An Inca girl sacrificed high in the mountains was preserved for five centuries by freeze-drying. These children apparently gave up their lives voluntarily on important ritual occasions, firmly believing that dying this way would grant them instant immortality *(Stephen Alvarez / National Geographic)*

Chachapoya mummy bundles from the Peruvian Andes were completely enclosed. Many have a stylised face embroidered to the surface of the bundle where the real face was encased *(Adriana von Hagen)*

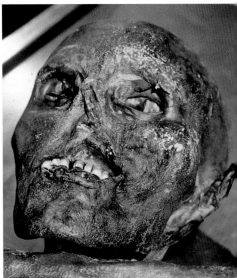

Many people consider the Ice Man of the Alps to be the single most important archaeological find of the century. Intense examination of his body and the artefacts found with him have revolutionized scientific understanding of European culture 5000 years ago *(Sygma)*

a way that they evidently considered more aesthetically pleasing than the natural shape. The Quiani usually wrapped the heads of their dead in well woven cotton turbans. Second, in some Chinchorro and Quiani graves the head has been removed. Archaeologists have found both bodiless heads and headless bodies in separate graves. This appears not to have been as a result of later disturbance of the grave, but a deliberate action taken at the time of burial. As both these practices play important roles in the cultures of the later mummy-makers of the Americas, it is worth noting that they both seem to originate in these coastal oases.

After the demise of the Chinchorro there is no evidence of the emergence of new societies who intentionally mummified their dead until around 800 BC, 1,000 years later. As I mentioned at the beginning of Chapter One, this apparent gap in the record may be illusory – we may not yet have found the remains of the cultures who continued the traditions, or the mummies from this period may not have withstood the test of time. But when mummy-making cultures did reappear, they did so in spectacular fashion.

The Paracas peninsula is about three hours' drive south of Lima. At first sight it is the very soul of desolation: not a plant to be seen anywhere and a fierce wind lashing at the sands and rock for most of the year. The sands on the peninsula are very varied in colour – pinks, greys, browns and many shades of yellow. One particular hill, known locally as Cerro Colorado, the 'Painted Hill', contains many of these colours. In the 1920s, the Peruvian archaeologist Julio Tello noticed regular indentations in the side of the hill and began to excavate. He soon uncovered a series of boot-shaped tombs, each containing thirty to sixty mummified humans. There were 429 of them in all; around 200 had been interfered with some time in the past. The rest were untouched. It turned out that nearly all of them were elderly men, and their skulls had been deformed by binding during infancy. They had been placed upright in the fully flexed position, their knees pulled up to their chins so that they were squatting in the way that most contemporary native South Americans sit to relax, chat, and eat or chew coca. The bodies had been placed carefully on thick cotton pads then wrapped in copious layers of textiles. One mummy had so many textiles draped round him that his entire mummy bundle weighed 150 kilos.

Controversy still rages as to whether the Paracas bodies were artificially mummified before being wrapped up. Tello was convinced that they had been very elaborately prepared, and gives precise details of how the bodies had first been eviscerated and much of the flesh removed. The head was then removed and the brain extracted through the opening at the base of the skull. An incision across the sternum permitted the removal of heart and lungs, then the body was smoke-dried by a fire and possibly, according to Tello, also treated with chemical preservatives.

Subsequent examinations of a few of the unwrapped Paracas mummies do not confirm any of these findings. As early as 1932, two archaeologists published a paper arguing that environmental conditions in the subsoil of the incredibly arid and salty peninsula were sufficient to preserve the bodies without recourse to elaborate human intervention. Re-examinations of some of the bodies in the 1940s and 1970s also failed to find any evidence to support Tello's descriptions. As other mummified remains have come to light throughout Peru over the last fifty years it looks increasingly likely that mummies can survive in well preserved states without artificial preparation in these conditions.

The key to the successful preservation of the Paracas mummies, and the successive generations of mummies which were produced elsewhere right up to the Spanish conquest, may actually be the result of two quite different factors: gravity and cotton. Sonia Guillen explained to me that by placing a body upright in the tightly flexed, squatting position you create a gravitational drainage system. Existing body fluids and those generated as a corpse decomposes will run down inside the body cavity and out via the anus or vagina. Paracas mummifiers were clearly aware of this – hence the thick cotton pad placed under the mummies. Scientific examinations of these pads have confirmed that this is precisely what happens. If you then choose to wrap the body in many layers of cotton – as the Paracas mummifiers did – then you create an extremely dry microclimate surrounding the body. The cotton layers will both absorb moisture emanating from the body and prevent any moisture which might exist in the exterior atmosphere from reaching it. Sonia also made the point that this technique is not always successful. In many cases the enzymes and micro-organisms in the body at death have destroyed the internal organs and 'eaten away' the lower part of the body or caused it to become carbonized. It may have been this natural carbonization process which Tello mistook for heat-drying of the bodies.

It was not so much the bodies in the Paracas necropolis which amazed first Tello then the world; it was the wrappings. Although the layer in contact with the corpse was usually made of plain cotton, many of the outer layers were fine woven textiles with dazzling colours and designs. They have subsequently proved to be some of the finest textiles ever found anywhere in the world. Some of these textiles were clothes – ponchos, tunics and turbans like the ones found on the bodies of the Quiani in Chile which are a thousand years older. There were also huge cloaks or mantles, many of them covered in the most intricate and perfectly worked designs. These were woven in several colours in block patterns, with the edges and blocks embroidered with the figures of people, animals and supernatural beings.

The sources and inspirations of this sudden explosion in artistic activity are said to originate in other parts of Peru, on the north coast and in the highlands, but nowhere else did the people put such huge energy into producing funerary goods of such superb quality and profuse quantity as in Paracas. Mummy bundle number 310, for example, contained fifty-six garments. It was covered with twenty-five wrapping cloths and contained five ponchos, two tunics, thirteen turbans and eighteen mantles. There were also ten pieces of gold strewn amongst the layers. Others had shell and gold necklaces and elaborately worked gold plates placed on their faces. Besides the mummified bodies there were also mummified animals – parrots, cavies, foxes, cats and even deer.

The textiles were so beautiful, so elaborate and so perfectly preserved that they soon attracted international attention. Textile specialists first noted that many of the clothes in the mummy bundles were new, unworn, and made so that they would fit the mummy bundle but not the corpse at its centre. So this was not a case of burying the deceased's normal clothes with him; the clothes had been specially prepared for the burial. Further expert scrutiny revealed that the clothes were probably made in workshops. A specialist designer marked the patterns and figures on to the cloth then other workers filled in the outlines with embroidery in many different colours and stitches. It seems likely that several embroiderers worked on any one mantle, which probably took months to produce. Recalling that mummy 310 was adorned with 18 mantles, along with 38 other items of clothing with a total weight of 150 kilos, then the scale of the operation becomes clear.

By 400 BC the people of Paracas had developed an entire industry dedicated to preparing for the afterlife on a scale comparable to ancient Egypt. Thousands of human work-hours and huge quantities of raw materials were being consumed solely for the benefit of the dead.

Walking around the site with Tara, it was hard to believe that any sort of 'industry' could have existed in this place more than 2,000 years ago. All that remains are a few rough holes and some dilapidated concrete shuttering which must have been put up as a wind-break when the excavations were under way in the 1920s. Not far from the necropolis, Tello had excavated some other holes dug in the sand and found them to be subterranean houses. To escape the wind and heat on the surface, the people had hollowed out homes in the hard-packed sand. But from all that Tello could find the community was very small, no more than a few hundred people at most. Perhaps they lived there primarily as guardians of the sacred ancestors interred nearby.

Near to the necropolis, the Peruvian department of antiquities has put up a little museum, simple but clearly laid out. It has been Peruvian policy for many years to keep at least some of their incredibly rich archaeological heritage on display where it was found, rather than concentrating everything in Lima. A policy to be lauded as it is so much more evocative to first meet these ancestral relics in the world where they once lived, rather than behind a glass screen in the middle of a seething Third World capital city. Stepping from the glare of the desert outside into the cool gloom of the museum gave just a hint of how it must have felt to the people of Paracas entering their homes or visiting their ancestral tombs 2,000 years ago.

Life and death on the Pacific coast had clearly moved on a long way from the times of the quiet little villages of the Chinchorro. The people of Paracas were farmers, hunters, fishermen, gatherers of shellfish, metalworkers and potters. Their weavers were among the most accomplished ever to have lived and were highly skilled at spinning and dyeing, and embroidered with astonishing precision and imagination. That most of the richly adorned mummies found in their burial chambers were adult males suggests that a hierarchical society had arisen dominated by senior men – chiefs, lineage heads or priests. As many of the mummies were of older men it seems that either life-expectancy was good or only those who survived to maturity had amassed the large quantities of goods necessary for their elaborate preparations for the afterlife. They were clearly producing considerable surpluses of food, enough to support a large workforce which spent much of its time preparing funerary goods. As many of the fine textiles were made from the wool of camelids (alpaca, vicuna, and so on) they clearly had extensive trade relations with the peoples of the sierras inland. This point is endorsed in the motifs embroidered on their clothes, which depict animals from the sierras and possibly from Amazonia, as well as the local fauna. There is also ample evidence from inland sites that coastal products were in constant use far inland, so by this time we can assume that permanent trade networks were well established between the coast and the mountains.

The men carried on the tradition of the Quiani in binding the skulls of babies and children to distort the shape of the head, sometimes so severely that it took on an almost cone-like form. They decorated their elongated skulls with wrap-around turbans, another tradition they probably inherited from coastal forebears such as the Quiani. A new development was the use of trepanning. This extraordinarily widespread practice is an early form of surgery. It entails cutting away a piece of the skull with a stone knife. This was sometimes done with a simple sawing motion, sometimes by drilling a series of little holes then removing the piece of skull bone at the centre. It is usually assumed that this surgery was undertaken to relieve pain or fluid pressure on the brain caused by illness or injury. This was certainly the reason for its use in classical and medieval times in Europe. I would just add in passing that it does seem to occur frequently in cultures who also chose to deform their crania, as the Paracas people did, so the two practices may be related. Most Paracas skulls which have been trepanned show clear signs of bone growth around the hole created by the operation, indicating that the patients had both survived and stayed alive for quite a while afterwards.

Most people consider trepanning to be a purely medical procedure. This is certainly true when the operation is associated with traumatic head injuries. Even today, if someone suffers severe head injuries leading to inflammation and fluid pressure on the brain, surgeons will drill a hole through the skull to relieve the pressure. However, there is also a well-established tradition, in Europe at least, of trepanning in the pursuit of pleasure. Even today a few people have been filmed using a large hand-drill to remove pieces of their crania. They report powerful sensations of euphoria, even ecstasy after the operation. In cultures where altered states of consciousness played a major role in religious life, it is possible that trepanning may have been performed with similar goals in mind. At any rate the extremely high number of trepanations among the Paracas mummy skulls, which had no signs of head injuries, suggests that they either suffered a hell of a lot from headaches or they had something else in mind altogether!

What might they have intended? We know that as long ago as the later days of the Chinchorro culture, the people had started to use hallucinogenic snuffs. They inhaled them through wooden tubes from little wooden dishes which have been found in their graves. The San Pedro cactus, which contains mescaline, is indigenous to this region and several hallucinogenic plants grow wild in the tropical forests of western Amazonia. In the scant literature published on Paracas, I have not been able to trace evidence for the use of hallucinogens but to me their artwork is suffused with the influences of mind-altering experience.

Their abstract designs are all highly patterned, mostly in very complex forms. Anyone who has taken visual hallucinogens will know that a primary and continual effect of these drugs is to generate patterns which we do not perceive in 'normal' consciousness. Stare at a blank white wall and within seconds patterns will emerge. They may move, change shape, colour, form or 'feel', but they will not go away. Looking at other people or scenes, the patterns may recede to the peripheries of the visual field, rather like the abstract designs round the edges of the Paracas textiles.

IN SEARCH OF THE IMMORTALS

Whatever is the focus, the centre of attention will be altered too. Extreme intensification and alterations of colour are common. Distortions and exaggerations of scale, shape and form also occur easily. Small objects may seem massive, minor details may seem to dominate an entire object. People, animals, plants, spirit-beings may seem to be attached to each other, intertwined, one form transforming itself into another.

I looked closely at one piece of Paracas textile (see photograph in second colour section). At a glance, it looks like two strips of orange cloth with a series of identical designs of monkeys embroidered on them. One set of monkeys is the right way up, the other upside down. They are reproduced in three colours – yellow, green and black, then another set of yellow, green and black. Looking closer, I realized that there is a baby monkey perched on the head of each adult animal. Its thick bushy tail curves round and appears to be clinging to its parent's throat, or perhaps to a little beard on the adult monkey's chin. At first, they seem to be the same but they are not. The yellow adult monkey has black eyes and a green mouth. Its baby has green eyes and a black mouth. The green adult has yellow eyes and a black mouth, its baby has black eyes and a yellow mouth. The black adult has green eyes and a bright yellow mouth, the baby has a green mouth and glowing yellow eyes. All the adults have three toes, the babies have two. While the babies' unrealistically thick tails are attached to the parents, the adult tails all end in a very clearly designed hand with five fingers. These clearly symbolize prehensile tails, the fifth 'hand' which some rainforest monkeys use as they move around in the forest canopy.

There are relatively few New World monkeys, and I am familiar with most of them. Squirrel monkeys look most like the yellow monkey design, with their dark eyes and mouth and long bushy tails. But the squirrel monkey does not have a prehensile tail. Woolly spider-monkeys are the only monkeys with prehensile tails which look vaguely similar to the design animal, but they live in the tropical rainforest which runs down the Atlantic coast of Brazil, on the other side of the continent from Paracas. So this design is not an attempt to represent any particular species of monkey, it is an idealization, a representation of 'monkeyness' rather than any particular individual or species. It is, in essence, a symbolic image, not a real one. By repeating the image in different colours and varying the colour content between adult and young, the design tells us of the great variety of monkeys and how they change over time, even perhaps how they cluster together in troupes as they range through the forest. This is a design deliberately loaded with symbolic meaning.

There is another very interesting aspect to the design. As far as I can tell, New World monkeys never occupied the river valleys which cut across the Atacama between the Andes and the Pacific, where the people of Paracas lived. The closest real monkeys lived in the Montana forests of the eastern slopes of the Andes. So it may be that the Paracas designers were copying designs which had come down from the mountains to them, or they may have been working from tame animals which had been passed along the trade network which we know linked the rainforest to the coast in those times. But whatever the source of inspiration, the designer has chosen to depict an animal which he or she may never have seen, but which held some special importance or power which might benefit its 'owner' in the afterlife.

So what at first seems to be a regular simple design is in fact full of fluid transformations. And this is just one tiny design in the thousands of metres of stunning handiwork that the Paracas people adorned their deceased with.

Many other animals are depicted in the designs, along with people, anthropomorphic creatures and purely imaginary beings, spirits or deities. One particularly prominent and striking being is known as the 'Big-eyed One', a cat–human creature with enormous eyes, the see-all of the spirit world. As there are no records of the belief systems associated with these symbolic designs, we can only guess at their specific meanings. But, in my view, the people of the Paracas peninsula, themselves already directly linked to many other parts of Peru, were creating in textiles a set of values and beliefs which remained fundamentally the same right through until the coming of the Spanish and beyond. Although the specific symbols and ideas varied from culture to culture and across time, the underlying perception of the forces which control people and their destiny remained the same.

Attributing special supernatural powers to specific animals, birds, snakes, insects and plants is a basic characteristic of the belief systems of virtually all of the surviving native peoples of South America. They believe that human life is so intimately bound up with the natural world that, for example, all Maku personal names are also names of living creatures or plants. My adopted Maku father-in-law was called 'alligator'; his brother was 'grass'; his sons were 'palm bush', 'fish head' and 'hawk'; his wife was 'tinamou', and so on.

My Maku friends never said explicitly that people were once animals, but their myths revolve around the idea that people take on animal-like qualities and vice versa. The most important story is an Aesop-like tale where the two culture heroes, twin brothers, have to tackle and defeat owl-people then toucan-people, then jaguar-people, porcupine-people, eagle-people and a host more. To succeed, the heroes in turn have to transform themselves into a variety of different animals, birds and insects. All the animal characters can talk to each other and much play is made of onomatopoeia, where the actual calls and songs of animals, birds, even frogs, are given vocal meaning. In one part of the story the new-born twin heroes are given to frog-women to hide them from their old jaguar grandfather who wants to eat them. The frog-women are called '*Bak-ai*', which literally means 'poison women'. '*Bak-ai*' is also a transliteration of the sound they make at night, '*bak-ai, bak-ai, bak-ai*'. They are, in reality, poisonous frogs whose skins can be used to make arrow poison. In the story, they take the twins down to the stream and wash them, pouring the bitter juices of the gourd plant over them. This transforms them into the 'bitter children', unpalatable to their cannibal jaguar grandfather. The sound of the water being lapped up in the gourd then poured over the children is '*bak-ai, bak-ai, bak-ai . . .*'

After I had learnt this story, whenever I lay in my hammock deep in the rainforest and heard the '*bak-ai*' frogs begin their night chant, I knew I was listening to the sound of their magical protection, the anointment of the twins who would one day create us people. In this way, mythology lives in the here-and-now, not just in some remote imagined past. Its symbolism is both entirely mystical and concrete and tangible at the same time. This type of thinking is not confined to mythology. As I got a reasonable grasp of their language, I began to understand that dreams played an important role in the way we were living. The Maku describe their dreams not as narratives but as single images. So in the morning, people would wake and sometimes say, 'Ah I had a dream of caterpillars last night' or 'I had a dream of tobacco' or the like. People took these dream-images seriously, even if the dreamer was just a child. It turned out that all these dream-images had a meaning in waking reality. To dream of tobacco meant that we would kill peccary; to dream of carrying roofing leaves meant that we would kill a tapir; to dream of caterpillars meant that we should harvest a specific type of wild forest fruit; to dream of teeth falling out meant that somebody would die soon, and so on. These associations were not random – my friends explained that the peccary's nose is the same shape as a tobacco leaf; bundles of roofing leaves are very heavy, as is the meat of a tapir; and leaf bundles are sometimes pointed like the tapir's snout. Caterpillars live on the trunks of the fruit-bearing trees and so on.

IN SEARCH OF THE IMMORTALS

~~~
~~~

People often acted on information received in dreams. If a hunter dreamt of roof leaves he would go out and check for signs of tapirs over the next few days. He might not find one – they are very shy and not very numerous in Maku territory – but he would certainly check all their known haunts, follow tracks and the like. The most startling case of dream 'prophesy' that I came across involved my good friend Chai. We had gone on a hunting trip deep in the forest for three days. On the third morning, Chai almost fell out of his hammock muttering, 'tobacco, tobacco'. The tobacco dream refers specifically to the white-lipped peccary, the larger of the two Amazonian species of wild pig which roam the forest in herds of 100 animals or more. These herds are hard to find and we had not seen any signs of them in our hunting grounds for more than a year. When they are located the people make a communal hunt and usually kill several large animals, creating a glut of meat.

After Chai's dream-signal we hunted our way cautiously back to his house. On the way, we caught a glimpse of a family of the other species of peccary, the collared peccary. I loosed off a shot at one of them, but didn't kill it. We reached Chai's place about two hours before dark, to find it deserted except for his ancient mother-in-law. Having greeted us, she brought cassava bread and a pot of boiled water with salt and pimienta, the traditional greeting. Once we had broken bread, Chai asked the old lady where everyone was. 'Oh, they've all taken off to hunt a big herd of white-lipped peccary. They found them early this morning,' she told us. We had had no contact with anyone from Chai's village for three days before this all happened, but Chai's dream prediction had come true.

I never asked Chai how he thought he could make these intuitive connections between the human and natural world because I don't think he would have been able to explain it. He could just do it. I have discussed some of these experiences with other native Americans and they have cautioned that to seek to 'explain' these types of events is both irrelevant and potentially damaging. They believe that if we try to discover how and why these mystical links can be made, we risk destroying their efficacy. Seeking to explain them is not the point. The point is to accept and act upon the mystical links between the human, natural and supernatural worlds.

Returning to Paracas, I think the imagery depicted in the wonderful funerary textiles, along with the presence of many mummified real animals, demonstrates that the people of Paracas shared the broad view that the human, natural and supernatural worlds are all deeply interconnected and that these connections stretch beyond the bounds of life and death. In death, the human soul will be enhanced by the company of spirit-animal companions, helpers and protectors. It is both set free and absorbed into the greater, timeless forces which cocoon the fragile, myopic waking world of everyday consciousness.

In these respects, the people of Paracas gave expression in their funerary art to a set of beliefs which are broadly adhered to by most native Americans today. These, as I have mentioned before, revolve around the central idea that ordinary human waking experience is only one aspect of a broader cosmic consciousness which stretches beyond the bounds of wakefulness into sleep, beyond life into death and beyond linear time to timeless immortality. Preserving the remains of the dead is, in a sense, an affirmation of these notions, proof that even the physical being can persist into eternity. These basic ideas were extremely widespread thousands of years ago, in the Old as well as the New World. In my view they provide the ideological framework which explains why the people of Paracas should choose to preserve the dead and send them into the afterlife in the company of specific symbolic helpers and guardians. But the people of Paracas also made mummies of a very different sort.

We have already noted how some Chinchorro and Quiani graves contained only heads, others only headless bodies. Some of the Paracas mummies were accompanied by specially prepared heads which are now known as 'trophy heads'. The brains have been removed from the skulls and the face carefully preserved by making small incisions to remove subcutaneous soft tissue. The resultant holes have then been refilled with cotton wool padding to retain the shape of the face. The scalp and hair were left in place as there is little soft tissue under the scalp. The remaining head was then carefully dried, probably using hot sand. The makers then pierced a hole through the frontal bone of the skull and passed a cord through it. The cord was, in effect, a handle that allowed the 'owner' of the head to carry it round with him. There are several depictions of this on Paracas funerary mantles – a man in a turban holds a large stone knife in one hand and a trophy head in the other.

It has long been held that these heads were the spoils of war – the heads of warriors killed then preserved by the victor. Endorsement for this idea came in the form of the famous shrunken heads made in recent times by the Jivaro or Shua, natives of the Peruvian tropical rainforest. Until a few decades ago, the Jivaro periodically raided each other and killed anyone they could find. They returned home with the heads of their victims, removed the skulls, then smoke-dried them until they had shrunk to about the size of a tennis ball. Doing this gave the spirit-power of the victim to the victor. (The Jivaro were also, incidentally, deeply involved with shamanism, using extremely powerful hallucinogens derived from the *Datura* plant. One of the greatest non-native-American shamans alive today, Michael Harner, received his initial training and initiation with Jivaro masters.)

Because head-hunters were still active in Peru when the first archaeological 'trophy heads' were discovered, people quickly jumped to the conclusion that these, too, must be bizarre trophies of war. But closer scrutiny called this assumption into question. Trophy heads date back to about 1000 BC and are relatively common in Paracas. The related cultures, which continued the Paracas traditions in the Ica and Nazca valleys, also made trophy heads. Yet none of these societies appears to have been very belligerent. There are few weapons found in their graves, few artistic depictions of combat or battles and few detected injuries on skeletons, mummies or even the trophy heads themselves. Many of the heads are of women and children, not warriors. Although the Jivaro would take and shrink the heads of women and children in their raids, warfare in pre-Hispanic South America was generally highly ritualized. There is little evidence of indiscriminate massacres involving all ages and both sexes.

This leaves three possible explanations as to who lost their heads in those days. First, the victims may have been executed criminals. Second, they may have been sacrificial victims. Third, they may simply be the heads of people who had died naturally. There is little supporting evidence for the idea of capital punishment from these times, so that explanation seems unlikely. There is, however, a lot of evidence of human sacrifice in the cultures which followed the people of Paracas, right through to the arrival of the Spanish 1,500 years later. In some cases, the victims were war captives or slaves; in others, they were close relatives of a deceased person, or children chosen for their beauty and purity. In general, death by sacrifice was seen as an honour which conferred supernatural power on both the victim and the sacrificer. The Paracas images of men holding trophy heads certainly convey the idea that the holder's power and prestige is being enhanced by the head he holds. The knife he holds in the other hand also implies that he has used it to acquire the head. So the idea of trophy heads being sacrificial victims is certainly possible.

The final explanation, that these heads are the preserved remains of revered relatives, also seems possible. The Quiani and the Chinchorro evidently separated the heads from the bodies of some of their dead, so there is ancient precedent for this practice. The latter groups were not at all warlike and – as with the Paracas heads – there are no signs of injuries or wounds on the preserved heads of the Chinchorro and Quiani. There is also no evidence that they practised human sacrifice, so the heads they kept were probably those of relatives or members of the kin group.

Exactly who was singled out to have their heads specially preserved and displayed we do not know, either among the people of Paracas or their predecessors, but there are good reasons for preserving a head on its own. In purely practical terms, the head is easier to mummify than other parts of the body (except for feet and hands), especially if the brain is removed. It contains little soft tissue, and what tissue there is can be removed relatively easily. More importantly, the head is the locus of consciousness, awareness, communication and identity. Our bodies portray our age, sex, fitness and so on, but it is primarily our faces and hair which single us out as unique. The people of Paracas took great care to preserve the facial features of their 'trophy' heads, making small incisions to remove soft tissue and inserting padding to fill out the eye sockets, cheeks, etc. They wanted the preserved heads to be as life-like as possible.

In my view, this contrasts rather sharply with the shrunken trophy heads the Jivaro produced. Their shrunken heads are deliberate deformations, symbols of one human's destruction of another. The shrinking of the head symbolizes physical and spiritual conquest. But the people of Paracas, and their successors in Nazca and Ica, were keen to retain the living identity of their heads. This implies that the retention of the head, probably after the body had been buried, was an act of reverence rather than a symbol of aggressive power.

We will probably never know the exact relationship which existed between the 'trophy' head and its owner, but ultimately this may not matter. The head may have been of a vanquished enemy or a revered forebear. Either way, by retaining its identity it enhanced the identity of its living 'owner'. It seems to me that if I was a member of Paracas society and saw someone carrying a trophy head, then I would know straight away that he was a special person, maybe a famous warrior or the descendant of a renowned chief or shaman. I might also be able to recognize the face of the trophy and thus know, without asking, exactly who I was looking at. The trophy head acted as legitimation, concrete proof of the enhanced status of the trophy's owner. Some aspects of the identity of the dead person have been transferred to the living owner.

A final clue comes from the depictions of the trophy heads: they are being carried around by a living person. Paracas mummy bundles were far too heavy to transport, but individual heads were light and easily portable. The heads furnished the bearer with enhanced status – and proof of identity. The trophy, dangling on its string, was almost a human ID card – because being in possession of the head meant that others could identify the person holding it as somebody who was in a 'known relationship with the dead head', whether that relationship was that of 'son', 'grandson' or 'killer'. This notion of using the remains of the dead as a means of identifying the living may have originated with the Chinchorro, whose mummies played such an important role in defining their society. The Paracas people refined and individualized this notion, just as their own society had become more individualized with the advent of farming, craft specialization and social stratification. And what, after all, could better endorse an individual's identity than the head of a fellow human being?

About an hour's drive to the east of Paracas is the ancient town of Ica situated on the river of the same name. It is some way inland, where the river valley is quite wide and where the land has been extensively farmed for at least the last 1,500 years. Another two hours' drive down the Pan-American Highway takes you to Nazca and the world-famous Nazca Lines. In the age when people walked, I guess it would have taken two days or so to walk from Paracas to Ica, maybe another four days to Nazca if you kept up a good pace. There is a lot of dry desert between these river valleys, but the distances are not so great as to prohibit communication between them.

Tara and I reached Ica in the evening and went straight to the regional archaeological museum – a small, well-kept building on the edge of town. We could immediately see the continuity in tradition from Paracas: mummies in the fully-flexed position with hugely elongated crania, forced to grow almost vertically upwards so that the skulls were ten, maybe even fifteen centimetres taller than normal. One display showed the set of boards used to bind the child's head. It reminded me of a North American papoose with extra wood and woollen bindings to hold the baby's head in place.

Some of the textile designs were simpler, more geometric than Paracas work; others displayed the same elaborate patterns and bizarre anthropomorphic spirit-beings we had seen there. Pottery, however, was much more complex and elaborate than the relatively simple pieces found in Paracas. Hairstyles, too, had taken on a life of their own. Many of the mummies had incredibly long hair, elaborately braided and bound. I assumed that animal hair had been mixed in with the wearer's real hair as some mummies' headpieces were longer than I have ever seen natural hair grow. One particular exhibit was only the skull and scalp of a male, but the hairpiece must have been nearly two metres long.

Fascinating though the individual pieces were, it was clear that most of the displays were remnants recovered from cemeteries after looters had ransacked them. Despite this, there was still little doubt in my mind that the cultures of Nazca and Ica, dating from around 400 AD to 1000 AD, were in essence a continuity of the Paracas tradition, periodically modified by new ideas, technologies and art forms from other parts of South America.

VALLEYS OF THE DEAD

〰️

From Ica, our next destination was the cemetery at Chauchilla, about twenty kilometres the other side of Nazca. The road took us right past the little airport at Nazca where you can hire a light plane to overfly the famous Nazca Lines. The Lines have been the focus of much controversy ever since Von Däniken published *Chariots of the Gods*. In this book, he claimed that the Lines are some sort of cosmic UFO-port. Others have claimed that they are astronomical observations and more recently that they are aligned with the principal mountains in the region. This last theory postulates that as mountains were also water sources, at times of increasing aridity the people made the Lines as a ritual appeal to the mountains to release more water, a sort of rain-dance. In the face of all these conflicting views, my own interest was first to take a look at them, then to try to see what they could tell us about the people who made them.

We clambered into the waiting Cessna, and the enthusiastic pilot explained that, as we were such important visitors who wished to film the Lines, he would take us on a special extended flight so we could see everything perfectly. Roughly translated this meant 'I would like a large tip, which will be most of what I earn from this flight.'

The little plane hopped effortlessly into the air and skimmed out over green irrigated fields which abruptly ended in flat stony desert. Water courses, made by flood run-off on the very rare occasions that it rains there, have carved a maze of vine-like patterns on the surface. It must have been these flood channels which gave the people the original inspiration to make the lines. The running water had washed away the surface grey-brown crust, revealing the lighter sands underneath.

A few minutes later, the wavy flood-channels were suddenly overlaid with dead straight lines, criss-crossing each other and apparently pointing in all directions. Some of them were very long, maybe as much as a kilometre. Sometimes two lines ran parallel; sometimes they gradually converged. I could pick out triangles and funnels and a set of lines which seemed to form a huge arrow, its triangular tip offset at a slight angle to the 'shaft'. The scale of the monument is impressive. The whole site covers thirty square kilometres or more. But it is also essentially chaotic. There is no overall design concept; it looks much more like a whole series of separate inspirations which led successive groups or individuals, probably over hundreds of years, to mark out their own lines and designs in the sand. In many places the designs overlap each other or are cross-cut by unrelated lines.

As well as the maze of lines there are also more than forty designs of animals, birds, fish and a single human figure. Our pilot, somewhat inevitably, called him 'El Astronaut'. He is actually a rather crude representation of an ordinary mortal with no arms. He is etched on to the side of a low red sandstone hill so that he appears to be standing, surveying the scene. The animal figures are magnificent, executed with tremendous confidence and precision, most of them very well proportioned. There is a monkey in profile with a wonderful spiralled tail and, curiously, either five legs or four legs and an extremely long, backward pointing penis; a brilliant long-legged fox or dog, a pair of llamas facing each other, a perfect top view of a spider and a magnificent fish, its body curved and fins spread. Then there are the birds – two superb humming-birds hurtling, like darts, through the air, a pelican in flight, its neck drawn up and huge beak pointing forwards, a bird with a very long neck and bill like a crane or egret, a parrot in full flight and a bird with a huge wingspan, probably an eagle or a condor. There are also more abstract designs – single and double interlocked spirals, flower-like patterns and a radiant sun-like symbol with one long ray protruding like a stick from it.

The natural figures are not very big – maybe twenty to fifty metres across – nor do they seem to be arranged in patterns or particular alignments. One thing is obvious though – they were all designed to be seen from the air, not from the ground. There are no mounds or hills nearby where a person could get an overview of the site. The local authorities have built a rather rickety observation tower at one of the highest points on the edge of the site, but you can only see the two nearest figures clearly from its platform. So, in a sense, these works of art are acts of faith. They have been created in such a way that no ordinary mortal would be able to see them. Yet to jump from this self-evident fact to the idea that they were created to attract passing spacemen requires an act of faith I am not prepared to make! It also overlooks some other very basic explanations derived from the belief systems of the people who made the Lines.

Almost all native South American cultures maintain that the cosmos is a multi-layered structure with our layer or 'land' somewhere in the middle. As previously mentioned, my Maku friends maintain that above the visible level of our land – above the sky, sun, moon and stars – there is a belt of rocks. Above the rocks is the land of the ancestors, above this the lands of the mythical heroes, and above these, at the top of the cosmos, is the land of the creator, Bone Son. In special circumstances these spirit-beings can move between these levels, travelling up or down invisible 'strings' like the lianas which dangle down from the top canopy to the floor of the rainforest. They also believe that in special circumstances some people can do the same thing. In shamanic training throughout the Americas, initiates are taught to 'fly' high above the ground and look down on our world below. Carlos Castaneda's epic flights under the tutelage of the Yaqui shaman, Don Juan, are just one well-known description of a very widely practised principle. In essence, the initiate is being taught perspective, how to look at things from a different point of view. Looking down from above is the way that the ancestors and the spirit-beings in the sky must look down on us.

We have already seen that this point of view also occurs in the Near Death Experience, at the moment just after the victim loses consciousness.

IN SEARCH OF THE IMMORTALS

When I was researching the Out of Body phase of the Near Death Experience a few years ago, I soon found that this was not confined to people on the verge of death. People with high fevers often feel themselves slip out of their bodies and the experience can certainly be drug-induced. Just a few hours after a major operation, my father told me in great detail that when he had first regained consciousness he had found himself at ceiling height, looking down at the nurses bustling round his body in the bed below. Similar experiences are reported by many anthropologists who have been introduced to hallucinogens by native South Americans. In the shamanic initiation rituals I filmed in the Peruvian rainforest, the express 'target' of the apprentice undergoing the rites was to experience the flight of the condor and look down on the world. So there is no need to conjure up alien space visitations to explain why the people of Nazca should want to create images best viewed from above.

The presence of so many bird images is also no surprise. Birds are seen as messengers of the gods, able to mediate between heaven and earth in most cultures. In South America large high-flying birds, such as vultures, eagles, condors and kites, are almost universally credited with super-natural powers; and the spider, dog and monkey are also said to possess supernatural powers by many native South American groups. There are other animals, though, such as the jaguar, which are more generally acknowledged as spiritually powerful, but these are not depicted in the Nazca Lines.

One feature which caught my attention in this geoglyphic menagerie, was that the animals came from all the ecosystems the people of Nazca had knowledge of – monkeys and parrots from the rainforest, fish and pelicans from the coast, and llamas and condors from the sierra. As we had seen on the ceramics and textiles it was quite clear that by the time these lines were laid down, the people who made them included in their 'pantheon of animals' many species which were not a part of their local ecosystems. It seems that in many cases exotic animals were being credited with exotic powers in the world of supernature, beyond the bounds of life and death.

Once the plane had bounced down to earth and the pilot had received his 'bonus', Tara and I drove on to Chauchilla, reaching the cemetery around two o'clock on a hot, blustery afternoon. At first, we didn't know we were there. There was nothing but an old tin board marking the site and a few dozen stones marking paths across the sand. No guardians, no perimeter fences, no explanatory notices – nothing. Following the stone trail, we came to a rectangular pit about two metres deep and lined with mud bricks. Propped against the brick walls sat two human mummies, empty eye sockets staring up at us. They had no skin on their faces and their bones looked bleached by the sun. Both had copious hair flowing from their skulls and spreading out over their plain cotton tunics. Wisps of hair and folds of loose clothing flapped in the hot wind. It was one of the eeriest sights I had ever seen.

After staring for some minutes at these mute 1,000-year-old faces, we moved on to the next pit to find more mummies looking up at us. These had scraps of skin still in place on their faces, one with his jaw dropped in a menacing scowl. In other pits the mummies were still wrapped in their bundles, although their faces and hair were exposed. There must have been forty pits, all open-topped, all occupied by men, women and children. Imagine going to any graveyard in the world to find all the graves open, all the corpses staring up at you. That's how it was at Chauchilla.

As we looked around further, we realized that there were fragments of clothes, pots and bodies scattered all over the surface of the cemetery. Here lay a shin bone with a well-preserved foot attached, skin and even toe-nails still in place; there a pile of skulls. I picked one up, leaving the lower jaw in the sand. The cranium had been deformed, pulled out into the long conical shape the people seem to have held as a mark of beauty. It had a neat hole cut in one side. The edges were thick and smooth, not jagged – a successful trepanation, the bone regrowing round the opening. Another had two large trepanation holes, also with clear signs of regrowth. I jumped down into one of the pits and looked very closely at its occupant, peering under its shroud wrappings. His hair was long and coarse, heavily braided, henna-coloured, probably as a result of his long exposure to the sun. Beside him lay a little painted bowl holding three brown maize cobs.

This was the first time I had been in a totally unsupervised mummy graveyard, with no one to tell me not to touch. Itching curiosity blended with a vague sense of unease. This was a sacred place and these strange ghoulish figures had once been laid to rest there with great care and dignity by their living descendants. I climbed carefully back out of the pit and looked around.

Miguel Pazos, Head of Regional Archaeology in Lima, had told us about this place. The whole cemetery had been comprehensively looted many years ago. The covers of all the graves had been ripped off, the mummy bundles torn open and anything of value stolen. When the authorities got to hear about it, there was little they could do except tidy the place up a bit and place the surviving bodies back in their graves as neatly as possible.

Miguel also told me to look carefully at the cemetery's setting. He has seen almost all of the known pre-Hispanic cemeteries in Peru and is convinced that the locations were chosen for their beauty and their proximity to hills or mountains. Chauchilla is no exception. Like the necropolis at Cerra Colorado on the Paracas peninsula, the Chauchilla cemetery is set at the base of spectacular coloured hills. Here, the shades are purple, grey and green, orange, yellow and reddish-brown.

VALLEYS OF THE DEAD

〰
〰

Before the looters wrecked the cemetery, it must have been a beautifully serene place to wait out eternity.

Our final destination was a little valley running back from the coast of southern Peru, just north of the port of Ilo. The Algarrobal Valley was home to the Chiribaya culture around 1000 AD. Sonia Guillen has been based there for many years, studying what may well prove to be the most extensive network of mummy cemeteries anywhere in the world.

The valley mouth hosted one of the northernmost Chinchorro settlements thousands of years before the awakening of Chiribaya culture. By the time this culture grew to prominence, the valley was densely settled for at least twenty kilometres inland. I arrived in the valley late at night, met there by Fran Cole, a charming British mummy-conservationist. We talked still further into the night about this extraordinary valley which almost nobody outside of Peru had ever heard of. Apparently there were mummies almost everywhere. Only a few days before I arrived, workmen had dug a narrow trench right alongside the museum and research centre where we were staying. They had unearthed 11 mummies in the 200 metres of trench they had dug. The research centre already housed more than 200 mummies, most in excellent states of preservation. It was hard just sitting there in the dark, waiting to see what the morning would bring.

It brought Gerardo Carpio, curator of the museum. A quiet local man, he knew the valley like the back of his hand and was keen to show me around. We piled into his pick-up and drove a kilometre or so upriver. He stopped in the boulder-strewn dry stream bed and pointed across the valley to a thin straight line cutting along the lower slopes of the hill opposite. It was the ancient aqueduct the Chiribaya had constructed to carry water to irrigate their fields. A little further on, he showed us the shallow terraces the people had made to regulate the water flow across their fields.

IN SEARCH OF THE IMMORTALS

Rounding another bend, a cliff face loomed up in front of us about ten metres high. A metre or so below the top, the cliff was pock-marked with little holes. I could just make out what looked like fragments of cloth in some of the holes. Gerardo explained that at the height of *El Niño* just six weeks earlier, a huge flood wave had rushed down the valley and washed away much of the cliff. We were looking at the cross-sections of mummy graves exposed by the 1998 *El Niño* rains after more than a millennium of tranquillity. Many of the mummies had fallen into the flood waters, others were found dangling by their shrouds on the cliff face. Seeing this made me realize yet again how easily just one natural disaster could wipe out priceless archaeological evidence which had survived for millennia. How often must this process have taken place all over the world – a single freak event destroying vital evidence about ancient cultures for ever. Add to that human avarice and the appalling conditions faced by most of the rural poor in countries like Peru, and it is a wonder that any mummy heritage has survived at all.

Sadly, there is also ample evidence of the latter form of archaeological holocaust in many parts of the Algarrobal Valley. Gerardo drove us back up the valley to a settlement site where we could still see the bases of walls constructed out of rush or cane matting – a small village, houses perched on terraces just above the cultivable land. In front of the houses was a great mound of debris – seashells and other rubbish scattered all around. A hundred metres above the houses, a cemetery had been totally ripped apart by looters. Long conical skulls, deformed like the peoples of Paracas, Ica and Nazca, lay strewn around on the surface. Brown fragments of clothes, knots of human hair, arms, legs, ribs, pelvic girdles, were scattered over the hillside. Gerardo explained that the sites had been looted decades, even centuries, ago, although he still looked sadly at the pitiful remains.

VALLEYS OF THE DEAD

Above the settlement, the valley curved to the right while the road went straight on up the valley side to the desert above. We stopped on the crest where we could see up and down the valley. It stretched away in both directions, a lush green stripe cutting across lifeless sandy wastelands. We crossed a field of boulders and came to what looked like a huge rubbish tip. The rubbish turned out to be human remains. Thousands of graves had been opened and their contents spilled out across the desert. It was like some ghoulish battlefield which had become frozen in time – the battle of the dead, won by the desecrators. We picked our way through the cemetery for twenty minutes or more and still did not reach the far side.

I asked Gerardo if this was the principal graveyard for the valley and he chuckled. He wasn't exactly sure how many cemeteries there are, but he estimated that the entire valley contains around 200 of them, many as big as this one. Most had been looted, but not all. He knew of several sites which were well enough disguised on the surface to be missed by looters. Despite the massive destruction, the Algarrobal Valley must rate as one of the most important sites for human mummies anywhere in the world.

We returned to the research centre and museum so I could look more closely at the Chiribayas and their culture. Here again was a people richly endowed by nature, with a fertile river valley to provide cultivated plants for food, clothing and housing, and the sea nearby yielding ample sources of protein. An environment rich enough to support a dense population who, like the Paracas people, had developed their own mortuary industry.

The mummies were wrapped in thick bundles with many superbly woven textiles among the plain cotton shrouds. The Chiribayas were particularly keen on frogs, humming birds and monkeys as icons. Their motifs appear in many designs and they also tattooed them on to their bodies. One man had a little frog tattooed at the base of each of his thumbs and scroll patterns across his fingers. Besides many clothes they also carried finely designed coca bags, all made new for the grave, to accompany the dead into the afterlife. Many men had lavish hairstyles and hats designed to complement their elongated skulls. A few mummy bundles contained little replicas of balsa-wood rafts, superbly modelled, with built-up sides which would have been used at sea. It is assumed that these individuals were fishermen in life, so they had been equipped with their 'means of production' for the afterlife. Others, perhaps chiefs, had finely worked gold masks covering their faces – hence the looters' interest in the graves. As in Paracas, food offerings, ceramics, household goods and tools had been placed in the graves beside the mummy bundles.

After we had looked at the dressed mummies and their bundles, Gerardo took me round to the storage area where several hundred mummies were housed. Some of the mummies had been completely unwrapped, giving me the chance to look closely at their bodies. Gerardo selected two from the catalogue and pulled down a couple of cardboard boxes from the shelves. The mummies were certainly well preserved, crouched in the foetal position, their skin wrinkled, muscles heavily reduced by desiccation. Somehow, though, squatting naked like strange shrivelled-up little dolls, they looked much less human than the dressed mummies I had seen. The two I saw were naturally mummified with no signs of incisions for the removal of soft tissue or insertion of padding. However, Gerardo assured me that they had found mummies in the valley who had been eviscerated, their organs removed through cuts in the side of the abdomen. So, even though the Paracas mummies may have been left to dry out naturally, by 1000 AD the Chiribaya had discovered that the bodies of their ancestors stood a better chance of perpetual survival if their internal organs were removed.

〰〰

VALLEYS OF THE DEAD

〰️

A pattern was beginning to emerge. From as early as 800 BC the peoples of the Peruvian coastal desert had discovered that the cotton they wrapped their dead in would protect their bodies in the afterlife. Placing their bodies upright in the flexed position also helped to ensure their survival. They sent their dead into the next world with good supplies of all the essentials of life, many adorned with the protective images of animals who would act as spirit guardians, perhaps even guides. The Nazca Lines and most surviving native South American oral tradition suggest that the 'land' of the ancestors and the spirit world was up above, in the sky or perhaps in the high mountains.

There was little sign of the need for a journey to reach this place, as there are in many other mummy-making cultures. Rather it seems that, in essence, the destination of the dead was essentially a different, expanded dimension of the world of the living. Perhaps one reason for this was because the world of the living already contained objects, concepts and ideas which lay beyond the reach of ordinary experience. On the one hand, hallucinogenic drugs had been broadening the consciousness of these people for hundreds of years; on the other, the network of human relations clearly stretched from the Pacific coast right across the highlands, onwards into Amazonia and back again.

Plants, animals, people, works of art, tools, weapons, drugs, medicines and much more had circulated throughout this region. With them had come new stories, ideas, ritual practices and observances. This sense of being part of a larger world order must have given the people of the coast an ability to accept the unknown, to come to terms with the fact that strange and incomprehensible forces lay beyond their own physical and social world. They also knew that periodically even the known world could dissolve into chaos, with earthquakes, landslides, floods and tidal waves engulfing all that was safe, familiar and orderly.

IN SEARCH OF THE IMMORTALS

They were also living in an environment where the natural preservation of the dead was an observable fact. It seems that even in the times of the Chinchorro, people had begun to look upon the bodies of the dead as symbols of the continuity of society, beyond the trauma of natural catastrophes, beyond the trauma of death itself. That they sought and found ways of enhancing the natural preservation of the dead should come as no great surprise. The peoples of Paracas, Ica, Nazca and the Chiribaya perfected their techniques over two millennia. Throughout that time, they were in constant contact with the peoples of the mountains where conditions were far less favourable for the preservation of the dead.

By the end of March I had finished my survey of the mummy-makers of the coast. The weather had cleared up and Peru's transport infra-structure was beginning to recover from the lashing meted out by *El Niño*. It was time to head for the mountains to investigate Sonia's spectacular new finds.

Chapter 9

Peruvian Andes
in the
sacred mountains

By the time we got back to Lima, our travel agent, Miryam, had good news. The weather had improved sufficiently for the resumption of flights to Chachapoyas and one was due to leave the next day. It was already full, but I was number one on the waiting-list and Miryam knew the charter operator personally. This meant that if the flight did go ahead – which was far from certain – I had a good chance of being on it.

Ever since I had heard about the discovery of the Chachapoya mummies six months earlier, I had developed a real yearning to see them with my own eyes. This was by far the largest and most significant find of preserved bodies in South America for at least twenty years. Furthermore, having been made by a group of people who had not been known as mummy-makers, an air of mystery surrounded them and their creators, the Chachapoya. This mystery was also fuelled by the beauty and extreme remoteness of the place where the mummies had been discovered. Recalling Miguel Pazos' advice about the importance of seeing the chosen site with one's own eyes, I was determined to get there. But there was also something deeper, luring me off on this madcap venture. I seemed to be responding to a 'call', an inner restlessness which I did not yet fully understand.

IN SEARCH OF THE IMMORTALS

Miryam decided it was time to let me know what I was letting myself in for. She explained that I would be met from the flight by a friend of hers who owns a hotel in Chachapoyas. He would fix up transport on the dirt road from Chachapoyas to Leymebamba, the little village where the mummies were now stored. The road had suffered a lot of damage from mud-slides and I would not know if it was passable until I was actually on it. If I made it to Leymebamba, then I should ask for Dona Adriana, Sonia's friend and co-curator of the mummies who would be waiting there for me.

Forewarned that I would have to go on horseback for about ten hours along a difficult trail to reach the site where the mummies were found, I went back to the hotel, switched my tropical clothes for warm mountain riding gear, and collected a sleeping-bag and tiny tent. At dawn the next day we made our way to the airport where I said farewell to Tara, who was flying on to Chile for her best friend's wedding. My flight was posted, and the usual scrum of anxious people were desperately trying to secure places on the plane. Miryam bided her time, then slipped to the front of the mêlée and had a few quiet words with the check-in manager. Sixty bucks changed hands and my place was assured.

All went pretty much to Miryam's plan after that. I was met at the airport by her friend, who fixed up a private taxi to drive me over to Leymebamba that afternoon. The car was a large comfortable Toyota and the driver seemed careful – and sober. Just as well, because as soon as we left Chachapoyas we were on a dirt road which was little more than a ledge running along the side of a cliff. The cliff wall was liberally adorned with metal crosses, each one signalling a lonely death where a vehicle had plunged off the ledge and fallen at least sixty metres on to the rocks below. Also, every few minutes we would round a bend to find a large truck bearing down on us with nothing like enough space to pass. Each time, there was a lot of reversing, fiddling around and tucking into tiny rock-face nooks before we managed to get free again and move on to the next obstacle.

IN THE SACRED MOUNTAINS

〰

At first all this manoeuvring deterred me from taking in the beauty of the place, but after about twenty minutes the road wound down to the valley floor and there was no longer a sheer drop on my right. We were now in high country, at about 3,000 metres. The air felt thin, but it didn't make me gasp as it does at 4,000 metres. We were in a fairly wide river valley, following a gushing silt-laden torrent. On each side the mountains rose steeply, covered in scrub. In many places vertical cliffs stood out boldly in greys and yellows. Potato fields dotted the valley floor and the less steep slopes. We regularly passed through little hamlets of clustered sun-dried brick houses. The people were small and ruddy-faced, the elderly stooped from decades of carrying heavy loads. They looked distinctly Andean, but were not wearing the hats and ponchos which distinguish the Quechua and other native Andean Americans from the more ethnically mixed (*mestizo*) farmers of the mountains. When we stopped at a police checkpoint I could hear the local women chatting in Spanish with strong local accents. Unlike rural areas further to the south, they were not talking in Quechua, the language of the Incas. The people of this region had evidently lost their original languages.

There were lots of landslides on the road, and one really big one. Huge boulders and thousands of tons of black mud had parted company with the hillside above and careered down across the road, pulping two houses near the river bank. My driver explained it had happened around six in the evening and the families had heard it coming. They got clear just in time to see everything they owned and loved crushed, ripped to pieces and buried. A local bulldozer arrived a few days later and cleared the road. I could see that the families had already started to level a piece of ground and dig holes for new house posts, right in the line of the big slide. Perhaps they figured that lightning (or landslides) never strikes twice. Personally, I was not so sure. But then what else can you do if you are destitute and live in rural Peru at the end of the twentieth century?

IN SEARCH OF THE IMMORTALS

A few miles further on, the driver pulled up. Pointing through the windscreen he explained that up there, on the cliff, was the house of a Chacha, the chief of this valley before the Incas came. I climbed out to take a look. Perched thirty or so metres up a cliff face was a brilliantly worked stone structure. Parts of it were curved, making the whole look like a huge swallow's nest. The only way to reach it was up an incredibly steep narrow path, which in past times had obviously made it very easy to defend. The Chachapoya, the 'Cloud People', were renowned warriors who had put up stiff resistance to the Incas in the fifteenth century AD. This house had doubtless doubled as a fort and watch-tower, just as the castles of medieval Europe had at that time.

I wanted to climb up to the fort but my driver insisted that the path was very dangerous and it would take too long, so we went on to Leymebamba, arriving in the late afternoon.

Adriana von Hagen greeted me in perfect English and took me into the house – a lovely old building set around an open courtyard. Several local women were working in one of the ground-floor rooms, meticulously cleaning, labelling and storing the objects found with the mummies the year before. The room next to them emitted a constant humming sound – a dehumidifier was at work to keep the mummy storeroom as dry as possible in the cool damp mountain air.

Adriana offered tea – real English tea – and we exchanged pleasantries for a while, but I could hardly contain my curiosity. Here I was sitting with her in a house high in the Andes with more than 200 mummified humans just a few metres away. At the first opportunity, I asked her how all this had come about.

Her reply was brief and candid. Early in 1997, she and Sonia Guillen were watching TV in Lima when an item appeared on the regional news. It reported that the police had intercepted a cache of looted artifacts in Leymebamba, a small town in the Andes. While being questioned, the looters had revealed that they had found the objects in a strange open-air tomb on a cliff face overlooking a beautiful lake, the Lake of the Condors, high in the cloud forest. They had found many of the objects wrapped inside bundles which also contained human bodies.

At first this had seemed implausible, as the chances of human bodies surviving for hundreds of years in the high humidity of the cloud forest was remote. But both Adriana and Sonia are extremely well versed in the pre-conquest history of Peru, and they knew from Spanish chronicles that the Incas had mummified important people and kept them intact for centuries until the Spanish ordered their destruction. They also knew that this region lay within the territory of the Chachapoya, a sophisticated and well-organized people who built impressive cities such as Kuelap, a huge fortified city which rivalled the Inca capital, Cusco, in size and complexity. The Chachapoya had remained fiercely resistant to Inca domination until about seventy years before the arrival of the Spanish. Adriana was especially fascinated as her father had explored the region in the early 1950s as part of his study on Inca roads.

So the two of them had gone to visit the chief of police in Leymebamba, who allowed them to examine the artifacts he had confiscated. Having examined them, they were immediately able to confirm that they were indeed Chachapoyan, although there seemed to be some Inca pieces too. What, then, was the situation at the site, they asked? The chief of police had explained that the site was so remote that he had not been able to post guards there, but he had warned the people living near to it not to touch anything else. And, yes, he said, there were lots of mummies up there...

Adriana and Sonia decided that there was only one thing to do: get up there and take a look for themselves. They were warned, but to no avail, that the trail was extremely poor and that it was a long and arduous trek, quite unsuited to elegant city ladies. Nevertheless, they set about organizing horses, guides, provisions and camping equipment and within a few days had set off.

IN SEARCH OF THE IMMORTALS

'I don't want to tell you too much about the trip up, Howard,' Adriana said. 'It was the dry season then and the trail wasn't as bad as it is now after all this rain, but it still took us about eleven hours to get there. We're better at it now. We can do it in eight or nine hours if we're not too heavily laden. I've got a video with some shots of the trail. I'll show it to you tomorrow.'

I saw it next morning. It showed horses struggling desperately through a quagmire of black mud, sometimes up to their bellies in peat bogs. The commentary solemnly related that, at one point, a horse got so embroiled it broke its leg trying to get free, and had to be shot on the spot.

Once they had arrived and set up camp, Adriana and Sonia set off to inspect the mausoleum. What they found was both exhilarating and disappointing. It really was a big cache of mummy bundles – not tens but hundreds – and much else beside. There were designs on the walls and the rock face and artifacts scattered all around. There were also frames made from wooden boards that presumably had been used for carrying the dead to their final resting place, and some still had mummies inside them. But the whole place had been ransacked by the looters. Mummy bundles were strewn all over the place, many of them slashed open by machetes. The damage was horrendous.

This was a totally unique find – nothing remotely like it had ever been found in the Andes. There was so much to learn from it, yet so much had already been destroyed. Adriana recalled that Sonia had been especially upset by the way everything had been pulled out of the mausoleums and strewn around. This meant it was impossible to determine in what order the mummies might have been placed and if there was any particular layout in the funerary rooms.

Having seen for themselves how things were at the site, Sonia and Adriana had struggled back on horseback to Leymebamba then returned to Lima to organize a full-blown expedition to the Lake of the Condors to retrieve the mummies. They had also contacted the Discovery Channel, which readily agreed to send a film crew to cover their mission.

By the summer they were ready to go again and a string of more than thirty horses set out from Leymebamba in July. It took over a month to carry all the mummies and artefacts down from the cliffside mortuary and ship them back from the lake to Leymebamba. Sonia and Adriana then recruited a team of local women to undertake the major task of cleaning, cataloguing and conserving the finds, and they were still at work on this when I arrived.

Adriana offered to show me the mummies next morning, explaining that, as it was her last night there for a while, her team of conservators were coming round with their families that evening for a little farewell party. The evening passed sweetly. One of Adriana's conservators had a beautiful clear voice and sang the songs of the mountains with such purity it moved all of us.

In the morning, Adriana opened up the climate-controlled store to give me my first sight of the mummies. As with the peoples of Paracas, Nazca and Ilo, the Chachapoya had conserved their dead in the flexed position, their knees pulled tight up against their chests, arms folded with hands pointing upwards. Most of them were still inside their bundles. The outermost layer was generally plain cotton with a simple circular face embroidered on to the surface where the real face was positioned. Sonia and Adriana had X-rayed all the bundles, but left most of them intact. The bundles that had been damaged or unwrapped by the looters had provided plenty of exposed human material for them to work on.

Adriana introduced me to several of the mummies, almost as if they were friends. Everyone, it seems, was fond of 'Big Ears', a mature man with extended ear- lobes whose face had been left exposed by the looters. As I lifted him from the shelf, I was astonished by his lightness. He could only have weighed a few pounds. We looked, too, at a newborn child. Its skin was puffy and loose-fitting, reminding me of my own children's first few days of life when their skin had seemed a size too big, until their mother's milk had filled them out.

There were mummified animals too: a small cat, probably an ocelot, a dog-like animal and an opossum. In some mummy caches people have found animals which have obviously crept into the mausoleum and died there of natural causes, but there was no doubt that these animals had been deliberately mummified. The ocelot's nose was pierced with a piece of bone through the septum. The dog-like animal's mouth had been sewn up in a highly elaborate embroidered style. These animals were clearly of special significance to the mummifiers.

We moved on to the grave goods. There were gourds in string bags, pottery, a perfect pair of sandals made from fibre, little woven bags – called *chuspas* – used for carrying coca leaves, and some sleeveless shirts. One of these was superbly woven in bright colours with anthropomorphic designs of supernatural beings. One set of objects, new to the archaeological record, remains a mystery: bamboo tubes about thirty centimetres long, some of them decorated with burnt-on designs, and each with a carefully shaped opening at one end. There were also some pan-pipes and several wooden carvings of people. Some were quite crudely made; others, about a metre high, were very stylized, apparently armless, and had long jaw-lines and noses. They reminded me of the great stone statues on Easter Island.

Finally there were many long strings with much shorter strings attached to them. Adriana explained that these curious things were called *Quipu* by the Incas, who had used them when they carried out population censuses in newly-conquered domains; when she and Sonia were first trying to figure out exactly who the mummies were, the strings had provided them with important clues. From these – and some of the ceramics and clothing – they were able to detect objects from both the Chachapoya and Inca traditions. Their initial conclusions were that this was a culturally-mixed mausoleum which contained both Chachapoya and Inca mummies. 'When you've seen the lake, Howard, I think you'll realize why even Incas would have been happy to be buried there,' Adriana mused.

To get me used to the altitude, we spent the afternoon strolling along a dirt track above the town collecting wild orchids for the courtyard. Adriana had quick eyes and a very detailed knowledge of cloud-forest flora. As we rambled, I realized that she was an expert on this part of Peru. When she was a child, her father had roamed these hills in search of the Inca road, and had clearly instilled in her a love and fascination with pre-Hispanic Peru which she has carefully cultivated ever since. Although not technically an academic, she is as well versed in the complexities of Peruvian archaeology as any of the top scholars in the field.

That night we ate in the town's only 'restaurant', then I got my pack ready, choosing only bare essentials – sleeping-bag, warm jersey, one complete change of clothes, spare socks, torch and toothbrush. As I dressed next morning, I felt a few sinister cramps in my stomach, but ignored them and set off for the rendezvous with my guide and horse. The horse, it turned out, was a pony of about fourteen hands. He was called Moro and Adriana knew him well. He was fine, she told me, very sure-footed but slow. I would have to keep forcing him on. That did not sound encouraging, but the die was cast. I was genuinely concerned that I was much too heavy for him, but Adriana insisted that he would cope. So, tying on our saddlebags, we said our farewells (Adriana was travelling back to Lima later that day) and set off at around 7.30 a.m.

The saddle, which consisted of a wooden frame and a lot of felt padding topped with a brightly coloured saddle rug, was fine. It was deep at front and back and fitted me well. Thank God.

Although there was a lot of cloud about, the morning was dry and mild. The first half-hour took us down an ancient, uneven, stone-paved track which caused the horses to stumble a lot. There were gardens on either side, mostly potato patches, and we passed many people walking and riding to or from the fields. We took a bridge over a roaring torrent and I looked up at our first ascent. The track was alternately deep orange clay, very slippery, and jagged rock, making a series of natural uneven steps. The gradient was hard to believe. The only way that Moro could tackle it was to scramble through the mud then take a series of cat-like leaps from rock to rock. Leoncio, my guide, was off his mount, and leading it, but I knew I would not make ten metres upwards at that altitude without collapsing. Moro struggled gamely on, panting like crazy and stopping to rest every few minutes.

It was one of those distant hilltops that you never seem to reach. You look up, think you can see the summit about fifty metres in front, then struggle on, get there, look up again and see that there is another fifty metres to go, and so it goes on. After about half an hour, we finally made it to the crown of the hill. Looking back there was a fine panorama, with Leymebamba nestled in among rolling hills, fields in the valleys, the higher slopes covered in scrubby forest. The trail ahead was level for a while, but very boggy. In some parts there was a walkway made from logs laid flat, but many of these were rotten, causing the horses to stumble and lurch whenever they gave way under foot.

As we started to descend into the next valley, Leoncio once again dismounted and this time I did the same. We let the horses go and hopped, slid and slurped along beside them. Here the black mud was mingled with whitish clay. Reaching a point where the path crossed a stream in the valley floor, we remounted and set off once more uphill.

This climb was longer than the first, but not quite so steep and rocky, just a mass of sticky mud. Near the top was an isolated farmhouse, no sign of people but two enormous ferocious dogs. We skirted round the dogs and crossed some waterlogged fields. The horses plodded on, reaching a part of the trail that was pitted by a series of holes about a metre apart with ridges in between. At each step, the animals had to lift their legs up over the ridge before setting them down in the next trough. Moro found this especially tough and kept slowing almost to a halt. Leoncio had to wait on his horse until we were almost past him, then lash Moro hard on the rump, yelling 'yaaaaah' at the same time. This quickened him for a while – and also showed me what to do.

The land gradually opened out and we found ourselves on a broad upland plain rather like British moorland. At a glance, the surface looked like grassland but it was in fact an enormous peat bog, with occasional patches of slightly firmer turf.

At least I could see a horizon and get a sense of direction, unlike the gruelling slog up and down the mountains which now lay behind us. On those slopes the torture was just not knowing when the climb was going to end, when we were going to get somewhere – anywhere. In the easier terrain of the moorland, I began to relax a bit and to appreciate that I was on a journey into the unknown – a journey to the ends of the earth to reach the final resting place of the Cloud People. A journey which many of them may well have made after death.

Gilgamesh and his search for his lost beloved friend came to mind. My lost beloved friend Robin floated in front of my eyes and Gilgamesh's words rang in my ears:

'How can I rest, how can I be at peace? despair is in my heart . . . I will go as best I can to find the Faraway, for he has entered the assembly of the gods.' . . . so Gilgamesh travelled over the wilderness, he wandered over the grasslands, a long journey . . . to the garden of the sun.

The horses plodded on over the wasteland and across a plain, and I could see that we were about to enter a pass between the hills. Halfway up, it opened out into a pleasant meadow. It was midday.

IN SEARCH OF THE IMMORTALS

Leoncio called a halt to rest the horses and eat. I slid to the ground to find that my legs and back were fine, but my belly was not. Great white swirling clouds descended on us, blanking out the view of the plain below, and it began to rain. I donned the red saddle-poncho Adriana had given me and clambered back aboard Moro. It was getting cold; dampness was everywhere.

The pass took us to another wasteland of peat bogs, this time peppered with huge boulders. The trail wound round, through and over these. In some places we came upon large holes, presumably where the peat had been eroded away by underground streams. While Leoncio's horse stuck mainly to the track, Moro preferred to pick his way clear of the churned ground and stick to firmer untrodden turf. This slowed things down, but I guessed he knew best and left it mostly to him.

At the end of the boulder country we came out to one side of a big mountain. In front there was an almost sheer drop, but I could not see the bottom for swirling clouds. To our right the trail went steeply up the side of the mountain. No peat here, just rock and loose stones – and a hell of an incline. Leoncio got off his horse, his felt hat pulled down against the biting wind and rain, and walked resolutely upwards. I guessed we were at about 4,000 metres. I stayed on Moro. He strained and heaved, stumbled, snorted and strained and heaved again. Twice, loose stones slid him backwards. I got off. But after only a few minutes, just as I had feared, I was gasping for air, my heart thumping like a Gatling gun. I waited a bit, then pressed on upwards. More gasping and thumping. Moro kindly stopped and waited so, when I got alongside him, I grasped the saddle's pummel and let him tow me up the remaining 200 metres to the pass at the top of the rock climb. Adriana told me later that the pass is at about 3,800 metres above sea level.

As I clambered back on Moro, the rain increased, bringing with it a biting chill. Under my poncho and layers of jerseys, my body, drenched with sweat, suddenly turned cold and I began to shiver. We snaked our way across the pass, then came to the descent into the Valley of the Condors. The track just seemed to drop straight down the mountain. In places the only way forward was for Moro to make yet another cat-like leap – using both his front legs to get him off a ledge, then bucking out with his rear legs to clear the ledge behind him. To help him support my weight, I had to stick my legs out as far forward as I could and lean right back over his rump. The problem came when he kicked his rear legs clear. At that moment the saddle jerked upwards into the small of my back, delivering a rabbit-punch to my kidneys. It was a bit like riding a slow-motion bucking bronco down the side of a cliff.

Moro stumbled many times and I had to keep yanking his head up to keep him on his feet. Fear began to creep in. If either of us fell and broke a limb, it would be fatal. But I was determined to fight this nightmare trip, do battle with it and deny its supremacy over me. Slowly, a rhythm set in. I began to understand Moro's tactics in this diabolical terrain and worked with him. In extreme conditions this is the only thing to do: go with the flow, blend and mould yourself into events which must inevitably take place. Once acceptance is achieved, calm can be restored.

I had learnt this lesson the hard way two years earlier when making a film about caves in Romania. Our hosts had insisted that I accompany them into a very special cave which, until 1986, had been sealed from the outside world for five million years. The way in was first to descend twenty metres on a rope, then to roll forward into an extremely narrow tunnel where I had to wriggle like a worm. In parts the roof was so low I had to keep my head sideways. In one of the narrowest sections, Serban, the group leader, stopped to offer me some words of encouragement. I could not move in any direction. I panicked. Every cell in my body wanted me out of there, right away. I felt as if I was exploding. Then a quiet inner voice said: 'What can you do? There are two boots right in front of your face and another human face just a foot behind you. You can't go forwards, can't turn, can't go back. All you can do is die, or just carry on.' Calm set in, and a few minutes later we emerged into a chamber where we could sit up, chat, breathe.

Fear of the descent into the shadowy Valley of the Condors induced the same resignation, followed by calm and acceptance of the madness I was trapped in. Towards the bottom, the trail followed a stream course which had cut its way through the peat to the bedrock below. At times the peat walls on either side were as high as my shoulder, making me feel that we had somehow time-warped into the trenches of the First World War, soaked to the skin and covered in mud in an endless desolate sea of black filth.

After a final titanic struggle through deep brown slimy mud, we reached the valley floor at three o'clock. The lake lay at the top of the valley, another two hours' ride away. The going was never easy anywhere on that trail, but at least the ground was now relatively flat. Trees in the valley were draped in weird mosses, lichens and bromeliads, all dripping wet. We were in the cloud forest. I dismounted and walked for a bit. Around four o'clock, the sun broke through the clouds, casting a huge rainbow across the valley, so close I could almost reach out and touch it. It felt like a good omen.

A little further on, the trees and underbrush had mostly been cleared, the sodden ground planted with *pasto*, the coarse grass used as cattle fodder all over South America. Barbed wire, a gate, dogs barking and a cow lowing. We had made it to the homestead next to the lake: a low sun-dried brick hut with three rooms and a zinc roof, smoke oozing out from under it. The barking dogs brought a curious child and a shy, thin young woman out of the kitchen. She was wearing a basketball cap, jeans and a grimy sweatshirt; the boy had on an old jersey and rubber boots, but no trousers or pants. His nose was running. The woman greeted

IN THE SACRED MOUNTAINS

Leoncio quietly then shook my hand. 'Does the Gringo speak Spanish?' she asked. *'Mas o menos'* ('more or less'), Leoncio replied.

I handed over gifts of rice, beans, potatoes and fruit to our hostess who, smiling her thanks, retreated to the kitchen. Leoncio turned the horses loose in the paddock, then called me to come with him to see the lake, claiming it was only five minutes' walk away. The farmstead was set into the side of a steep slope with a ridge about a hundred metres above it. This entire hill was a glacial terminal moraine, a vast pile of rubble pushed out by a glacier in the last ice age. It was this barrier which had caused the formation of the lake.

We set off uphill again. The ground was squelchy but passable, and ten minutes later we made it to the ridge. About 100 metres below us was the black glassy water of the Lake of the Condors. It lay in a delve, surrounded on three sides by majestic limestone mountains. Waterfalls cascaded down sheer rock faces, making slashes of white on the grey and brown outcrops. Wherever it could gain a footing, vegetation clung to the steep slopes. Puffy white clouds scudded down the mountains and across the lake, causing the light to change constantly. One minute there was deep shadow, then a shower of rain engulfed the far shore. A few moments later, it was in full sun and we were in shadow. A truly magnificent place.

'Look straight across the lake, *señor*. You see that cliff with the grey line down it, about 100 metres up. That's it, that's the *chullpas*, the mausoleum.'

I could just make out some irregular features on the other side of the lake and a faint streak of red on the rock, but it was too far away to see any detail. That would have to wait until tomorrow.

The night was distressingly uncomfortable – and cold. I ate only boiled potatoes but my belly still churned. Every hour or so, I had to get out of my sleeping-bag, pull on all my clothes and boots, and struggle round the back of the farm to the open-air privy. I slept fitfully, a sleep full of strange dreams and visitations. At one point I was certain that a great mystery of the universe was about to be revealed to me. I woke sweating and the secret slipped away. One of the farm dogs decided to go out and bark at the deep, dark night. Images of a jaguar's amber eyes caught in torchlight danced before me.

The morning, however, was clear and fresh and I felt okay. After another potato, Leoncio and I set off for the *chullpas*. To get there we had first to walk along the ridge, which took us through the remains of the Chachapoya village. The homesteaders had cleared the area so it was easy to see the stone circular walls of the houses, with their carefully placed stone door-posts and lintels. Sonia and Adriana had counted over 200 structures, which meant this had been a large village, perhaps even a small town. The houses were pretty close together. It must have been a bustling, almost crowded place 600 years ago.

Beyond the village the land sloped steeply down to the mouth of the outflow stream at the eastern end of the lake. We forded the stream on a semi-submerged foot-bridge made of a few bamboo poles and I scooped up a handful of water as we passed. It was cool and clear with a slight brackish tang from the peat it carried.

On the other side we passed the camp where Adriana, Sonia and the mummy-rescue team had stayed the previous summer, then we plunged into the forest. A partly overgrown trail snaked its way along the edge of the lake through dense bamboo thickets. We ducked and weaved, breathing the pungency of decaying vegetation until the trail turned inland, virtually straight up the rock face. Here the rescue team had built wooden ladders up the steepest parts, which were slippery but sound. For the rest of the climb we had to heave ourselves up from trunk to trunk, gripping shrubs and liana as 'anchors'. The ladders had made the 100 metre ascent easy and we were soon on a narrow ledge, moving laterally across the cliff face. Then I put one foot wrong, stepping on to a rotten log which simply disappeared down a ten-metre drop. Managing to twist round as I fell, I landed with both elbows on the ledge, with just enough grasp left to stop me going over.

Rounding a bend, I looked up and there was the *chullpas* nestling under a big limestone overhang. Water was cascading down from the overhang, forming a liquid curtain in front of the mausoleum. We scrambled round the waterfall on to the small space in front of the funerary houses and sat down to catch our breath. At once, I realized there was something very odd here: the ground was incredibly dry. It was littered with crispy bamboo leaves which – almost as if they had been toasted – snapped when I crushed them between my fingers. At the time of writing, it is still not known *why* there is a tiny super-dry spot within a climatic area of vegetation which is wet almost all the time. But this extraordinary micro-ecosystem exists, and there is no doubt that the Chachapoya discovered it and realized its potential for the preservation of their ancestors.

The *chullpas* were a collection of small rooms with front and side walls made of limestone blocks, the back wall being the cliff face. Some of them had been plastered and painted white with red and yellow designs added to them. Others had zig-zag stone friezes on the front, a characteristic feature of Chachapoya architecture. Two deers' antlers had been fixed into the walls of one of them just above its central windows. They all had windows, but no doors, so presumably the dead were hoisted through the windows. The roofs were made from thick, rough-hewn planks. Apparently, when they were first discovered, there were a lot of mummies stashed up on the roofs as well as inside the houses. Everything, including the roofs, was extraordinarily dry.

After I had scrambled around a bit and looked more closely at the *chullpas*, Leoncio got out his bag of coca leaves. Scattering a few of these as an offering to the spirits of the place, he filled up his cheeks with leaves and passed the bag to me. We added lime from his little gourd and settled back to chew. I looked out over the lake, the same direction in which the mummies had 'looked' for centuries. A light buzz, created by the coca leaves, gently enhanced the profound sense of peace and tranquillity of the place. Perched high on the cliffside, I could survey the world rather as a harpy eagle or condor might. The glassy waters of the lake mirrored the forest and mountains and the deep blue sky. Puffed-up white clouds whizzed by, the breeze that carried them stirring great whirls of ripples on the surface of the waters below. The time had come to try to 'see' the Chachapoya, the 'Cloud People', as they once were.

A tough, hardy mountain people, early chronicles report them as being tall and good looking, the women sought after as brides by the Incas. They are said to have had fair skin, possibly even fair hair. This has led some people to speculate – erroneously – that they were linked to the Vikings or Phoenicians. They lived by farming but also had great skill in weaving, and were accomplished architects, city-builders and renowned warriors. They were doubtless also traders. Their lands possessed one of the most important 'gateways' in the central Andes: the gateway to Amazonia. The peoples of the Andes had long prized the products of the tropical rainforests – the medicinal and hallucinogenic plants and herbs; the dazzling feathers of birds such as macaws, toucans and hummingbirds; and materials such as the super-hard wood of the *chonta* palm. The Chachapoya held the keys of access to these prized goods.

Although some of their homelands, like the Lake of the Condors, were quite isolated, trade linked the Chachapoyas to their neighbours in both the Andes and the rainforest. In a broad sense, they were one among many similar autonomous 'states' found throughout the Andes at that time. Like the others, they expressed a distinct sense of identity in their clothing, artwork and architecture. Doubtless, they also held their own beliefs about the supernatural world and the afterlife, expressed in their own mythology and rituals. As the contents of the *chullpa* revealed so startlingly, the need to preserve their dead must have lain at the heart of their world-view.

The archaeological record shows the emergence of their culture around 800 AD. They do not seem to have had any single paramount leader, rather a loose federation of independent chiefs. The Spanish said they would come together in times of war. Above all, they seemed to value their independence and autonomy. When their neighbours, the Incas, began their imperial expansion early in the fifteenth century, they used subtle techniques, trying to negotiate first allegiance then fealty to the Inca emperor. The Chachapoya would have none of it. They rebutted the Inca overtures and only succumbed after a very costly military campaign. The Incas were so riled by Chachapoya resistance that they are said to have moved half the population to other parts of the empire in an attempt to break the spirit of resistance. They then implanted their own colonists and administrators, which may explain the strong presence of Inca artifacts, maybe even Inca mummies, at the Lake of the Condors.

Looking out over the lake from the ancestral eyrie, I could just about make out the Chachapoya village site on the other side. Understanding this ancient people, I mused, would have been so much easier if the stone houses still had their conical thatches and plumes of smoke rising from them. Certainly, the playful shrieks of their children, men and women calling to each other, snatches of pan-pipe music drifting over the water, would have assured them that all was well for the living. And the ancestral shrines, where I was sitting, would have been easily visible, a concrete assurance that the ancestors were watching over them. As the light trance induced by the coca set in, some key words of Adriana's came back to me: 'If you really want to get to grips with the Chachapoya view of death, then you have to account for one key factor: they didn't bury their dead; didn't put them down into the ground out of sight. They kept them up, visible, actually physically above the living. For me, this means that they didn't see their ancestors as "dead and gone" in the way we do. They saw them as a part, an essential part, of the world of the living.'

Sitting up there in the clouds, trying to 'see' the world as it had been 600 years ago, I sensed that she was right. Her vision had ancient echoes – thousands of years before the Chachapoya came to be, the Chinchorro had kept their dead close to them, wrapped themselves in the protection of their forebears in much the same way. It seems to me that, by the time the Chachapoya came to mummify their dead, they were following an ancient, widespread and deeply revered procedure.

Exactly what this procedure was we do not really know, but the discovery at the Lake of the Condors has provided many vital clues. Once Sonia and Adriana had removed all the mummies from the *chullpas* and hauled them back to Leymebamba, conservation work was able to begin. As already mentioned, many of the mummies had suffered badly at the hands of the looters and needed immediate treatment; some had been unwrapped; others needed to be unwrapped because of the damage they had sustained. This, however, gave Sonia and Adriana the chance to make their first detailed examinations.

They found that all the mummies were sitting on thick cotton pads, and the pads showed signs of having absorbed fluids which had run down inside the mummies' body cavities. One adolescent had a wad of cotton, like a large tampon, inserted into her body cavity from the region of her vagina and anus. There were no signs of desiccated internal organs in her body cavity. X-rays confirmed the absence of entrails in any of the bodies. X-rays do not reveal soft tissue, but if large organs, such as the liver or heart, had remained in the body they would at least have cast shadows. There were none to be seen. There were also no signs of incisions in the stomach or chest areas of the bodies. So Sonia and Adriana came to the conclusion that the Chachapoya eviscerated their dead by extracting the internal organs through the anus and/or vagina. There were no obvious signs of removal of the brain, but the mummies' heads were fixed in their bundles in a position where brain fluids would run down inside the body cavity and out through the anus on to the cotton pads they were sitting on.

Removal of the internal organs is certainly essential if you want to preserve a body in less than ideal conditions, but on its own it is not sufficient to ensure that other soft tissues – muscle, skin and sinew – do not decay. As climatic conditions were far from ideal for body preservation in most of Chachapoya territory, they must have used other techniques. Elsewhere in South America, especially in Colombia, the bodies of important people were often preserved by heat-drying. Spanish chronicles contain many references to this practice, even in areas of tropical rainforest near the Darien Gap in Colombia, although no bodies have survived from these cultures.

In other Colombian communities the bodies were smoke-dried by being kept close to a fire for several months. Some of these bodies have survived. Although well preserved, several of them carry evidence of the drying process in the form of scorch-marks on the skin. Although, so far, Adriana and Sonia have not found scorch-marks on any of the Chachapoya bodies, it may yet emerge that the Chachapoya used this method very carefully. It does however seem unlikely – given the absence of any trace of ashes, burns or presence of fire close to the bodies and their wrappings. In my view, this leaves only one alternative method – freeze-drying. For centuries the people of the High Andes have been freeze-drying crops such as potatoes, and they still do so today.

As we shall see later in this chapter, the Incas certainly knew that if human bodies were left exposed high in the mountains, they would be well preserved even if they had not been eviscerated. Recent finds of sacrificed Inca children bear witness to the efficacy of this method. So it could be that the Chachapoya took the bodies of their dead to some high, dry spot in the mountains to desiccate them before transporting them to the holy *chullpas*, their final resting places.

The Chachapoya mummies were not as heavily or elaborately wrapped as the mummies of the coastal desert, but none the less they were carefully and extensively enclosed in cotton shrouds. The shrouds were bound firmly in place with string, and in some cases the outer covers were sewn up to 'seal' the bundles. As we have seen in Chapter Seven, shrouds and wrappings were important because they engender a 'micro-climate' which absorbs any fluids emitted by the body. They may also inhibit the penetration of any external humidity, and insects attacking the body. On the other hand, cotton also absorbs moisture and it is actually more likely that, in the very humid conditions of the cloud forest, the shrouds would have become saturated, wet rags. In that case they would have contributed to the decay rather than the preservation of the bodies.

These thoughts brought me back to the site – the rock ledge where I was sitting. Yes, it was weirdly, uncannily dry. If I had sat down anywhere else on that mountain, it would have been soaking wet. Although, as mentioned, we do not know why this ledge is so dry, there is no doubt that the Chachapoya knew that it was and chose this site for their mausoleum. There were doubtless other reasons, too – reasons we may never know, but can try to guess. As mentioned before, it is a common belief throughout the Andes (and in many other parts of the world) that mountains are sacred places, the homes of the gods; and that placing the dead there brings them closer to the deities which control the lives of the living.

Looking at the empty *chullpas*, I remembered the photos Adriana had showed me of the site when it was first discovered and tried to imagine how it had been before the looters ransacked it: neat rows of mummy bundles, all in the foetal position, wrapped and cushioned for eternity, all with their stylized faces looking calmly out over the lake. They were like time-capsules – a fertile nest of cosmic human eggs, patiently waiting for the next coming, the new awakening. How sad that people in our modern world had ended their vigilance; how sad that their destructive urges had forced these patient immortals into captivity far from their holy lake in the mountains of the gods.

Leoncio roused me from my reverie, offered more coca, and said we should be moving soon. I scattered a few more leaves to the spirits of the place, offering my thanks. This, then, was the turning point. I had come as far as I needed and made it to the house of the dead. I felt peaceful and calm and wondered if something had changed within me. Going back along a path is always much easier than going forward into the unknown. We slipped quickly down the mountainside, then skirted the lake. When we reached the outflow stream, the sun was shining, making the water glisten – and beckon. I murmured to Leoncio that I was going to swim and slipped out of my clothes. The water was bracing, but not shockingly cold. I splashed and dipped my head under the surface, saw a trout rise to catch a fly a few metres away. The sweat, filth and fear of the journey melted away, leaving me feeling purified. It was, I suppose, a kind of private baptism, a moment of rebirth.

Scrambling back up the sodden hillside, we picked our way through the ghostly Chachapoya village and reached the farmhouse an hour or so before dark. That evening two men came into the kitchen where we sat. One was the father of the child I had met on arrival, the other a neighbour from a farm several hours' ride away. They were shy at first, but the conversation soon grew. They were the ones who had first spotted the *chullpas* (so they were probably also the first looters). We skirted that issue, and listened as they talked about the great team of people Sonia and Adriana had brought out to evacuate the site. At one time there had been more than thirty horses, an inflatable canoe on the lake and a lot of gringos with cameras. The gringos, they told me, were really clumsy and fell over all the time. They and the other helpers had carried the mummies down the mountain on their backs, transferred them to the canoe and rowed round the lake to the campsite. The rancher's wife had been cook at the camp, making huge meals every day. Everyone had obviously had a great time, out here in the middle of nowhere.

We talked of the difficulties of living in such an isolated place, and the woman explained that when the children were older she would have to leave them with relatives in town, so they could go to school. The land, it turned out, was not theirs – it belonged to their patron, as did the cattle. They were just ranch-hands, paid next to nothing. Little wonder, then, that when they spotted the mummy cache, they had set about it with machetes to see if there was gold in the bundles. We talked till late, I ate a few more potatoes and fetched the last of the whisky I had brought in a little plastic bottle. It disappeared quickly.

In the morning we woke to steady, heavy rain. The clouds were low and dense. Leoncio brought the horses down to the house and we packed up lethargically, but the rain showed no sign of abating. So we slung on the saddle-bags and cloths, pulled the ponchos down over our backpacks, and set out. The rain did not let up. It trickled down my poncho into my rubber boots; ran off my cap down the back of my neck, and fanned out across my shoulders, wrists and forearms. I walked a lot to keep warm, most of the way down the valley, in fact, to where the track turned uphill. There we remounted in order to clear a really deep bog at the base of the climb. Leoncio hopped off and walked the entire way up the 600-metre ascent to the high pass. I didn't. Moro hauled himself and me up the climb, choosing his footing with care.

At the top, the rain drove straight into our faces, carried by a fierce wind. My chin and cheeks went numb; sodden feet started to lose all feeling, and my hands turned blue and stiffened, making it hard to hold the reins. The rain lashing my face blurred my vision. But by then we had crossed the pass and were standing at the top of the steep, gravelly descent down to the edge of the mountain to the peat bog and boulder moor. Dismounting, I set off down the pass, using my legs as brakes and letting gravity do the rest. I slid and stumbled a lot, but didn't fall. I had always enjoyed scree-running as a child, where you sort of ski down loose stones on steep slopes. That early practice held me in good stead. By the time we made it to the bottom I was warm again. The worst was behind us, just six hours of peat bogs in front.

Leoncio chose a different route from the one we had followed on the way up. It was firmer and easier going. We urged the horses on and they broke into a trot, then a canter. They knew that they were headed home and began to pull, trying to race each other. A sudden wave of elation shot through me. All the misery of the mud, rain and cold evaporated and joy coursed through my veins. Suddenly, clear as bell, I heard my dead friend Robin say: 'That's it, Howard, you've done it. You've done your time, the grieving is over. Turn away from death, come out of the shadows, look at the light, return to laughter and life.' I heard him laugh with me, just as he always had in life.

We chased on across the moor at full speed, Moro surging ahead. Suddenly I sensed I was alone. Glancing back over my shoulder, all I could see was a horse's head and two front legs, no Leoncio. I swerved round to find that Leoncio and his horse had gone full tilt into a concealed hole. Seconds later Leoncio's head appeared, cursing and swearing at the horse. He hopped out of the hole, unhurt, cursed again, then turned to me and grinned. I looked at this 'horse in a hole' and shook with laughter. Together we hauled him out.

The rest of the ride back was uneventful, just a plod through the endless sea of churned mud. It was more downhill than up, so I walked a lot of the way. Despite the lack of sleep and food, I felt stronger and fitter than on the way up to the lake. On the outskirts of town the horses, sensing home, broke into a skittish trot. But, just as it all seemed over and done with, we came to a party of workmen digging trenches for water pipes. As they were adamant that we were not allowed to jump their ditch, we had to make a detour round another valley and then come back into the town by a different route. Altogether, this added an extra hour to the journey.

Smiles from the conservator ladies greeted me at Adriana's house and, having taken one look at me, they immediately set two large kettles on the stove. I was filthy from head to foot, and damp all over. The simple joys of sluicing myself with warm water, having a shave and changing into clean dry clothes signalled the return to normality. Pleasure came in the form of the whisky kindly left for me by Adriana who had known I would need it. A deep, peaceful sleep followed.

Next morning the sense of pure joy I had felt the day before came flooding back to me. Life's sweetness had returned, and I knew then that something had changed irrevocably within me. At that very moment I caught a slight whirring sound as a hummingbird whizzed into the courtyard, hovering just a few feet from my head. It seemed to look at me for a second then darted over to the wild orchids to sip nectar. Hummingbird, messenger of the gods, ball of bright light, flashing like a crystal in the sun. It seemed to confirm that an inner transformation had taken place.

Back in Lima, I had time to gather my thoughts. The Chachapoya were certainly sophisticated mummy-makers. For several hundred years they had been in contact with neighbouring Andean societies and with the peoples of the rainforests on their eastern borders. They were in touch with the Inca empire and eventually conquered by them. The evidence from the *chullpas* at the Lake of the Condors suggested that even after the

IN THE SACRED MOUNTAINS

Inca conquest the Chachapoya had continued to mummify their dead. They may even have mummified their Inca masters. If this were the case, then it seemed likely that the Inca and the Chachapoya had shared a religious ideology which advocated the preservation of the dead. As many chroniclers had referred to it, I already knew that mummy-making was practised all over Colombia at the time of the conquest. So did the Incas mummify their dead, too? I telephoned Adriana who immediately confirmed that they did.

Mummification in Peru was a widespread and comparatively well-documented practice at the time of the conquest. Early chroniclers had reported that most senior heads of lineages and village chiefs were mummified after death and their bodies kept and revered by their families. They even described individuals holding conversations with the dead, as if seeking advice from an oracle. The mummies also had their clothes washed and changed regularly and were given food to 'eat'. The retention and occasional display of mummified ancestors essentially legitimated the social status of their custodians. To have mummified ancestors was to confirm one's place in society and one's rights to use land, build houses, levy taxes and the like. Mummies were somewhat akin to title deeds in our own society.

The Spanish conquistadors soon came to realize that mummies played an important symbolic role in binding Inca society together. They doubtless also realized that if they could destroy the power of the mummies then they would be able to subject the Incas to even greater Spanish domination. Their chroniclers, many of them priests, condemned the reverence of ancestral mummies as idolatrous. The elevation of a dead kins-person to divine status was a profanity to them. One chronicle referred to 'the beastly act of venerating the bodies of the dead'. A more perceptive chronicler noted that when the Spanish ordered the Incas to bury their mummified ancestors, the people were horrified and protested that the mummies would suffer terribly from hunger and thirst if they were placed in the ground.

So the ancient notion of venerating the ancestors, interacting with them and keeping them close by, was in evidence all over the Andes at the time of the conquest. This core idea had its roots with the Chinchorro and endured in South America for at least 7,500 years – more than three times as long as the ideologies of Christianity or Buddhism have so far survived.

In essence, this notion relies upon concepts of life and death which are fundamentally different from our own. For many of us, life has a finite, biological beginning and an absolute end in death. Yet many people who have experienced the loss of someone close to them have come to realize that it is not as simple as that. We are social beings: our lives operate within a fabric, a network of interrelated and emotional relationships which bind us all together. When someone dies a physical being may cease to pulse, but the network which sustained the deceased does not disintegrate. In a very real sense, we live on in the hearts and minds of those who make up the social fabric of our being. On my ride up into the High Andes, I have no idea whether anything external communicated with me; whether I actually heard Robin's spirit-voice. But I am totally convinced that part of Robin lives on in me, and it was that part of 'him-who-is-now-me' which spoke to me.

In general, people living outside our highly individualistic, alienated, 'modern' Western world are much more aware of the social fabric which binds them together. The Incas, following a tradition thousands of years old, expressed their belief in the continuity of their society by preserving their dead. They clearly believed that their reverence acknowledged the semi-divine status of their ancestors – hence the Spaniards' insistence on the destruction of the mummies to stop them worshipping false idols. Even so, the Spanish did not destroy the mummies of the Inca emperors at the beginning of their conquest. This was probably because they realized that they were such potent symbols that any attempt to destroy them would ferment rebellion. Some of the Spanish were also fascinated by these royal bodies. Pizzarro's secretary, Pedro Sancho de la Hoz, described the mummy of the emperor Huayna Capac, who died in 1525, as being in near perfect condition in 1543. One of the first detailed descriptions of the royal mummies dates from 1559, written by the chronicler Garcilaso de la Vega:

> The bodies were so intact they lacked neither hair, eyebrows nor eyelashes ... They were seated in the way Indian men and women usually sit, and their eyes were cast down ... I remember touching the finger of Huayna Capac. It was hard and rigid, like that of a wooden statue. The bodies weighed so little that any Indian could carry them from house to house in his arms or on his shoulders. They carried them wrapped in white shrouds through the streets and plazas, the Indians dropping to their knees, making reverences with groans and tears, and many Spanish removing their caps.

The mummies were taken from the royal funeral sepulchre during special religious and state ceremonies, such as the accession of a new emperor and the two annual solstice festivals. The Inca chronicler Guaman Poma made a drawing of one of these events, showing the mummies of Emperor Huayna Capac, his wife and a retainer being carried through the streets.

The Incas certainly believed that after death their emperors became gods and, following ancient funerary practices, they also sacrificed and mummified some of the emperors' wives, concubines and retainers. They also believed that it was not only royalty who could be transformed into gods. Recently, Inca altars have been discovered on the peaks of the highest mountains in the Andes, and excavations have revealed many offerings in these holiest of shrines. These have included little animals and ornamental dollies made from silver and gold, some dressed in fabrics adorned with feathers from the tropical forests.

There were also near-perfectly-preserved bodies of children, both boys and girls, confirming the chroniclers' descriptions of Inca child-sacrifice. According to their writings, when a major natural disaster occurred or a new Inca emperor was crowned, children would be selected as sacrificial offerings. For the coronation ceremony, 200 children were sacrificed. The girls were drawn from the 'Chosen Women' – girls who were specially selected for their beauty and physical perfection at the age of ten. They spent the following four years being trained in special 'convents'. Some of the Chosen Women were then married to nobles or officials, others became priestesses known as 'The Virgins of the Sun'. But the most coveted role for the Chosen Women was to be selected for sacrifice.

They believed that death, as a sacrificial offering, ensured happiness in the afterlife. Each child had to be physically perfect and of noble birth – the son or daughter of a *curaka*, a chief or lineage head. When his or her time came, the child, accompanied by her family and fellow villagers, was taken in pageant to the Inca capital, Cusco. Feasts were held for the child, who was presented to the Emperor in person. Blessings and praises were heaped upon them. One such child, a ten-year-old girl named Tanta Carhua, was said to have been 'beautiful beyond imagination'. The chronicler who witnessed her sacrifice records that, after the feasting, she turned to her villagers and said: 'You can finish with me now because I could never be more honoured than by the feasts they held for me in Cusco.'

Priests, village chiefs and her family led her up to the mountain's peak-top altar, gave her a strong draft of *chicha* (maize beer) then walled up her burial chamber while she was still alive. Other children were knocked unconscious with a blow to the back of the head. Some were buried, others left exposed on the mountain top. All the living believed that the children would achieve instant immortality by becoming benign deities who would guard and protect the villages and families in the valleys below.

Ever since the 1950s, high-altitude archaeologists have been finding the remains of these children on the high peaks of the Andes, at altitudes from 5,500 metres to as much as 7,000 metres. In recent years, many of these discoveries have been made by Johan Reinhard. In November 1998, he found seven children's bodies on the top of a volcano in southern Peru, and three more were recovered in April 1999. In the light of these discoveries we can safely assume that the Incas knew that the children's bodies would be preserved by freeze-drying. So, given the use of deliberate mummification as a means of ensuring immortality in the population as a whole, the natural mummification of these children must have provided the Incas with 'proof' that their sacrificial victims had achieved immortality too.

All round the world this seems to be a primary reason for preserving the dead. Mummies act as testament, bear witness to the continuity of humanity beyond death. In many societies they clearly comfort the living, cushioning the trauma of a life lost, both for individuals and for society as a whole. Being able to see, speak to and feel for a deceased person certainly softens the blow of death. In South America it is clear that mummies were also a source of legitimacy, a way of asserting that individuals or groups are who they say they are and retain rights to land, property and the like – a sort of human will and testament.

At a more profound level, mummies blur the boundaries between life and death. In South America the embodied ancestors mediated between the worlds of nature and supernature, aiding the living through catastrophes such as natural disasters and the deaths of their leaders. In ancient Egypt – and perhaps in other parts of the Old World – afterlife beliefs became interwoven with the cyclical nature of the world. The preserved body was in itself a seed, a life not terminated but in suspension, awaiting rebirth with the rising of the sun or the coming of spring. Underlying both the Old and New World visions is a simple idea: life is not necessarily 'nasty, brutish and short' nor necessarily of finite duration. Rather, the boundaries between life and death are much more blurred than we sceptical Westerners would have it.

It is easy for us to dismiss these elaborate afterlife constructs as just so much fantasy, assigning them to their proper time and place in the evolution of human thought and society. But occasionally events take place which give us food for thought, making it less easy to dismiss all these ideas, beliefs and practices as illusions. One such event took place in my life over twenty years ago, and only in the last few months have I begun to understand what it might mean.

I have only recently got to grips with the nature of ancient Egyptian cosmology and concepts of the afterlife. As this happened, I was struck by the number of parallels between their views and those of my friends the Maku. Like the ancient Egyptians, the Maku believe that there are several spiritual aspects to human life, and that two of these endure beyond life. They believe in an underworld with a river running through its centre. The sun passes along this river every night in his sun-canoe from west to east, rising once again to our world in the morning, just as the sun-god Re does in Egypt. Although in Maku eyes the underworld is not associated directly with the dead, night-time is. The human ghost, when it quits the body after death, can be seen and heard at night. Its name, *baktup*, also means darkness. And the ultimate resting place of the Maku ancestors is in the sky, just as it was in ancient Egypt. The pharaohs reached this ultimate resting place by flying up the sun's rays from the heart of their mausoleums, the pyramids; the Maku, as I discovered, achieved their transition to immortality in a rather strange way.

IN THE SACRED MOUNTAINS

〰️

After I had been living with the Maku for about a year, I had accrued sufficient skill as a woodsman to travel through the forest on my own, following the network of small paths linking village to village. I knew the lay of the land – which way the streams flowed and where there were swamps, hills and other landmarks. I liked travelling alone and sometimes stopped off in the forest overnight, making a little leaf shelter and roasting a fish or two by the fire.

One day I set off early on a trip that I knew would take ten hours if I walked fast. I was returning to Chai's house after visiting some of his relatives, all went well until about midday. At the furthest point between the two settlements the game was abundant, so groups of people often came there, made hunting camps, and stayed for as long as it took to amass a good surplus of meat. As a result, a whole network of trails had fanned out from the campsites in every direction, criss-crossing the main trail. And it was here that I somehow picked the wrong way out of the campsite. After half an hour or so, the trail just petered out. The sensible thing to do in such a situation is, of course, to back-track, but I thought, no, I've been in the woods now for more than a year and ought to be able to navigate my way home cross-country. I knew there was a big rock to the north, called 'Vulture Rock', and that all I had to do was track round its base to the left, and go westwards until I picked up the trail for home. I had once seen it from the air – a huge granite volcanic plug which reared up like a massive pyramid from the forest floor.

Having reached its base, I started to head left. The vegetation was very thick, forcing me to crawl and wriggle through tangles of liana and thorny shrubs. Around three o'clock, with three hours of light left, I stopped for a smoke. I had just one cigar butt left, three matches, four bullets for my rifle and a small piece of bread. My canvas boots were rotten, the sole almost off one of them. As I sat smoking I suddenly heard a voice saying 'You're going up, Howard, up to the top.' To this day,

277

IN SEARCH OF THE IMMORTALS

I cannot honestly tell whether this voice came from within or from somewhere else, but I got up, slipped my pack on and set off upwards.

The rock was lightly covered in forest so I hauled myself up from trunk to trunk. About an hour later, I came to an opening in the forest cover. A bare granite slope fell sharply away to the forest floor several hundred metres below; a huge green sea spread out before me. I could see distant rivers and the columns of smoke where my Maku friends were burning off small garden patches. It was as if I was looking down on the world from on high.

Further up, the forest had grown over the peak but it was thin up there and easy to get about. As darkness fell, I reached the summit and peered down through the trees on the other side in the thickening light. There was no water at the top so I made my way down a little until I found a spring. I drank the pure, peaty water and slung my hammock between two trees. It was too late to make a fire so I smoked the last of my cigar and chewed on the last morsel of bread. As darkness enveloped me, I lay back in my hammock and drew my blanket round me.

I didn't sleep, but fell into a kind of reverie, thinking about my life — all of it. I wasn't afraid, although there were some unfamiliar noises in the dark. All night long as I lay there, I seemed to relive everything that had happened in my life, almost from the moment of my birth. I saw all my family, friends and lovers, and remembered all that had taken place between us. Sleep did not come.

As the first rays of light began to filter through the trees, I felt blissful, totally relaxed and calm. I rolled up my hammock, threw away my shoes and headed down the slope barefoot. I knew exactly where I was going, walked in a straight line, and about an hour later cut across the trail to Chai's house.

When he returned from hunting that afternoon, he sat down beside me and asked why I was back a day later than expected. I told him nonchalantly that I had lost the trail then made my way to Vulture Rock, climbed it and slept the night there. Chai was astonished and told me I was a dumb fool. Didn't I know by now that Vulture Rock was crawling with big, angry jaguars? I giggled, shrugged my shoulders and told him about the fresh tapir tracks I had seen on the way down. We agreed we should, perhaps, check these out the next day. A deep peace settled down inside me.

A few weeks later Chai and I were talking about the soul. I knew by then that the Maku believed that people have a body, a ghost and a soul. A new-born baby's body is enveloped by its ghost and its soul is tiny. As we grow up, the soul grows too, displacing our ghostly aspect. By maturity it is the soul which envelops the body, creating an aura that shamans can see. The ghost gets smaller and smaller as we grow, until it, too, is tiny. At death, the ghost wanders off into the forest and sometimes hangs around, spooking and annoying people.

'What, then, happens to our soul when we die?' I asked Chai. 'When we die, How,' he replied, 'our soul shrivels up into a little ball, then it flies off to the top of Vulture Rock, the place where you slept out, you idiot. That's where Bone Son [creator of the universe] comes down to our souls. He gives us a draft of flower pollen and we inhale it like snuff. It makes our soul rise up and grow again, ascending to the land of the Birth People, our ancestors, who live above the sun and moon and stars. That's why you shouldn't have been messing around up there on Vulture Rock, How.'

So in Chai's terms, I had accidentally followed the path of the soul after death to the point on the sacred mountain where Bone Son causes the souls of the dead to be reborn and to rise up to the land of the immortals.

I thought little more about this strange experience until twenty years later when I began to work on Near Death Experiences. I realized then that when I had stumbled on to that sacred rock I had unwittingly undergone some of the key stages of an NDE in a state of normal consciousness with no sense of imminent death. I had seen the world from above and found myself out of touch with normal waking reality. Although I had not travelled down a dark tunnel, in the darkness of the night I had undergone a very thorough 'total life recall' which had left me unnaturally calm, purified. Then with the first rays of the sun, I had returned, as if from another world, to the world of the living, almost as if the Beings of Light had ordered me to do so.

In Egyptian terms, I had unwittingly travelled a long way down the path beyond life. Stumbling upon the sacred pyramid, I had ascended to its zenith, just as the *ba*, the immortal soul, must do after death. In the darkness of the night, as the sun-god Re crossed the underworld in his golden barque, I lay in the darkness, surrounded by the ferocious beasts of the night. As the night passed, so my *ba* had made its way to Osiris's Hall of Judgement. There, my soul had recited my confessions as Anubis, jackal-headed god of mummification, weighed my soul against the feather of Ma'at, goddess of truth, divine order and justice. Had it been found too heavy, doubtless the gods would have cast me to the jaguars of the mountain. Had it been too light then I would have risen on the sunbeams to take my place in the heavens. But the scales must have balanced because I was permitted rebirth and, with the first blood-red rays of the sun, a return to the world of the living.

A few weeks later, I left Chai's genial company and travelled downriver by canoe to meet up with my field supervisor, Peter Silverwood-Cope, who had pioneered field research with the Maku in nearby Colombia. Besides being a brilliant academic, Pete was also a deeply spiritual person, with keen shamanic insight. We met in a remote outpost of the Brazilian government's Indian Agency. After eating, Pete produced some coca and I rolled a cigar with a banana leaf and local tobacco. As we smoked and chewed, I told Pete that I had had a strange experience a few weeks earlier.

IN THE SACRED MOUNTAINS

Before I could explain, Pete interrupted, 'You got lost in the forest, didn't you?' I assented. 'Then you climbed to the top of a mountain, didn't you?' I said yes, feeling a little alarmed. 'You spent the night up there and had many visions. You saw your whole life unravel in front of you, didn't you?' I asked him how on earth he could possibly know all this. 'Same thing happened to me when I was doing my fieldwork, exactly the same. Welcome aboard,' he added with a chuckle.

Like Robin, my other soul-brother, Peter is dead now and I, for the time being, live on. But neither of them is gone, lost forever. They live on inside me and in the hearts of all those who loved them. In life there is death, in death life. As many of our ancestors realized so long ago, the two forces are deeply entwined.

The Importance
of mummies

My main aim in this book has been to seek the deeper meaning of mummification practices, both for those who made mummies and for ourselves. Many of the scientific aspects of mummy studies lie beyond the scope of this book, but this is not because I think they are uninteresting. For me, human mummies are *the* most important part of our archaeological heritage. Artefacts, clothing, jewellery, works of art and architectural remains provide us with important clues about our forebears, but they do not provide us with anywhere near the same quantity of information as one preserved human body.

Furthermore, we are only just beginning to discover ways of decoding the priceless information that mummies contain. A single hair, for example, can now tell tales and, as I write, the sampling of hair from a Guanche mummy – given to Joann Fletcher – will soon tell us a great deal about Guanche health and diet; a small bone sample will give us the mummy's DNA structure, providing population geneticists with invaluable data for assessing the ethnic origins of the Guanche people. These are just two of the scientific techniques now available to mummy scientists. Thirty years ago neither of these was available.

If we can learn so much from a fairly non-invasive investigation taking place in 1999, imagine how much more we will be able to learn about our ancestors in fifty or a hundred years' time.

IN SEARCH OF THE IMMORTALS

Mummies are a unique and vital part of the heritage of mankind. Left undisturbed in the ground, thousands of them have survived to the present day. The moment humans disturb them, however – be they grave-robbers or archaeologists – the mummies are seriously imperilled. The beautiful woman I described in Chapter One had lain in her tomb for 3,500 years before He Dexiu and his team exhumed her in 1991. Her face was perfect then, as contemporary photos attest. But when I filmed her just six years later, long cracks had opened up in her cheeks from just below the eye sockets almost to her lower jaw-bone. This was not surprising; she was lying in an unsealed glass case in a museum in the centre of Korla, a town of several hundred thousand people almost all of whom cook every day on coal fires and travel in vehicles which emit destructive fumes. The polluted air was undoubtedly responsible for damaging this wonderful mummy.

Elsewhere in China I saw mummies with skins covered in white fungus, and many others lying in filthy storage conditions with no climate or humidity control. Similar problems abound in South America and Egypt. And even in the most august institutions of the affluent Western world, many mummies are stored in far from ideal conditions with no adequate measures taken to ensure their conservation.

This is not the fault of those charged with looking after the mummies. In my experience they are deeply dedicated and, where relevant, acutely aware of the inadequacy of the resources at their disposal. But if you live in a country such as China or Peru, the choice may be as stark as preserving the long-dead or saving the now-living.

So, over the millennia and centuries since they were created, mummies have on the whole had a rough time of it. Of the 200 or more bog bodies that have been discovered, all but a handful have been reburied or simply cast away. Thousands of Guanche and Egyptian mummies have been destroyed – even consumed for their so-called medical properties by Europeans. All the known Inca mummies except for a few child sacrificial

THE IMPORTANCE OF MUMMIES

offerings on the mountain tops have been destroyed, and tens of thousands of mummy graves have been ransacked and looted along the Pacific coast of Peru.

In all, I would say that more than ninety-five per cent of all the mummies ever made have now been lost to us – a few through natural causes, the vast majority through human ignorance and prejudice. A truly unique heritage has been destroyed or left to decay.

This is a great tragedy, because although our understanding of the mummy peoples of the world has come on in leaps and bounds during the last few decades, the scientific techniques for understanding these gifts from our ancestors have advanced and there are still many more wondrous discoveries that could have been made.

Mummies may be mute and bandaged, but they can still speak volumes: they are priceless resources for us and for future generations to learn from. They are also uniquely fragile. If we do not start to care for them properly, they will rapidly revert to the ashes and dust they have managed to evade for thousands of years.

The Ice Man
of the alps

No book on mummies written in the 1990s can be complete without reference to the Ice Man of the Alps, discovered on the Austrian – Italian border in 1991. Many archaeologists consider him to be one of the most important finds of the century. He was discovered emerging from a glacier by a German couple on a walking tour. At first the authorities assumed him to be the body of a climber, probably no more than fifty years old. But when archaeologists were called in they soon realized from the clothing on the body and the equipment spread all around him that he haled from prehistory. In the end he turned out to be 5,300 years old, by far the oldest ice mummy ever discovered and the oldest European mummy found to date.

The discovery of this excellently preserved body revolutionized scientific understanding of the era in which he had lived. Before 1991 it was assumed that copper smelting and casting began in Europe around 4,000 years ago. The Ice Man, however – almost certainly a coppersmith himself – put that date back by more than 1,000 years.

Likewise, before he was found, it was assumed that the only inhabitants of the high Alpine valleys were hunters and herders, but his clothes contained two grains of domesticated wheat which had been threshed and husked, and his stomach contents revealed that his last meal was of bread and meat. So his people were certainly farmers as well as herders.

The Ice Man is a paradigmatic example of how much can be learned from just one relatively intact human and his belongings. But from the point of view of this book he cannot tell us much about his people's attitudes towards death and the afterlife as his death was clearly an accident. As far as we can tell he had no desire to die, let alone become mummified so that his physical being would endure for more than 5,000 years. Yet there are some aspects of his story which chime with the themes I have been exploring in this book.

To start with, when he died the Ice Man was on a journey – and was well equipped for it. The journey took him high into the mountains, doubtless sacred places to his people, just as they were to most of the mummy-making people we have met in this book. A solo journey high into the mountains is always a risky undertaking, even for those who know them well. He certainly did, but he still took steps to ensure his safety. He wore a thick waterproof cape made from dried grasses and leather boots stuffed with more dried grass. He had on a conical fur hat tied with chin straps. Beneath the dried-grass cape he wore a fur cape, probably made of deerskin, and leather leggings. He covered his private parts with a loin-cloth held in place by a leather belt.

He carried a wood-framed backpack bound with string. This – and the pouches on his belt – contained an amazing assortment of kit: burning embers wrapped in damp moss and encased in a little birch-bark pouch; a small flint-bladed knife and equipment for resharpening it if it got blunt or chipped. His most prized possession was a superb copper axe set on to a wooden shaft and bound in place with leather thongs. He also carried a long staff-cum-bow, a quiver, two whole arrows and all the equipment necessary to make more arrows. His bow string was probably also in the quiver, along with feathers for making flights and sinew for binding them on to the arrows. A net found near his body may have been used for snaring birds. He had supplied himself with ibex meat for the trip and his belt pouch even contained dry tinder to help him get a fire started. Two pieces of birch fungus had holes drilled through them and leather thongs inserted. These he wore round his left wrist. Birch fungus contains bacteriological agents so these were presumably his 'medicine'. He also had a tassel with a single drilled piece of marble attached to it. The tassel, made from twisted leather thongs, may have been his supply of thongs for running repairs, but the piece of polished marble looks like an ornament, or perhaps a charm.

So this forty-five-year-old was well equipped with a thick cape-cum-blanket, warm clothing, food, fire and weapons for his journey through the high mountains. And many of the durable objects he carried have been used to corroborate where he came from and which culture he belonged to.

In this region the only artefacts which usually survive are stone, metals, ceramics and bone found in graves. The unique thing about the Ice Man is the wonderful profusion of organically derived equipment and clothing which have survived with him. His wooden tools and weapons were made from a variety of different trees and shrubs, his clothes and quiver made from many different wild and domestic animals. He carried tools which showed that he was skilled at both knapping flint and forging, casting, hammering and polishing copper. He made his own arrows, axe shaft and many more fine tools. He probably also tanned and sewed his own leather gear, and knew how to make, carry and conserve fire. In all, he was a highly accomplished individual.

These discoveries paint a much clearer picture of a life than any information that has been gleaned from the scant objects found in graves dating to that period. Ironically, though, had he died from natural causes the contents of his grave might have given us an accurate picture of the afterlife beliefs of his fellows at the time he was laid to rest.

IN SEARCH OF THE IMMORTALS

We have seen throughout this book that the urge to send people into the next life properly equipped for the journey to the after-world was very widespread. It seems highly likely that the people inhabiting the Alps 5,000 years ago – people used to making regular journeys with their animals to the rich high-summer pastures then back to the valleys for harvest time and winter – would certainly have wanted to give their dead all the help they could with the migration of their souls to the afterworld.

Bibliography

Adams, D.Q. 1995, Mummies, *Journal of Indo-European Studies* 23, 3–4, p.399–413

Allen, T.B. 1996, The Silk Road's Lost World, *National Geographic* 189, no.3, p.44–51

Allison, M. 1985, Chile's Ancient Mummies, *Natural History* 94 (10), p.74–81

Anton, R.G., Behrmann, R. de B., Ramirez, P.B. & Aguilar, C. Del A. 1994, *La Piedra Zanata*, Cabildo, Tenerife

Arriaza, B.T. 1995, *Beyond Death: the Chinchorro Mummies of Ancient Chile*, Smithsonian Institute Press, Washington & London

——— 1995, Chile's Chinchorro Mummies, *National Geographic* 3, p.68–9

Aufderheide, A., Munoz, I. & Arriaza, B. 1993, Seven Chinchorro Mummies and the Prehistory of Northern Chile, *American Journal of Physical Anthropology* 91, p.198–201

Badham, P. 1990, *Near-Death Experiences, Beliefs about Life After Death, and the Tibetan Book of the Dead*, International Buddhist Study Center, Tokyo

Badham, P. & Badham, L. 1984, *Immortality or Extinction?* SPCK, London

Bahn, P. 1995, Last Days of the Iceman, *Archaeology* 48 (3), p.66–70

Bahn, P.G. & Vertut, J. 1988, *Images of the Ice Age*, Winward, Leicester

Barber, D.J.W. 1995, A Weaver's-eye View of the Second Millennium Tarim Basin Finds, *Journal of Indo-European Studies* 23, 3–4, p.347–355

Barber, E.W. 1999, *The Mummies of Urumchi*, Macmillan, London

Barber, P. 1995, Mummification in the Tarim Basin, *Journal of Indo-European Studies* 23, 3–4, p.309–318

Bittmann, B. & Munizaga, J. 1987, The Earliest Mummification in the World? A Study of the Chinchorro Complex of Northern Chile, *Folk* 18, p.61–92

Blackmore, S.J. 1982, *Beyond the Body: An Investigation of Out-of-the-Body Experiences*, Academy Chicago Publishers, Chicago

Blackmore, S. 1993, *Dying to Live: Science and the Near-Death Experience*, Grafton, London

Bloch, M. & Parry, J. 1982, *Death and the Regeneration of Life*, Cambridge University Press, Cambridge

Brier, B. 1996, *Egyptian Mummies: Unravelling the Secrets of an Ancient Art*, Michael O'Mara, London

—— 1998, *The Encyclopedia of Mummies*, Facts on File Inc., New York

Brothwell, D. 1986, *The Bog Man and the Archaeology of People*, British Museum Press, London

Campbell, J. 1987, *Primitive Mythology: The Masks of God*, Penguin, Harmondsworth

Chapman, R., Kinnes, I. & Randsborg, K. (eds.) 1981, *The Archaeology of Death*, Cambridge University Press, Cambridge

Cockburn, A. & Cockburn, E. (eds.) 1980, *Mummies, Disease and Ancient Cultures*, Cambridge University Press, Cambridge

Cockburn, A., Cockburn, E. & Reyman, T.A. (eds.) 1998, *Mummies, Disease and Ancient Cultures*, Cambridge University Press, Cambridge

Coles, B. (ed.) 1992, *The Wetland Revolution in Prehistory*, Prehistory Society/ WARP, Exeter

BIBLIOGRAPHY

〜〜

Coles, B. & Coles, J. 1989, *People of the Wetland: Bogs, Bodies and Lake-Dwellers*, Thames & Hudson, London

di Cosmo, N. 1994, Ancient Inner Asian Nomads: Their Economic Base and its Significance in Chinese History, *Journal of Asian Studies* 53, no.4, p.1092–1126

Davis-Kimball, J. 1996, Tribal Interaction Between the Early Iron Age Nomads of the Southern Ural Steppes, Semirechiye and Xinjiang, *Proceedings of the Bronze Age and the Iron Age Mummies of Eastern Central Asia*, University of Pennsylvania (April)

—— (in press), Sauro-Sarmatian Nomadic Women: New Gender Identities, *Journal of Indo-European Studies*

Davies-Kimball, J., Bashilov, A. & Yablonsky, L.T. (eds.) 1995, *Nomads of the Eurasian Steppes in the Early Iron Age*, Zinat Press, Berkeley

Doore, G. (ed.) 1988, *Shaman's Path: Healing, Personal Growth and Empowerment*, Shambhala, Boston

—— 1990, *What Survives? Contemporary Explorations of Life after Death*, Jeremy P. Tarcher, Inc., Los Angeles

Dunand, F. & Lichtenberg, R. 1994, *Mummies: A Journey Through Eternity*, Thames & Hudson, London

Duncan Baird Publishers 1997, *Egyptian Myth: The Way to Eternity*, Time-Life Books, Amsterdam

Eliade, M. 1989, *Shamanism: Archaic Techniques of Ecstasy*, Arkana/Penguin, Harmondsworth

Fletcher, J. 1999, *Ancient Egypt: Life, Myth and Art*, Duncan Baird, London

Francalacci, P. 1995, DNA Analysis of Ancient Dessicated Corpses from Xinjiang, *Journal of Indo-European Studies* 23, 3–4, p.385–397

Franck, I.M. & Brownstone, D.M. 1996, *To the Ends of the Earth: the Great Travel and Trade Routes of Human History*, Facts on File, Oxford

Frazer, J.G. 1970, *The Golden Bough: A Study in Magic and Religion*, Macmillan, London

Glob, P.V. 1969, *The Bog People*, Faber & Faber, London

Good, I. 1995, Notes on a Bronze Age Textile Fragment from Hami, Xinjiang with Comments on the Significance of Twill, *Journal of Indo-European Studies* 23, 3–4, p.319–345

Green, M.J. 1993, *The Legendary Past: Celtic Myths*, British Museum Press, London

—— 1997, *Dictionary of Celtic Myth and Legend*, Thames & Hudson, New York

Guillen, S.E. 1992, *The Chinchorro Culture: Mummies and Crania in the Reconstruction of Preceramic Coastal Adaptation in the South Central Andes*, PhD thesis, University of Michigan

Gwei-Djen, L. & Needham, J. 1980, *Celestial Lancets: A History and Rationale of Acupuncture and Moxa*, Cambridge University Press, Cambridge

Habenstein, R.W. & Lamers, W.M. 1960, *Funeral Customs the World Over*, Bulfin Printers, Milwaukee

Hadingham, E. 1994, The Mummies of Xinjiang, *Discover* (April), p.68–77

Von Hagen, A. & Morris, C. 1998, *The Cities of the Ancient Andes*, Thames & Hudson, London

Harner M.J. 1972, *The Jivaro*, Robert Hale, London

—— 1980, *The Way of the Shaman*, Harper & Row, San Francisco

Herodotus (trans. de Selincourt, A.) 1996, *The Histories*, Penguin, Harmondsworth

Huntingdon, R. & Metcalfe, P. 1985, *Celebrations of Death*, Cambridge University Press, Cambridge

Ingerman, S. 1991, *Soul Retrieval: Mending the Fragmented Self*, HarperCollins, New York

Kamberi, D. 1994, The Three Thousand Year Old Charchan Man Preserved at Zaghunluq, *Sino-Platonic Papers* 44 (January), University of Pennsylvania, p.1–15

BIBLIOGRAPHY

~~~

Keating, W. & Chauchat, C. 1988, *Peruvian Prehistory*, Cambridge University Press, Cambridge

Lanning, E.P. 1967, *Peru Before the Incas*, Prentice-Hall, Englewood Cliffs, N.J.

Lichtheim, M. 1973, *Ancient Egyptian Literature, I: The Old and Middle Kingdoms*, University of California Press, Berkeley

McIntyre, L. 1975, *The Incredible Incas and Their Timeless Land*, National Geographic Society

MacCormack, S. 1991, *Religion in the Andes: Vision and Imagination in Early Colonial Peru*, Princeton University Press, Princeton

Mair, V. 1995, Prehistoric Caucasoid Corpses of the Tarim Basin, *Journal of Indo-European Studies* 23, 3–4, p.281–307

—— 1995, Mummies of the Tarim Basin, *Archaeology* (March/April), p.26–35

Mallory, J.P. 1989, *In Search of the Indo-Europeans: Language, Archaeology and Myth*, Thames & Hudson, London

—— 1995, Speculations on the Xinjiang Mummies, *Journal of Indo-European Studies* 23, 3–4, p.371–383

Ma'sumian, F. 1995, *Life After Death: a Study of the Afterlife in World Religions*, One World, Oxford

Meisch, L. 1997, *Traditional Textiles of the Andes: Life and Cloth in the Highlands*, Thames & Hudson, London

Menon, S. 1997, The People of the Bog, *Discover* (August), p.58–67

Mercer, J. 1980, *The Canary Islands: Their Prehistory, Conquest and Survival*, Rex Collings Ltd, London

Morton, C. & Thomas, C.L. 1997, *The Mystery of the Crystal Skulls: Unlocking the Secrets of the Past, Present and Future*, Thorsons, London

Moseley, M.E. 1992, *The Incas and their Ancestors: The Archaeology of Peru*, Thames & Hudson, London

Murphet, H. 1990, *Beyond Death: The Undiscovr'd Country*, Quest, London

Needham, J. 1959, *Science and Civilisation in China*, Vols. I–III, Cambridge University Press, Cambridge

Opie, J. 1995, Xinjiang Remains and 'Tocharian Problems', *Journal of Indo-European Studies* 23, 3–4, p.431–437

Ovid (trans. Innes, M.M.) 1955, *Orpheus in the Underworld*, Penguin, Harmondsworth

Paul, A. 1991, *Paracas Art and Architecture: Object and Context in Southern Coastal Peru*, Iowa

Pirazzoli-t'Serstevens (ed.) *The Han Civilisation of China*, Phaidon, Oxford

Polosmak, N. 1994, A Mummy Unearthed from the Pastures of Heaven, *National Geographic* 186, no.4, p.80–103

Prescott, C. & Walderhaug, E. 1995, The Last Frontier? Processes of Indo-Europeanization in Northern Europe: The Norwegian Case, *Journal of Indo-European Studies* 23, 3–4, p.257–278

Pulleyblank, E.G. 1995, Why Tocharians?, *Journal of Indo-European Studies* 23, 3–4, p.415–429

Reid, H.A. 1979, *Some Aspects of Movement, Growth and Change Among the Hupdu Maku Indians of Brazil*, unpublished PhD thesis, Cambridge University

—— 1988, *The Way of Harmony: A Guide to the Soft Martial Arts*, Unwin Hyman, London

Reid, H. & Croucher, M. 1983, *The Way of the Warrior*, Century, London

Reinhard, J. 1992, Sacred Peaks of the Andes, *National Geographic* 181 no.3, p.84–111

—— 1996, Peru's Ice Maidens: Unwrapping the Secrets, *National Geographic* no.6, p.62–81

Ringe, D. 1995, Tocharians in Xinjiang: The Linguistic Evidence, *Journal of Indo-European Studies* 23, 3–4, p.439–443

BIBLIOGRAPHY

Ringe, D. 1992, *The Tibetan Book of Living and Dying*, Rider Books, London

Rogo, D.S. 1989, *The Return from Science: a Study of Near-Death Experiences*, The Aquarian Press, Wellingborough

Rowe, J.H. 1946, Inca Culture at the Time of the Spanish Conquest, *The Handbook of South American Indians II*, Steward, J. (ed.) Bulletin 143 Smithsonian Institute Press, Washington, p.183–330

—— 1991, Behaviour and Belief in Ancient Peruvian Mortuary Practice, *Tombs for the Living: Andean Mortuary Practice*

Rudenko, S. 1970, *Frozen Tombs in Siberia: the Pazyryk Burials of Iron Age Horsemen*, Dent, London/University of California Press, Berkeley

Rudgley, R. 1998, *Lost Civilisations of the Stone Age*, Century, London

Sahlins, M. 1972, *Stone Age Economics*, Tavistock, London

Sandars, N.K. (trans.) 1972, *The Epic of Gilgamesh*, Penguin, Harmondsworth

van der Sanden, W. 1996, *Through Nature to Eternity*, Batavian Lion International, Amsterdam

Schobinger, J. 1991, Sacrifices of the High Andes, *Natural History* (April)

—— 1995, *Aconcagua: Un enterratorio incaico a 5.300 metres de altura*, Inca Editorial, Mendonza, Argentina

Spencer, A.J. 1982, *Death in Ancient Egypt*, Penguin, Harmondsworth

Spindler, K. 1994, *The Man in the Ice*, Weidenfeld & Nicolson, London

—— 1995, *Human Mummies: a Global Survey of their Status and the Techniques of Conservation*, Springer-Verlag, New York

Stead, I.M., Bourke, J.B. & Brothwell, D. 1986, *Lindow Man: The Body in the Bog*, British Museum Press, London

Stringe, C. & Gamble, C. 1993, *In Search of the Neanderthals*, Thames & Hudson, London

Tacitus (trans. Mattingly, H. & Handford, S.A.) 1970, *The Agricola and the Germania*, Penguin Classics, Harmondsworth

IN SEARCH OF THE IMMORTALS

〜〜〜

Taylor, J.H. 1995, *Unwrapping a Mummy*, British Museum Press, London

Temple, R.K.G. 1984, *Conversations with Eternity: Ancient Man's Attempts to Know the Future*, Rider, London

Tierney, P. 1989, *The Highest Altar*, Bloomsbury, London

Torday, L. 1997, *Mounted Archers: The Beginnings of Central Asian History*, The Durham Academic Press, Durham

Turner, R.C. & Scaife, R.G. (eds.) 1995, *Bog Bodies: New Discoveries and New Perspectives*, British Museum Press, London

Urioste, G. 1981, Sickness and Death in Preconquest Andean Cosmology, *Health in the Andes*, Bastien, J. & Donahue, J. (eds.), American Anthropological Association

Wenkan, X. 1995, The Discovery of the Xinjiang Mummies and Studies of the Origins of the Tocharians, *Journal of Indo-European Studies* 23, 3–4, p.357–369

Winter, W. 1984, The Tocharians in Cultural, Historical and Linguistic Perspective, *Studia Tocharica: Selected Writings*, p.9–26

Wise, K. (ed.) The Chinchorro Occupation at Villa del Mar, Ilo, Peru (translation), *Gaceta Arqueolgica Andina* 24, p.135–149

Zaleski, C. 1987, *Otherworld Journeys: Accounts of Near-death Experience in Medieval and Modern Times*, Oxford University Press, Oxford

Index

INDEX

INDEX

〰

INDEX

INDEX